How Children Make Art

How Children Make Art

LESSONS IN CREATIVITY
FROM HOME TO SCHOOL

George Szekely

Teachers College, Columbia University
New York and London

National Art Education
Association

Published by Teachers College Press, 1234 Amsterdam Avenue, New York, NY 10027
and the National Art Education Association, 1916 Association Drive, Reston, VA 20191.

Portions of the book are reprinted with permission, with minor editorial alterations,
from the articles "Water Artists," "Dress-up Artists," "Flashlight Artists," "Art on
Wheels," "Pillow Artists," "Home Chore Artists," "Gift-giving Artists," "You've Got
Art Mail," "Phone Artists," "School Bus Artists," "Shelf Artists," "Hand Made Artists,"
"Disguise Artists," "Personal Container Artists," "Print Store Artists," "Block Play
Artists," "Doll Artists," and "Small-Scale Artists," all by George Szekely, in,
respectively, the June 2003, December 2002, February 2000, June 2002, December 2001,
October 2003, April 2003, April 2000, May 2001, October 2004, May 2004, February 2001,
October 2002, February 2002, November 2005, March 2004, February 2003, and January
2004 issues of *Arts & Activities* Magazine, 12345 World Trade Dr., San Diego, CA 92128,
www.artsandactivities .com

Library of Congress Cataloging-in-Publication Data

Szekely, George.
    How children make art : lessons in creativity from home to school / George Szekely.
        p.   cm.
    Includes bibliographical references and index.
    ISBN-13: 978-0-8077-4719-3 (pbk : alk. paper)
    ISBN-10: 0-8077-4719-X (pbk : alk. paper)
    1. Art—Study and teaching (Early childhood)   2. Creative ability in children.
I. Title.
    LB1139.5.A78S94 2006
    372.5—dc22
                                                                              2006012842

ISBN-13:   ISBN-10:
978-0-8077-4719-3 (paper)   0-8077-4719-X (paper)

Printed on acid-free paper
Manufactured in the United States of America

13   12   11   10   09   08   07   06   8   7   6   5   4   3   2   1

Yes, I typed this book myself! I finally learned to type after eight handwritten books that were typed by my wife, Laura. Having typed this book, however, does not mean I did it all by myself. Without Laura's encouragement and wisdom nothing gets done in our home. What I am trying to say is that Dr. Laura Szekely is the real teacher in our family. She is creative and completely devoted to her students in middle school, at the university, or on the supermarket checkout line, where she is ready to counsel and encourage every-one to pursue an education. She is my candidate for the teaching hall of fame and the muse for all my writing about children and the teaching profession.

Contents

Preface

In this book I share the stories in my diaries because I still use them as exciting references for teaching art in the schools. Parents and teachers who enjoy reading these stories and recognize their significance will strive not to separate children from their art at home—or in school art classes.

May I introduce you to my three children, Ilona, the oldest, Ana the little one, and Jacob in the middle. They are the stars of the book and most of my writings. I date my growing up as an art teacher and discovering the uniqueness of children's art from their early years. Spending time on the floors of their studios, their rooms, I was introduced to a world free of adult-conceived art exercises and adult views of child art. I never played the art teacher at home, but took voluminous notes and learned to champion the home players who completely redefined for me a unique art world never addressed by my art teaching. Descriptions in this book are from the many notebooks, films, and photos of the young Szekelys' home art and how it formed a new foundation for my art teaching. My three children taught me everything about art teaching, altering my former art lessons, a series of adult-planned and adult-guided events introducing adult art conventions and adult artists to children. My children are now grown, but the stories in the following chapters will be related in the present tense.

Perhaps inspired by my enthusiasm for their early artistic life, now as adults, my children all have their own students and classrooms. We talk each night on the phone, comparing our teaching days from different parts of the country, still discussing what we love best, amazing moments of children's discoveries.

I never resigned from the elementary classroom when I became a professor, but simply invited all future art teachers to join me, learning about the profession while playing on the floor in the company of school children. All of my 35 years as an art teacher, starting with elementary school and during the university teaching years, were spent with children. In 1973, I organized the nationally recognized Adopt-a-School Program, which relocated the site for art teacher preparation to public schools, learning by being with children in every art education class. I am in the schools all week, and throughout this book I refer to my teaching of art to children. These experiences include working side by side with future art teachers in every elementary school "adopted."

1

Learning from Home Studios

INSIDE THE GREEN CABINET

The bottom drawers of the large green built-in cabinet in my childhood bedroom were like a giant treasure chest. I can't recall the objects in the drawers, but I still remember the joy of taking things out, discovering objects one at a time, and hearing them drop on the hardwood floor. I remember the piles I created and my mom putting everything back, so I could start excavating all over again.

As soon as I could stand on a chair, my interest moved up to a large door opening to a cavernous closet in the center of the cabinet. I built steps, ramps, and elevators for my toy troops up to the ascending shelves on both sides of this closet. The closet had everything, including a light and a key, and I recall happy hours of arranging my Bakelite cars, plaster soldiers, and lead horses inside. The green closet was my discovery place, and later it became my design practice and museum to showcase toys and collections. It was a display forever in progress. I can still feel the fun of climbing inside the closet to set up scenes and stories that amazed my friends. The closet door had a glass window, and my friends peered through this window at the magic canvas set up inside. Children have many canvases—closets, floors, shelves—all places where they create displays as art, using their favorite articles. When I became the parent of three young artists, I found kindred spirits in my children's rooms.

I grew up as an art teacher when I learned to make art on the floor and to enjoy the fun of shopping for art materials everywhere in our house. Through the experience of parenthood I understood the essence of art teaching—to encourage children's playful and independent creations. As a frequent studio guest, I learned to listen to children's ideas without overwhelming them with an art lesson, or with my art views. In my children's rooms, I learned how to set up an inviting art room with fun shopping sites and unusual display spaces. Now I can walk into a school art class and describe why a particular art lesson may have little to do with children's experience, or if an art room feels like a child's art studio. I trust young artists and know they have great ideas because I became an art teacher by playing with children on the floor.

As a professor, I ask my college students to learn about teaching art by visiting and videotaping children's rooms. I explain to the children who are our hosts that we are looking for how children play, design, and decorate their rooms. I ask parents not to sanitize the room before our visit and assure them that it is the art encoded in the mess that we came to see.

WHY VISIT CHILDREN'S STUDIOS?

From elementary school to college, future art teachers study adult art. In darkened art history rooms they view art history. Visits to the shrines of the masters and studio art classes are the art teacher's inheritance. Future art teachers of children are introduced to an art world without child art. Adult art is presented as the gold standard—what to admire and work toward. Conventional formulas and wisdoms of art come to be adapted to school curricula, from elementary school to college. No wonder the subject of children's art classes becomes adult art.

At what point do art teachers come in contact with children's art? When do they meet refreshingly different art makers and learn about the unique materials and means children use to create? Visits to children's home studios are intended to introduce future art teachers to another art world—to be inspired by the wonders of childhood art and to experience a different setting than a college art studio.

In home studios we find children playing, inventing, and making art in un-adult-like ways. We see authentic play setups and many forms of children's art that the contemporary art world has only begun to explore. We witness creative inventions not tied to adult art or bound by art history. It is art that predicts the future; it is an art that has preceded earthworks, environmental art, and performance art and one that illuminates the path of contemporary art. In a child's room, we see novel uses of space and furnishings and of decorating over many unofficial canvases. We witness new ways to display and organize collections. We find children's creative supplies and discover what children use and need to make art, all before we write material lists or order from school supply catalogues. In children's homes we see what kids value, what they save and collect. We listen to children with boundless creative ideas, independently engaged in creative projects. A future art teacher who has studied home art cannot view children coming to class as blank slates, without ideas. Those who have studied home art do not see children as unable to function without an adult plan, having to be told what art is or how to make it.

For art to have deep significance to children's lives, home art needs to be connected to school art. Visiting children's rooms gets us to the source and enables us to understand the differences between homemade art and art in school. Young children start life as full-time artists and collectors. But they become part-time and secret artists as they find little connection between their home art and school art. We visit children's homes to be able to inspire full-time art.

Children continue being artists when their art dreams are supported in school, and the art ideas they bring from home are valued in school. A lifelong interest in art can be fostered when art teachers look beyond the brief art class period and see their role as supporting the home artist. Home and school art are interdependent. A school art lesson should be based on home art and the recognition that children already come to us as artists. The art made in school has significance if it becomes part of the children's life and has perpetuity at home.

We also make home visits to balance future art teachers' education between adult art and the study of child art. We introduce art teachers to their future colleagues—the children—who are the most likely to help build a sense of enthusiasm about life as an art teacher.

REPORTS FROM HOME VISITS

The following descriptions are observations from site visits videotaped by future art teachers on visits to children's homes.

A Door and Window Artist

The camera is rolling while Sandra walks upstairs. Sandra had babysat Laura, now age 8, when she was just 2 years old. Laura's room is still easy to find; it's the one with the exciting door decorations. Laura's name is written with colorful zippers on a raised marquee made from an altered lamp shade. Each panel of her door frames a portrait. One portrait is sketched with pink chewing gum. Other, more formal family portraits are presented on bumper stickers. The doorknob is covered by a head drawing over a white sock, extended by a body sketch over a hotel-room door sign. The door frame is decorated with stars cut from candy wrappers.

So this is what real door artists create! Even before entering the room, Laura's creativity is inscribed on the door. From school observations Sandra was used to seeing teachers decorating classroom doors with crafty, ready-made items. As the teacher's display space, classroom doors seldom are decorated by children. Laura's wonderful door is a reminder to turn over door decoration to the real experts: children.

Since Sandra and Laura live on the same street, she frequently walks by Laura's house and smiles at her unusual window displays. Sandra was glad to get a closer look inside and record Laura's art on film. Her window displays are clear soda bottles. Each has been decorated with colored markers. Laura has topped the soda bottles with balloon heads, and the entire display shimmers when seen from the street. Her room is tinted with hues from colored bubble wrap stretched across the inside of the window. The filtered light shines on her bottle collection and on the silver washers she has threaded around her acrylic blind pull. Laura's blinds are her loom for weaving wires and lace through the slats. Her display of white shells on the windowsill reflects a silver sky. Laura freely shops all over the house and outside for window transforming materials. It is exciting to see how she is so aware of the artistic possibilities of the window and light.

Laura's room feels very different from schoolrooms sealed off from the "distractions" of the outside. Imagination can open art room walls, ceilings, and even floors to fresh views and flights of fantasy. Sandra now realizes how doors and windows are important openings to an art room, pathways to keep in touch with the world as well as to shape the feelings and attitudes of the students inside.

A Film About Furniture

Melinda is a first-year art education major. She has an 8-year-old daughter named Hanna. "Cheese! Hi," Melinda says while beginning to video-tape Hanna's furnishings. The corner shelf with doll chairs on it was a big box that a floor lamp had come in. Hanna stickered and painted the sides, made shelves, and glued comic strips in the background. The furniture in this room was not selected from a store; it is not what parents would pick for their children. Hanna has a chair and coat hanger she rescued from the neighbor's trash and repainted with glitter stirred into house paint. Her acrylic shelf filled with tiny treasures was a pharmacy display. Hanna wanted the shelf for a long time, but the store manager said to wait until it was empty. A trash can covered with puffy stickers and a picture frame hot-glued with custom jewelry fragments fits the decor. Framing her art is important to Hanna, and the nontraditionally framed pieces certainly acquire prestigious exhibition spaces in her room.

Melinda decides that in her future art classes drawings and paintings will be extended by children's decorative framing. Her art room products will not be made to go on refrigerators; they will be prepared to hang on living room and museum walls. Melinda looks forward to using her art room to gather "homeless" furniture and to curating the art children craft from it. Inside refrigerator-box forts and under towel-covered chairs, children will set up their contributions to the art of interior design.

Amy, the Designer and Decorator

Dan is standing before Amy's corkboard. Beautiful stamps and bows frame the board. Movie tickets are taped together, hanging from the board like streamers. Amy displays postcards and greeting cards she receives, decorating them with puzzle pieces. A close-up look at the white pushpins shows miniature nail-polished canvases. The colorful pins hold a row of wallet-sized photos framed with colored tape. Before the video, Dan never considered a bulletin board as an artwork.

Seeing Amy's masterpiece reminded Dan of how much effort he used to put into decorating his own childhood room, although no one called it art. School bulletin boards are officially set up by teachers and are definitely not a party children are invited to. In the past, museums would never allow anyone to violate their walls either, but now many artists casually pushpin their art to the wall. Perhaps this is a hopeful signal to guardians of school bulletin boards. Dan says, "It would make sense to open all bulletin boards to children and organize shows of portable corkboard art."

Panning across Amy's room there are so many things to see. A good shot of her phone reveals a display of furry fabrics and a stickered handset. Her boom box is covered with stars, colored tape, and paint-marker dots. The pencil sharpener is dressed in a spider web of sparkly hot-glue strands. Few objects in the room lack Amy's decorative touch.

Following her logic, art rooms shouldn't have to look like other classrooms, especially if children have the opportunity to transform the bulletin board, clock, pencil sharpener, and trash can. Dan says, "An art class should be influential in giving life to young artists' interests in decorating every surface and beautifying their surroundings."

A Toy Maker's Workshop

Ben is videotaping his 8-year-old niece Ellen watching the Macy's Thanksgiving Day Parade and making her own float. Ellen tests and tapes different platforms on top of her brother's remote-controlled car. She decides on using a fruit crate. On film is a young hot-glue artist building with crackers and decorating her float with dried flowers pinned between hair curlers. The theme of Ellen's float is a moving dollhouse. It contains tiny dolls she makes from the fingers of an old glove. Ben, a former gallery director and now a first-year art educator, observes, "Ellen makes artworks to play with, yet I have not read about designing toys being part of an art curriculum. Play and toys are left out of the serious business of schooling."

The float reminds Ben how much fun art used to be, when he made school buses from chairs, with a pot-cover steering wheel and cardboard-tube passengers. Determined to make toys in his art class, Ben asks, "When play, toys, and childhoods are simultaneously discarded, how are children supposed to continue creating? Toys are basic to children's sculpture art and playing."

Ben's film also focuses on a handsome game in a painted box on display on top of Ellen's dresser. The game, a version of Monopoly, all in French, is a prized artwork his niece made in French class. It features an original game board with Sculpey clay pieces. Ben wonders why the art on permanent display was not produced in Ellen's art class. He asks:

> What does it take for an artwork to be honored by permanent placement in a child's room? What does it take to make art with students that becomes a "keeper," something that continues to provide inspiration and become part of a child's room? The treasured piece on display has a great deal of Ellen invested in it—it is art that she planned and constructed with materials she found. Perhaps art made in school needs to be something playable and the young artist left in charge.

Filming in a Home Studio

Angela's studio was recommended by her art teacher because the second grader always brings amazing things to class that she makes at home. When Helen started filming, Angela was preparing for a friend's birthday party. What's in the box will be her surprise—she is decorating the cover with patterns of colored glue accented with candy and pieces of colored ribbon. The inside of the box looks like a fine chocolate display, with rows of colored-pencil points, little round stickers, and an assortment of painted erasers. Angela's wonderful reason for art making is that it is her gift for special people. Our videographer and future art teacher Helen will remember how children create their artworks as presents. She says her art class will be called "Presents to Go." Helen says, "Parents need to understand that the art coming home is a special gift, and to receive the child's art as a great present."

Angela has a large cardboard box she opens up as her doll factory. Inside she made shelves and drawers to keep colored glue sticks, unusual buttons, and her fabric collection. Finished dolls are placed in cellophane-faced donut boxes. One doll's long hair is made from pretzel sticks. Children set up interesting spaces to make art at home. The videotape shows how Angela likes surrounding herself with material finds that inspire her art. Helen notes, "Children set up interesting home studios in a box, or a bathtub. If art making is to continue at home, teachers of school art have to demonstrate an interest in home studios and the children who shop for unusual objects and materials to stock them."

Renee with a Detailing Artist

Renee, a video and art education major, is filming Andrea, a fourth-grade student. Renee's first short video is about Andrea's computer. The video features a mouse pad cut like a doily and drilled with brightly colored hot glue. Andrea individually painted each key on her keyboard. She wove glow-in-the-dark threads into her computer's speakers. Her monitor is festively stickered. Andrea's printer case design, outlined with puffy markers, is in progress. The video's dramatic ending, filmed in the dark, shows the different fluorescent media used on the computer aglow. Reflecting on her video, Renee says:

> Everything children wear, their toys, furnishings, and school supplies are overflowing with ready-made designs. Children can hardly find a yellow pencil or plain notebook cover. It is exciting that they still find surfaces to decorate and canvases to make their own.

Aware of Andrea's ability as an artist to change, improve, and beautify any object, her parents wisely allow her to paint on many things. In the second video, Andrea tells a story of when she was younger and had Care Bears everything—sheets, pajamas, sleeping bag, slippers. Then she found a suitcase of old linens in the attic, which her mom said she could have. Andrea started to color over the sheets and pillowcases with fabric markers and special paints. The video also shows Andrea's unframed paintings in her closet—her painted white canvas sneakers with boldly painted shoelaces. Her painted lamp shades also star in the film. Andrea, like many children, has a broad idea about art and the possibilities of painting. Art teaching has to preserve this.

Harold's Art of Just Playing

The videographer David, a future art teacher, explains to Harold that he is filming his circus as an example of children's art. Wearing a drawing of a ringmaster on a long paper towel, Harold dances around the room. Filming Harold's room is not easy. It requires crawling through a dark tunnel with the video equipment and shooting a circus under a blanket staked by chairs. It is hard to adjust from the dark, to the flashlight-spotted scenes. Harold decorates the hula-hoop ring for the wind-up robot act. He makes tickets and holds a microphone, lending voices and applause to a large cast. Open desk drawers are balconies to seat a stuffed animal audience. Excited about his play being filmed, Harold wants to include everything.

Harold is interested to learn that it is important to learn how to set up play in an art room. While talking, Harold makes circles in the air with a "flying" Hot Wheels car. The video continues to capture his playful hands that hopefully will animate every tool and object in an art room. Toward the end of the videotape Harold is invited to bring his casts and scenery and demonstrate his performance art before other art teachers. Excited about the invitation, he throws out ideas. "Let's print money and set up a drive-through window. We can play bank or post office, or I can show how to make a fast-food restaurant in class." Harold manages a busy room, yet he is ready to explore every new idea for an interesting play site. Confident and active players are comfortable in seeing themselves as inventors and idea people. Art teachers can be sponsors of creative play settings, starting each art lesson with a preliminary play to generate art ideas from children.

And what does play have to do with art? Play is children's way of experimenting and remaking the world their way. It is how children try new things, break from known paths, and explore new possibilities. Playing is a license to handle, touch, take apart and reassemble their toys and any found object. It's a rich source of creative ideas. Playing encourages the inventing of new art media, surfaces, and tools—in a word, the inventing of future art. In our art class, play is a warm-up to every art lesson, promoting children's gathering of their own ideas, a way to break away from adult art plans. Playing in school reminds children of the freedom of home art making and moves their actions and thoughts beyond the bounds and possibilities of school and the traditions of school art.

Grace Documents a Cleanup Artist

In a multilevel tote are Lara's baby teeth, nail clippings, and sample curls from playing beauty parlor when she was younger. Grace is doing the camera work of this unusual portrait, visiting Lara, age 9, the queen of organization. In a gallery walk, Grace films Lara's design of items in the medicine cabinet, in her mom's jewelry drawer, and inside the refrigerator. Lara calls it "cleaning up," redoing every shelf and rearranging every magnet on the refrigerator. The video documents every home chore—polishing, vacuuming, setting tables, and watering the lawn—as an opportunity for Lara to explore, arrange, design, and beautify things. A new definition of art is needed for home chores.

To view a messy artist, Lara shows off her sister's room. A hand-painted door sign reads Beware Artists at Work! In a productive mess, ponies circle the top of the space heater, and combs are used as fencing and exercise hurdles. Everything out of place in this room is in service of a particular setup. There is obvious tension in how the room is supposed to look according to Lara, who is the "good child." "Sarah thinks she is just being creative and we don't understand her." She is assured, in the film's narration, that both girls are wonderful artists who simply create in different ways. Even art teachers who are neat and organized are called the "good ones," instead of considering what goes on in the room, not just the different modes of creating.

Jake the Futurist

Joe is a senior who has visited many art rooms as part of required field-work. He introduces this video by stating how unimpressed he was with the art rooms' displays of old exhibition cards, bad art posters, faded color wheels, and art vocabulary on the wall. He points the camera in different directions in Jake's room to show inspiring objects and interesting things to see everywhere. Jake's room is alive. He knows what's new and exciting to display and talk about. "You want to try the metallic color staples?" asks Jake, pointing to a stapler drawing he made. Look at the race car and the Lego toothbrushes. How can Jake decide which toothbrush to use at night? Jake mentions that a nurse saves pens for him, and in a close-up on the video is a folding bone pen and other unusual pharmaceutical advertising pens he collects. Jake is ready for the contemporary art world as a curator of the new and an interested collector of the latest.

Joe says that school art lives in the past. Children are taught old art forms, stale media tricks with stories of old masters. He hopes to welcome other Jakes to class, to share new finds and observations from the drugstore, the toy store, and the art world. When he is asked what other things in the room should be photographed, Jake shows his box of computer parts. To make art, Jake just empties his pockets. Jake is a constant shopper for supplies and ideas, which, he says, are everywhere. What a great attitude to preserve in young contemporary artists!

THE FINAL FRAME

With the camera lights on, children hold up their collections, perform their art, and demonstrate their lively setups. Each school year, our filmmakers find memorable samples of unique art in children's home studios. They also learn the importance of observing and listening to children's ideas, witnessing their plays, and seeing how children design and care for all parts of their environment. Recognizing how much there is to learn from home artists is the first step in creating art rooms and school art programs that preserve children's art and allow young artists to flourish.

A little red notebook was the first of many recording companions in my study of children's home art and home studios. Now many notebooks are filled with stories of children's playful adventures, performances, and unique inventions in restaurants, markets, toy stores, playgrounds and, of course, in their rooms.

2

Children's Rooms as Art Studios

BED ARTISTS

Art with my infants was a happy time. Above their crib I rigged elaborate trapeze acts, finding moving objects and creating sculptures overhead. There were no crib mobiles for this artist's children. My high wires extended from doorknob to the ceiling, until it was hard to enter the nursery. I still share photos of these creations with my art class and talk about what they would build above a baby's crib.

My adult children still complain about the purchase of their first beds. Jacob only wanted a race-car bed, and my girls dreamt of a playground-style bunk bed. Unforgiven for my artistic choice, we purchased simple beds, blank canvases. A bed is an important canvas for children's changing play creations. My kids transformed their faceless beds throughout their childhoods, creating memorable play settings about which I still write and lecture.

After a day of jumping and setting up action scenes over their beds, children are tired. Sesame Street sheets, accented by cartoon pillows, frame little bodies in superhero pajamas. I kept my children's sheets, sleeping bags, and pillows, but I have built on this collection with older samples and the latest finds in this rich visual arts history. In our classes we continue this history by contributing our own designs of bedding to the art room.

Even superheroes need to be reassured at bedtime with a storybook. As an avid children's book collector, I was eager to share my favorite American artists with my kids. The pace of the art appreciation lesson was slower than I envisioned in the syllabus, since my children wanted to see the same book over and over again until they memorized it.

Recalling beds and bedtimes in the art class brings back cherished memories for kids of any age. Art lessons need to flow from such warm feelings shared with children who are excited to respond with their own stories and creative thoughts.

Bed Transformations

Toys had to be removed from Jacob's bed before he went to sleep. Considering the bed had already been a racetrack, a schoolroom, and the site of the Battle for Beanbag Mountain, clearing it was not a small task. We negotiated about leaving the insulation-board side of his fort in place, and of course the playground beneath the bed remained undisturbed. Action figures under the bed would sleep standing up, waiting for the morning stage call. When Jacob couldn't sleep, you could see his lighted slippers illuminating a night game under the bed.

One day our blue camping tent soared above Jacob's bed. Inside it had comfortable accommodations, snacks, toys, and a portable television. One way children look at their beds is as houses. Bed designs are architectural and interior-design solutions that use objects gathered in the home. While children entertain themselves on their beds, they also dream of designs for privacy and beds that are homes with all amenities for eating and entertainment.

Our children turned their beds into forts when they were punished or angry with us. The bed became a place of resistance, their protected kingdom. Bed forts are also children's safe havens against unfriendly monsters and bad dreams.

In the art class, we use blankets, sheets, and pillows in a myriad of folds, clever dips, and peaks to create changing terrains and mixed landscapes on imaginary beds. In different setups, a bed becomes a place for landscape artists to arrange populations of figures and vehicles. Accomplished bed artists shape their linens to recreate the Tour de France with difficult passages for riding through the folds of sheets. In the steep hills of a sleeping bag, rock climbing and off-road events are featured. In a space theme, over pillow clearings, children land slippers converted into rockets.

Conceptions of the bed as a house, a protected domain, or a changeable landscape can be applied to art room plays. On sheets, blankets, sleeping bags, and pillows set out on my art room floor, children create bed setups accompanied by great performance art and storytelling. Ask children about their thoughts regarding an ideal bed and be ready to take notes on the extraordinary creations and features they share:

I want a bed with more cup holders than our car, a built-in fridge, and snack table.

A drink and candy dispenser would be good for my bed.

My bed is a great hiding place, but it needs safe and secret compartments.

I would buy a bed that has surround-sound speakers, a little drawer for my Gameboy cartridges, and a headboard that is the screen.

As children, we may share a room with a sibling, but our bed is the one place that is ours alone. It is our creative playground, a place to dream, the place to go for comfort. Children see their bed as a flying machine or a race car because they want it to take them to exciting places to have new adventures, very much the way they use art making. The bed becomes an extension of children's art—a supportive easel, a fantasy machine, and a natural place for art making. As adults we may not make forts underneath our beds, but we love to decorate them with beautiful sheets and pillowcases.

Bed artists go through many mattresses, each jump-tested upon arrival. In spite of parental urging not to jump, to keep the bed clean and uncluttered, it is the children who ultimately decide the uses of their bed. Jumping on one's bed demonstrates ownership of the place and sovereignty over what will be created on it. Bed art is important for young artists to assume independent responsibility over other art canvases. Experiences of playing in and around a bed are also beneficial because they promote a lively questioning of what a bed can be. Children who are allowed to play on their beds have impressive visions beyond traditional beds.

Small Beds

Children know who need beds, and they bring their bedless individuals to our art class. Teddy bears and blue monsters determine the features and scale of fantasy bed constructions. My college students like to tell stories about the play beds of their youth as the children create beds fit for our guests:

- For a spotted dog, a bed is designed from a strawberry crate with a bubble-wrap quilt. The space beneath the bed has drapes for the beloved toy puppy.
- Foil wrapped heat tiles cover a Smurf's bed, created for sleeping and space dreams. The cylindrical bed has an open back to climb in, and interior amenities like a sponge mattress for comfort in space travel.
- A doll rests inside a see-through high-heeled shoe. Golden bells, perhaps for room service, and a miniature Cracker Jack–prize phone are part of this bed's features. A decorated shoe box is fitted with a handle to use as a travel case for the doll and its bed.
- Inside a darkened box conducive to sleeping, a bird's nest made from rubber bands and tape is suspended by springs to the sides of the box. This unusual, nest-styled bed was created for a squeaky yellow Tweety toy. The nest-style bed was padded with cut leaves, and the interior of the box was decorated by painted branches.

Sleep Art

Children's dreams of giants, closet monsters, attic threats, or being kidnapped are reinforced by traditional bedtime stories and television. When children arrive at school, their napping days are over, but their sleep concerns—scary dreams and vivid nighttime fantasies—are freshly recounted in words and art. We spread fabrics and stuffed paper pillows on the art room floor as make-believe sleeping bags and dream catchers. Children find it amusing to nap in the art class, yet their make-believe naps collect interesting images on pillows, sheets, or dream notebooks. My collection of vintage night-lights, unusual slippers, and historic doll beds and doll quilts are used not only to establish a mood, but also to inspire the students with great American sleep art works.

At the End

I spent a lot of time next to my mother's sickbed, sitting beside a night table with ordered rows of pillboxes, assorted thermometers, and empty glasses. It was my turn to sit by the bedside, just as she had done or countless hours of the night when I got sick as a child. For 2 years I watched her erratic breathing and dreamt of the happy beds of youth. Instead of joy and laughter, her bed was silenced and moved only through our occasional hand holding. I was touched by a picture of my mom that my daughter was drawing in the back of her prayer book. On back of medication warnings, pillboxes, and nursing receipts I also constantly drew, trying to hold on, picturing the cancer visiting mom's bed now and remembering family visits before with our children jumping on the bed and piling up their pillows to watch a movie. I teach art lessons about beds because they are significant timekeepers, changing scenery witnessing our lives.

Often I walk into elementary art classrooms observing a lesson on values or perspectives drawing, and have the teacher apologetically tell me, "This is only an exercise." If an art lesson is to portray the essence of art, it cannot be an exercise devoid of meaning, regardless of the young artist's age. Art lessons need to be in touch with children's lives and center around things that have meaning for all of us. I tell my bed stories to students because they are sympathetic and understand them. Instead of exercises, art lessons need to be inspiring, tapping into universal experiences and memories. Art or art lessons are real because they are deeply motivated from the artist's heart.

ARTISTS ON THE FLOOR

Don't sit on the dirty floor.
Wear socks, or you will catch a cold.
Sitting on the floor gives you bad posture.

Parents warn against floor life without recognizing the value of this unique play space and art studio. To kids, floors that are cold, wet, or slippery are fun and feel good. Children's art careers begin on the floor as crawling explorers. Adventuring on home floors provides endless creative possibilities. Children taught modern artists how exciting it is to create on the floor, opening the way for Jackson Pollock to move action and invention to the ground. As kids get older, their art and play is confined to smaller desk spaces and modest explorations with limited art inspiration.

School desks are for schoolwork, not art making. In our art room hula hoops on the floor may mean the start of a circus. Play pools on the floor invite a visit to the ocean. Special islands are designated by large, torn–brown-paper forms. Black floors are for intergalactic adventurers, and white floors allow children to play in the snow. On floors, and with floor covers, children imagine and create art. A shiny drop cloth becomes a skating rink. A fancy bedspread is a picnic blanket. Children admire the cracks and textures of outdoor floors, the interesting patterns of indoor carpets, and they invent plays to compliment them. Moving art class activities from tables to the floor, the largest canvas in a classroom, is the first step in freeing children's imaginations and actions from a school frame of mind to playful art rehearsals.

Floor Attitudes

You meet a better class of people on the floor. Everyone is closer and friendlier. It's the coolest place in school; just take off your shoes to play here. Unlocked from the grids and rows of chairs, the floor is more like being at home. Even in the togetherness, one can dream and find a sense of privacy, choosing the amount of interaction wanted with an audience. When teaching moves away from a podium, relationships between the teacher and students become relaxed and conducive to informal talks and support. On the floor, goldfish (painted gummy worms) swim, and a decorated briefcase (a control tower) guides the safe descent of flying slippers. The floor has a magical sensibility, ideal for stories and make-believe plays that set the mood for art.

Floor Views

On an open floor you can see forever. One feels distance on the floor and a variety of viewpoints. Boarding toy helicopters, children get a bird's-eye view of miniature settings. They descend with parachutes (paper drink umbrellas) to their "base" below. They describe the unusual sights they see when looking up or beneath things. Sitting on the classroom floor feels

like the bottom of the room, the floor of the ocean. Unlike school art papers, floors have no boundaries, and "mile-long" artworks can be unfurled.
The floor space feels like a real canvas. In art room plays, we drive with
toys through construction sites and into parking lots. With hands and art
tools, we walk over floors and imaginary structures like playgrounds, indoor gardens, or Ground Zero. Children's senses of landscapes, of far and
near, of visions of being on the bottom or on top of the world, develop on
the carpets, grasses, and floors on which they play.

Floor Canvases

As if in an ancient Persian palace, children arrange fabrics and carpets
on the floor. Children use ready-made floor coverings such as tiles, cork,
carpet samples, and Astroturf, as canvases to paint and assemble into floor
art. In our art class, children handle antique carpets, vintage linoleum,
old sleeping bags, classic doormats, and the latest in beach towels. White
jean fabric is cut to towel- or rug-sized segments for children to create
their own towels, sleeping bags, or picnic blankets for floor displays.
Outdoors, bright orange yarn clings like Velcro to grass, allowing children to draw on a field of green. Watering cans, chalks, pebbles, and
surveyors' flags are our art class tools for children, the original earthwork
artists. Outdoor grounds and indoor floors challenge students to create
on scales seldom tackled in tabletop art.

Floor Furnishings

Kids set up their visions of the world on the floor in unique combinations
of toys and found objects. Children use pillows, carpets, books, and laundry baskets to furnish floors and create artistic play settings. Forts, scenic
train layouts, drive-through banks, and carpeted pastures are built under
beds or under a canopy of tables. In the art room, we use umbrellas as tents
and furnish the floor with what is available in school. Trash-can lighthouses
direct the passage of lunch-box barges and tankers that pass under bridges
constructed from rulers, pencils, and erasers. In floor sketches, children assemble imaginary cities, landscapes, and personal scenes inhabited by toy
people. Setups on the floor are home art that should be continued in the
art class.

Floor Moves

Whereas still art is produced on tables, action artists play on floors. Children gallop across the floor on stick horses they craft, taking advantage of

open spaces. They navigate the depth and breadth of the floor with long-reaching art-tool handles. They spin umbrellas with drawing tools at the tip. Children kneeling on the floor mark papers with drawing tools attached to the webbing of old baseball gloves. The movement options of the floor alter young artists' art-making moves. At a table, children's hands are anchored, limited in movement. On the floor, bodies become engaged; full arm and hand motions can apply a choice of pressures and extended marks to art. The floor allows for playful bodies to respond with a large palette of art-making moves.

Floor Appreciation

When I was a boy, the walls were cold in our apartment in Hungary, but the fanciful rug hanging next to my bed kept me warm. I recall selecting the carpet from the large roll carried on the shoulder of a Gypsy who sold carpets door to door. To leave Hungary, I carried the smallest roll of carpets and my parents the larger ones, as we lined up at the door of the Hungarian National Museum. Only four of our carpets, including my wall piece, were stamped for permission to leave the country, because all the rest were considered national treasures. I often come to class like that wandering Gypsy, with a carpet collection carried over my shoulder, unfurling a personal art history of beautiful carpets. Appreciation of "magic carpets" from around the world can be part of any art course.

Floor Memories

In the art room, we recall floor events and memories of times spent on the floor or on the ground outside. Children who appreciate small sidewalk cracks are amazed at the scale of cracks being repaired on a road; they tell the story of following a spray gunner moving along a truck of steaming hot black asphalt, and drawing enormous black, flowing lines over road cracks. Children recall discovering unlikely trash and treasures on the ground, and remember the teeming life beneath it. I show my photos of the artworks of children arranging pine needles and fallen petals into rooms furnished with leaves and rock gardens. My daughter Ana and I spent lots of time on the floor of her room, where I planned my best art lessons. Ana created great floor displays from all her birthday presents set up inside her jump rope on her carpet; and it became a tradition to wait to sample Halloween candies while Ana elegantly styled her haul over the patterns of her oriental rug. I simply sit with children on the floor and watch for amazing art ideas to appear.

Floor Plans

Don't call it a mess without carefully examining the thoughtful organization and careful planning that goes into kids' floors. Scores of extras are set up on the studio lot to play house, perform in a circus, present a figure-skating revue, or race on a Grand Prix track. In spirit, art room floors should not be far removed from the exciting floors found in children's rooms at home. The surprise layouts or fun shopping sites that are part of home-floor plays may look like a dump, but they exude the richness of possibilities in an active play site. Each art lesson needs a floor plan to illustrate the placements of floor coverings and props, to show where shopping and surprises may be found, where building sites or watering holes (pools) will be located. Floor plans can be outlined in tape, or defined as parcels of real estate, and filled in by student inventions. Floors can have a traffic plan of adding machine–tape runways or highways. They can suggest moods such as a festive dropping of confetti and petals. Floor plans can include a dig, an excavation, a treasure find, or a parade, all of which can be landscaped and further filled in by stories, signs, lighting, and sound design.

Come on Down!

Adults walk just as they drive, by looking ahead. But children look down, noticing mystical drawings in sidewalk cracks, treasures on the ground, changes in sounds and life that they pass over. Kids are drawn to floors on which they may easily bend down to investigate. Moving art instruction to the floor indicates a respect for children's creative interests. It acknowledges an understanding of the magical powers of floors that allow kids to relax, to let their imaginations interact with the floor surface. Building on children's natural interests, we can further build an appreciation for the richness of the many floors we daily traverse.

PILLOW ARTISTS

My daughter Ilona was born weighing 7 pounds, 12 ounces. I can tell you our children's birth weights because they are inscribed on their pillows. Grandma Ruth created a wonderful pillow for each child's birth. Our history can be deciphered from treasured pillows, handed down through generations. In the past, family members demonstrated their art on handcrafted pillows, with appliqués, petit point designs, or weavings celebrating weddings, births, and other occasions for which we now buy Hallmark cards. As our art class sorts through my pillows, children speak of making their own as presents and to celebrate special occasions. For children, who make art as a gift for special people in their lives and don't view art as a business, this traditional family art has great appeal.

Few objects are closer to children or possess more magical qualities than pillows. They donate their tooth, only to find a stash of cash in the morning under their pillow. This magical mailbox is also said to help absorb learning, so children insert their vocabulary words in their pillowcase to sleep on at night. Of course, pillows have wings to fly through dreams, and they are comforting and protective as we travel. Pillows can become important canvases for children to log nighttime journeys. In our art class, we create unusual pillows, share pillow dreams, and tell pillow stories which are recorded in a pillow book—and on the following pages.

Building with Pillows

There always seem to be more pillows on a child's bed than on anyone else's. All the pillows may not be necessary for sleeping, but they are essential for children's many construction projects erected over the bed site. Forts made of pillows may frame one bed, while towers rise from another. Pillows are children's earliest soft play blocks from which fantastic architectural ideas are created. Children stack pillows into magnificent mountains and valleys to conduct extensive army maneuvers, invite space landings, or set up a challenging terrain for off-road vehicles. Pillows are set up as cribs for bedtop nurseries or as desks for teddy bears and dolls to play school.

An art room should invite children to build and design with everything around them. To expand children's natural inclinations to build with all kinds of objects, we construct with school supplies such as erasers, pencils, rulers, and books. The contents of lunch boxes are opened for construction work, and umbrellas visiting the class on rainy days are inviting to building crews. Our class steamer trunk is always overflowing with pillows available to construction workers. Soft landscapes are built for soft trains to traverse. Pillows become playhouses for fast-food figures, and legendary pillow cities are the combined effort of individual pillow architects displaying visionary models.

Traveling with Pillows

It was a tradition. Trips in our family started at dawn, and we packed the night before. Packing was always supervised by the children who made sure their seats were properly set up for the journey. Most important, besides claiming a good spot, was the selection of travel pillows. Our children set them up for easy conversion from sleeping, to eating, to daytime activities. Travel companions such as dolls or stuffed animals got their own pillows. By the time we left, the house was emptied of pillows, and passengers were so well padded that airbags were overkill.

In the art class, we design travel pillows with supply pockets, handles, and Velcro for easy assembly. Children have created pillow tables for comfortable car rides, with compartments for snacks, art supplies, and changeable game-board covers. One side of the pillow table can be for sleeping, the other side for writing, complete with a stationery pocket. A young pillow designer in our class envisions a pillow with offspring—different sizes for parents, children, pets, and dolls, all inflatable and fitting into a small travel case. The tiniest pillow of the set becomes the driver's key chain.

Pillow Toys

My daughter Ana used to craft what she called "pillow dolls," each with unique facial features and wonderful hairstyles and clothing. Children frequently use pillows as cribs and playpens for stuffed animals and dolls. Our children often borrowed the large foam cushions from our couch to fence in horses, make a helicopter landing pad, or raise sturdy walls for a playhouse—furnished, of course, with the rest of the pillows from the couch. Pillows from the bed and from the living room converged on the floor. Children cast their pillows in different roles, creating a cake, pizza for a picnic, or seats on a skateboard.

The art class pillow container is never short of browsers. Our classroom's trash can, mounted on a pillow, became a large cement mixer truck. Other pillows have worn firefighter ladders or ridden atop a broomstick as a hobby horse. Commercial quality rubber bands, ribbons, duct tape, and other fasteners are made available for pillow sculpting, instantly turning a lumpy pillow into an expressively wrinkled dragon or an unusual backpack. Children couple pillows to make trains carrying toy riders. They equip pillows with moveable parts to create an amusement park ride. Children who create soft toys out of pillows are fascinated by the works of adult soft-form sculptors like Claes Oldenburg.

Pillow Furnishing and Design

After renting a movie, children design a home theater. A quick survey of the house is required to select pillows for seating sections on the floor. Children must have been the original inventors of beanbag chairs and soft home furnishings. A playhouse under the table or a clubhouse in a box would not be complete without a handsome selection of pillows to furnish it. Children's play space is the floor, and pillows are their official furniture. On the art class floor we continue to investigate soft-furniture designs with combinations of pillows and stuffed trash bags. Children use classroom chairs as a favorite armature to shape clusters of soft forms over them.

Just as adults move furniture around in the home to explore new configurations, children rearrange pillows to explore new design ideas in the living environment. Our family pillow collection stands proudly next to the many pillows our children made with Mom's sewing machine and excavated fabric scraps. Every piece of furniture in our home was made softer, and the rooms more colorful, with pillows that were constantly on the move. Pillows are a favorite household item to teach design because they allow for the testing of design ideas in a living space. Adults need to notice and encourage children's home redecorations. Moving pillows around can also become an important art room design game. Children construct many pillows in our class and arrange them on the floor, over chairs, and in displays on a bright orange couch.

Pillow Portraits and Pillow Figures

By placing hands inside the pillowcase and squeezing its perimeters, children animate and give great expression to a pillow. They notice the folds, wrinkles, and shadows in the "indoor rocks," and discover faces in them as they often do with the hard outdoor forms. Moving pillows before a mirror, or a video camera, or following pillows' rich shadows before a light source, rehearses the human qualities children ascribe to the pillow. Pillow plays also provide a wealth of figure studies for an art class. Molding figures from a single pillow, or putting together a string of pillows, creates unusual action figures.

In changing bed linen, our kids always loved to be in charge of pillow dressing. They virtually climbed into the pillowcase, wearing it as a headdress, mask, or body suit, all the while performing inside. In art room investigations, pillows have been transformed into wearable art such as hats, slippers, or soft vests. Discovering faces in pillows or creating figures from them are important artistic visions to practice.

Pillow Canvases

Some children treat their pillows as bulletin boards without pushpins. Others use them as a canvas for text. We have seen writings, and even an entire diary, inscribed over a child's pillow. Some children use pillows as picture galleries and feature portraits of family and friends. Evening pillows designed by children have flashlights, tissues, and other nighttime accessories in strategically placed pockets. My daughter Ana checked any old garment to be discarded in our home, looking for unusual buttons and pockets to be used in future pillow designs. She made shirts into pillows with dazzling buttons—and pockets, of course. Her art form was made possible by an early introduction to the sewing machine, a very exciting tool for any art room.

Some of the great artworks of our time may be in the form of illustrated children's sheets, sleeping bags, and pillowcases. Collecting, making, and playing with pillows and children's illustrated pillowcases suggest wonderful art lessons. These activities open up a new understanding of what art is and what it could be. A great art lesson should inspire new thinking about art: Could art be something to sleep on? Could a canvas be soft and fluffy? Could art be displayed on a couch?

PLAYHOUSE ARTISTS

To solve a case of the missing shoes, Ana's room always came under surveillance. Sometimes the entire shoe rack was commandeered and reincarnated as elegantly furnished high-rise apartments. There were young ladies who lived in my shoe. Fast-food figures were found as squatters in my loafers, and Barbies camped out in my dress shoes.

Entering school, my daughter could have qualified as an experienced builder and designer, having an extensive resume of furnishing and remodeling play spaces. Before she was 8, Ana had already moved into many unfurnished playhouses, building them with storage units, garment bags, her deceased fish Alfonzo's aquarium, and, of course, shoe racks. Children's inventions go far beyond track housing or Ethan Allen furniture; they foreshadow the most innovative ideas in building forms and interior designs.

Children's art is improvising with interesting containers and finding places in a home that suggest an enticing dwelling. Ana liked to move into our night table with her dolls, always seeking her own place. A drawer left open was a balcony, while others were furnished with ashtray Jacuzzis and soap-tray cots. In the space between twin beds, she built domed playhouses with pillows, sheets, and blankets. Children's tent designs are unique art forms, important to re-visit in the art room. During a dinner party at our house if you inadvertently stretched your feet under the dining room table, you might find an active playhouse beneath. In homes across the country, under tables, beds, and on shelves, luxury hotels and apartments are furnished and decorated.

Kids admire and collect living homes: birds' nests, wasps' nests, and tunnel dwellings beneath the ground. Natural openings in a tree or bush are discovered by clubhouse developers, who find ways to build with leaves, rocks, and twigs as furnishings. Great tree homes are not built by the

Berenstain Bears, but by children who lift playhouse artistry above the ground. How many toolsheds in backyards have been "borrowed" by kids who bring out the TV, card table, and snacks in order to furnish it as their playhouse? Most children have owned many summer homes on the beach, in the mountains, or by a pool where they wrap beach towels around chairs and arrange comfortable inflatables inside their towel tents. Children search for interesting parcels and views for playhouses on which to site pocket-sized to life-sized play spaces. In turn, children's playhouse activities are an inspired foundation for art room architecture and interior design practice.

Collecting Playhouses

Children are surprised that their art teacher collects playhouses. The great American art of classic playhouses are curated in my art room and appreciated by children who play in them. A vintage doll house is a way to give meaning to historic architecture and furnishing styles. We look at the Fisher-Price barn, school, and garage. We study Barbie's vintage "suitcase" plane, yacht, and RV. Polly Pockets are represented by such pieces as Polly's book, locket, pencil case, and home in a backpack. We look at the imaginative Curious George's tree house, Peewee's playhouse, and the Star Trek command room. We set up in playhouses that examine aspects of the environment, such as the Micro Machines service station or the Playskool dog-grooming parlor and ice cream stand. Our imaginary collection includes the Smurf Village and others based on films and television shows. The ready-made playhouse selection in our art room demonstrates great three-dimensional illustration and sculptural inventing, packed into beautiful cases by obscure artists, uncelebrated by Caldecott Medals.

It is fun to have a new box of crayons, but it is often more liberating to work with a set already broken in. This is also true of flea market playhouses that have missing parts and are in need of architectural restoration. I am always scouting for used playhouses for our art room that need to be refilled and redecorated by child designers. I look for nondescript playhouses that leave room for invention. Working in a ready-made playhouse, a handyman's special, or a computer simulation needs to be accompanied by experiences of building your own structure; selecting a container, modeling a facade, partitioning interiors, creating and arranging furnishings, making scores of complex artistic decisions.

A Unique Art

Over fields of carpets and grasses young children build sanctuaries for their figures and toys. This play becomes focused in a more compact environment inside a playhouse. All kinds of stimulating containers with unusual spaces can serve as abstractions for playhouses in the art class. From designing shelters for themselves and surrogate toys, children expand to designing public environments, planetariums, museums, and airports. Playhouses modeled by kids are based on experiences and interior investigations. In the art room, students are exposed to architectural models, important pieces of furniture art, and the works of other designers. We offer a unique design practice in school, where students meet clients, deal with "specs" and budgets, and invest in words and sketches the concepts found through playful investigation.

Art class experiences build on a fruitful life in playhouses and build connections between children's increasing interests in the world. Developing environmental awareness is enhanced by children's own environmental creations. A playhouse is a complete environmental art, requiring complex thinking, seeing, and understanding of relationships between exterior and interior, form and background, small details and the design of the house as a whole. Playhouse graduates develop a feeling for spaces, a sense of being in control of the environment and of being a contributor to the world.

Playhouse Inventors

With so many ponies, cars, fast-food and action figures to house and feed, no wonder kids are constantly searching for the most unusual object to move into. One child suggests a playhouse made from the giant shoes of basketball star Shaquille O'Neal. Thinking about possibilities is as important as building or playing in a playhouse. Mobile home players create living quarters on a circus train, a rock star's luxury tour bus, or in the leading lady's trailer on a movie set. Experiences such as designing in a pocket or in an eyeglass case lead to broad architectural ideas for designing a playhouse from a hat box, a suitcase on wheels, or an expandable tackle box featuring many floors and rooms. Planning homes inside a clear hanging garment bag can suggest discussions for other hanging playhouses. Designing apartments inside a box inspires students to make connections with the many containers in which we live, drive, or store things. When playhouse dreaming is encouraged, students envision new worlds of underwater housing, portable homes to wear, or homes that move with us.

Dreaming of Your Own Home

Finding the perfect house, remodeling, or building one's dream home begins in childhood. Even kids who have their own room search to establish their own play spaces. Before a long car ride, it was important for Ana to know who sat where, so that the traveling "apartment" could be suitably furnished the night before with an extra shelf and added table space. When arriving at the hotel room, our children always wanted to know which was their space, which drawer could they have to rest their dolls and create a suitable setting for them? From their playhouses our children grew up to decorate their dorm rooms and first apartments. An interest in homes and furnishings, making decorating a lifelong creative expression, begins in the playhouse. I recall Ana as a teenager spending hours looking at dollhouse furniture catalogues and spending a good portion of her first European trip going from one Ikea store to another, looking for accessories for her room. Those who have had a solid experience in playhouse art will always cherish the artistic moments of altering and rearranging the canvas of their homes, gardens, and communities.

The art room can carry playhouse dreams to new heights. We design our own innovative furniture and create catalogues for them. Learning to see furniture possibilities in everything leads to such high-style inventions as the famous banana couch. We write and picture interior design magazine spreads featuring our interior creations. Only the most unique containers will do, as we begin to plan our homes and consider different sites and landscaping plans. We look at the most modern Italian commercial lighting catalogues and study the incredible details and designs of stores in the mall. From playhouse designs, we expand our art room practice to store interiors, designing play fast-food places and ice cream parlors. Celebrated contemporary furnishings and architecture enters the art room through magazines and books, as students learn to speak the language of art deco, vintage, and arts and crafts.

An Open House

Video game enthusiasts often miss growing up in playhouses. Other children only experience creating in playhouses designed by adults. Contemporary playhouses are overaccessorized, leaving few options for players. Others are circumscribed by the fantasy of the film or television show they illustrate. Art classes are the important places to learn all about playhouses, to create one's own, and to conduct design experiments. For young artists growing up, playhouses act as a treasure chest for collections and creations. They are a game board to practice design, a showcase for ideas, a second home, a place in which to hide or find adventure. Playhouses help children contemplate how to improve upon a world defined by adults.

Future architects, interior designers, furniture designers, landscape architects, and set designers meet and rehearse in playhouses. In a playhouse kids groom their love for living in beautiful places, for collecting furniture and accessories, for appreciating architectural details. In a playhouse children can take charge of and fine-tune the visual world. In these plays children can form lifelong artistic tastes and interests in arranging fabrics, colors, and beautiful objects. From these magical homes children will carry the skills to visualize ideas in scale models, to arrange things in three-dimensional settings, to solve construction and environmental problems. Playhouses are as important as play blocks in building design skills and artistic understandings.

3

Art in Childhood Events

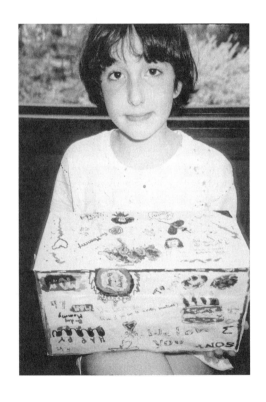

BIRTHDAY ARTISTS

Ana's Birthday Events

Disappointment, Age 7. A group of happy children are tucked away in the back row of the local fast-food restaurant. Wearing an ill-fitting clown mask, our table cleaner appears as the clown. Everyone is crowned in advertising gold, and favors are solemnly dispersed. In the crowded eatery, we guardedly party among a sea of annoyed glances. A disappointed child talks about how much fun her next birthday will be.

A Celebration, Age 8. We have a party room this year, a bunker without windows under the bleachers of the roller skating rink. The converted dressing room is decorated with partially inflated balloons. We are number 9 on the birthday list of 22 celebrants whose names are listed on the decorated chalkboard. Soon our cake enters, dressed in sporting goods advertisements, with matching plates. The server reminds us not to take food out of the bunker and to leave on schedule. The next anxious celebrants are already banging on the door. Our guests eat and quickly meld into the circle of skaters. A painless birthday for busy parents.

Partying, Age 9. The "Party Palace" at the ice center was under construction. The fading birthday sign above the door lost its glow among announcements for skating lessons and the latest in skate shop bargains. We are on our own, the final party of an evidently busy day. Mom brought the party pack—plates, cups, tablecloth, and matching favors from the latest Disney release. Gifts were torn open, as my wife took down vital information for each thank-you note. We had planned to play creative games next, but the kids wanted to go back to skate. My daughter Ana's printed birthday award from the ice center read, "Tell your friends about the fun of an ice skating party."

Revelation, Age 10. This year Ana wanted to have her birthday party in my art room. Children wore cool rubber slippers to the birthday party. The party took place around several water-filled play pools, where party guests were imaginarily transported on decorated floats they built on their rubber slippers. The birthday party on the water had every sea creature humming. Party decorators designed festive water canvases, detailed by fall leaves, Silly String drawings, Magic Sand sculptures, and tub-block towers. On the magic canvas of water, an inflatable cake floated, and presents on foam trays were pulled by tugboats.

The birthday party in the art room became the talk of Ana's school and changed birthday celebrations in her life. It is also the story of how birthday party designs ended up as part of my art class repertoire. We play birthdays in the art room regularly—fantastic birthdays that seldom occur in children's lives. Have the art class birthday experiences had an impact on the fast-food and roller-rink birthday industry? I hope so, because more children in our schools are asking for creative events, held at home, that involve the creative dreams of parents and children.

In spite of the sad diary above, when we recently looked at our albums of birthdays, our kids remembered them as happy occasions. After all, their parties were identical to their friends': these were the parties they went to and asked for. In designing our family birthday album, I saved and used the most unusual cards, fun shopping bags, illustrated plates, and gift wraps from each event. I looked for signs of beauty within the party-mold circuit. After each birthday party, our kids planned and fantasized about the next. I took notes on their great ideas and included them in the birthday book. Their party visions were always a cut above the event just completed.

Art Class Birthdays

It's Livia's birthday! Mom and Dad came to class: Dad sits on the floor narrating his PowerPoint presentation of Livia growing up, and Mom shares the family album. Livia's classmates become presents, acting out who they are, and giving themselves to Livia. "I am a toy that keeps on giving," says one gift. "I am a basket filled with kittens," says another. Our birthday girl is presented with a crown to which everyone added a sticker jewel. Every child would like to sit next to her this day; Livia is the star of our art class. Parents invited to art room birthdays make creative contributions to a memorable event.

We also invite other guests. A big furry blue monster with a red nose celebrates his birthday. The children are required to hold their noses because of the strange smells coming from pizza boxes surrounding the monster. The monster is obviously on a very unusual diet; only artistic children could dream up and create such yucky pizza toppings. Sitting high and proud on phone books are the children's teddy bears all dressed-up for the monster's party. Their owners had eagerly sifted the art room fabric trunks and created hats, jewelry, stylish suspenders, and cool sunglasses for their teddy bear guests. Children are dress-up artists who celebrate a Halloween spirit in the art room all year round.

We celebrate a horse's birthday and extend invitations to everyone's My Little Pony horses. We design extra-long, intricate straws to funnel colorful party drinks into festively decorated stalls. Students decorate pink spoons from the ice cream parlor with pony patterns. As part of the birthday celebration, we fill ice cream cones with painted Ping-Pong balls and embellished cotton toppings. Existing containers are often creatively filled during children's play acts. Students roll newspapers and shape them in the form of presents, and everyone is asked to guess what could be inside these improvised sculptures.

Perhaps the most unusual and certainly the quietest birthday celebrants in our art room have been the pet rocks children collected. It was difficult to determine their exact ages, but they were undoubtedly our oldest birthday guests. No paint or mascara was spared to make each rock look its best, and everyone worked with imagination to construct the hundreds of candles needed to adequately celebrate the rocks' ages. The rocks received fine, hand-crafted presents such as pillows, luggage, and cars made from Legos. At the party, we watched performances by "rock stars," using jeweled, play microphones. Party planning is children's art that includes the creation of party themes, the design of celebrations, and festive environments.

Children's talent is to decorate every surface in a room, every object and guest. The most unusual birthday cakes are created by junior pastry chefs. Part of their art is the design of fantasy foods and imaginative party plays. The biggest pastry we made was "Sam's cake," crafted from flexible crate dividers I hauled from a Sam's store. Working from inside this playhouse-like structure, children stacked and folded incredible cake sculptures. Flowers and shaving cream, surveyor's flags and plastic jewelry were on the decorators' palettes. Tasty pieces of "cake" were symbolically cut and displayed over garnished cardboard place mats, with customized plates and utensils attached with Velcro for portability. Decorating cakes and cupcakes and creating real or imaginary food designs are practiced by children from the time they are able to mount the kitchen counter. Art class party designers practice mixing colors for floral arrangements, in make-believe drinks, and by shaking salads in clear plastic containers. Children, of course, are the final authority on the design of their own party favors.

The Art Teacher's Birthday

Don't come in costume for this party. You will find your plain white paper poncho at the door. This outfit is transformed by children dancing and rhythmically crossing drawing tools around each other. The art teacher's birthday is an art occasion, new and different each year. Last year, students squirted water over giant birthday greetings that were drawn with watercolor markers. The cards covered an entire classroom wall. Yes, I get great birthday presents—someone's favorite found object attached to a card or something special a student creates. During the party, we "bake" and decorate sculptural "cookies." And old party games like Twister receive a new twist as we sketch body shadows or add bare hand and foot painting to the game board.

"Our art teacher will put on the funny hat we made him. He'll climb inside our cake tower." Birthdays change our relationship by providing a unique opportunity to have fun with students. Try it and you will find responses to every art lesson will be more playful and experimental. My birthday is not an art assignment; it is a time that students and I celebrate art by making things together. There are few people I would rather share my birthdays with than the kids. My art students are the most interested and excited about the subject, the most devoted experts. Sharing birthdays with students is also an important way of sharing one's art life, creativity, collections, and art interests.

I bring in presents I bought for myself such as a vintage toy ice cream truck. I share what my family has given me—an illustrated children's book, an old lunch box. I tell the class of presents I dream about. The class enjoys stories and pictures of childhood presents, like my first bike in bright metallic green with white tires, a combination scooter with a running board and a column fitted with a seat and pedal. Birthdays are occasions for art teachers to share their wealth of visual interests. With each birthday we celebrate in class comes the lesson that the art teacher is often interested in many of the same things the students are—and that our inspirations can have common sources.

The Final Balloon

To make inventive and playful art in class, young artists have to know and trust the art teacher. They get to know an art teacher by celebrating together. Birthdays build bonds of common interests; they yield opportunities to make art together, to share visions and inspirations.

For educational evaluation, I advise young teachers to picture a lesson they are about to teach and consider if the lesson will be as exciting as a child's best birthday party. But how good are children's best birthday parties in today's society? Are they close to kids' birthday party fantasies, the parties kids envision and dream about all year? The art class has to be the place for constructing the parties today's kids wish they could have.

PARADE ARTISTS

Children as Parade Artists

Inside a multilevel plastic tote lies a fun part of my childhood. On the top level of the clear container are my Hungarian plaster soldiers. As a child, I painted colorful uniforms on them, but no one told me that was art. I set them up in precise marching formations, like the military day parades I had to attend in Hungary as a Young Pioneer. On the bottom of the tote are my first American figures, plastic and flexible, but hard to force into precise configurations because each seemed to have its own preset joints.

After my first Thanksgiving Day parade in the United States, I was so excited that I could not wait to get home and get out all my toys. I had a different view of what a parade could be, and it changed everything. I used formations of play figures more like a celebration, cheerleading the new freedom that I felt. Replaying events on a small scale, choreographing rows of action figures, and rehearsing casts of fast-food figures are unique children's expressions.

Children are inspired by the public attention paid to parades and use the form to advertise their ideas. After learning about endangered species in school, my daughter decided to drum up support for the cause in the neighborhood. She tied together her brother's skateboards and arranged her stuffed animals for the ride. Each creature pulled in front of our house carried a sign and message relating to endangered species. Some of our recent art room parades, complete with marchers and floats, were about such diverse themes as "Save the Whales" and "A Celebration of Unrecognized American Artists." The latter parade celebrated artists who design hubcaps. Children marched in a lively end-of-class parade with plates and pot covers on which they had drawn original hubcap designs.

Since children like to play school at home, I ask volunteers to present a lesson to the art class. In those lessons, a parade is a frequently selected medium for bringing students together to celebrate art and art themes.

Idea Parade

In search of an inspiration for my painting, I take a morning walk. To find their ideas in the art class, my students join a parade. Since kids at home use active playing to make their plans, we don't sit waiting for ideas in our art class; we get out, parading with our objects, looking for new impressions. Today our school hallway is bustling with children pulling fragments of pink insulation boards, brightly colored detergent boxes, fruit crates, and unusual foam trays with string connections. What are these flatbed vehicles, and why are kids pulling them in the hallway?

Before we start an art project, we take our material finds and selections for a walk or a ride, testing them and actively engaging them. Students love to bring and share specially stamped "collectors bags" to class. They dig through their bags searching for interesting object and material finds for each art class. Our art lesson does not start with lectures or specific instructions on how to make a parade float. We start by sharing our object finds in an active way, sorting, stacking, and, of course, placing a handle, wheel, or string in front of an object to allow it to be pulled. Students engaged in active home-style playing don't need to be told how to make a float.

Parades Celebrating Art

When teachers come to pick up students from the art room, children at the quietest tables usually get to line up first. The classroom teacher just wants silent lines at the door, yet the children often fight to be near the front of the line so they can show their teacher their art. Kids who make art at home cannot wait to share it, for everyone to see it, especially the important people in their lives. But at school, as pieces of art are proudly carried to the classroom door, jubilant artists are not always greeted by a receptive audience. Classroom teachers more often inquire about the children's behavior in the art room than about their art. Busy quieting down the excitement, teachers often ignore newly created art and sometimes demand that it be put away or kept out of sight.

Instead of organizing dutiful lineups picked from the quietest tables, I lead students in a parade to make sure their art is celebrated and not ignored. Spiraling around tables, my children proudly hold up their art. The teachers picking up their children can hardly ignore the art on parade as it is heading toward the door. Just as adult artists party at gallery openings celebrating their work, we commemorate and share our art with a lively parade at the end of each class. Parades animate artworks, and the sculptures and paintings children have made come alive in their hands. Unlike critiques at the end of an art class, parades build confidence and pride in the artists' accomplishments.

Art History Parade

After looking at a great American century for pull-toy sculpture, including a 1936 Fisher-Price elephant, a yellow 1940s Slinky Bronco Buster, and a 1957 Gong Bell's Noah's Ark, the children hope to take art history for a spin. The students try on vintage parade marshals' hats, and their drum rolls dust off my antique drum collection. The parade begins.

Parades pull, push, and carefully animate items from my antique children's toy collection. Children develop a love for beautiful antiques by dusting and polishing items in a family display case or by handling and trying on precious items found in an attic trunk. During an art history lesson on children's umbrellas, students get to twirl and parade fine examples from the twentieth century. Every art lesson should be fun. It should break with school routines and awaken the artists' minds. Pull toys and children's umbrellas were not designed for the quiet contemplation given to wall hangings; they were designed to spark imaginative plays. A parade is a perfect way to engage students directly with these historical classics—a parade that leaves the classroom and brings a smile to everyone we meet in the hallway. Students can even take umbrella parades outdoors where the umbrellas' richly colored fabrics are seen in natural light. By using parades to highlight beautiful art from the past, I place art in children's hands to form lasting memories and appreciation for all artworks of the past.

Parades from Life Events

When the circus came to town, my daughter Ana was ready to decorate her red wagon and dress stuffed animals as performers. In wedding plays, she marched chess pieces in stately parades down a checkered aisle. In our art classes we also celebrate special events with parades, such as the Olympic Games. During Olympic week, the children crafted amazing trophy sculptures and celebrated their art by parading it before waving fans. I know the mark of a "good" teacher is how quietly their children march in hallway lines, but perhaps we can make an exception for marching artists showing off art works. After all, children are not inmates, and it is appropriate to expound on the excitement of art. Parading children who proudly wave their unique works can change the somber climate of any school.

Parades: The Great American Art

Some people try to ride all the great roller coasters. I set out to witness the best parades, from Pasadena's celebration of the Rose Bowl to the great Macy's Thanksgiving Day Parade in New York. In the study of American art, I enjoy showing the parade footage I took myself. During Thanksgiving week, I ask my students to watch the Macy's parade and return with souvenir drawings, an album of their favorite segments.

I have witnessed many great parades over the years, but I still get excited when children design parades. In art class parades students set up scores of play figures, taking charge of customizing, choreography, casting, and directing. We create found-object floats and use instruments or synthesizers to accompany our parade. We empty our trunk of flashlights to light the videotaped event. Children focus their daily home search on finding interesting objects to decorate and carry in a parade. Wearing costumes and masks from duct tape, children hold signs and pull floats, parading by every part of the school. For many forms of children's action art, a bulletin board display is inappropriate. Parades allow children who are action-art makers to take on active roles in presenting their work.

As the Parade Passes

I stand in the grandstand of a school hallway with thoughts of wooden soldiers in the *Nutcracker*s of my childhood. I remember other parades that brought joy to my life, including Dorothy keeping step with the Munchkins in *The Wizard of Oz* and Calder's entrance march to his wire circus. (Calder's Circus)

Soon I see our first row of class marchers, wearing elaborately decorated derby bonnets, constructed over plain straw hats. Children carry painted banners, which cover yard signs from a recent election. Next come the floats, rolling on golf-ball wheels, riding on the chassis of remote-controlled cars hidden by decorative skirts. Here comes a tricky car with sunglasses for a windshield. And last come the horses, the stars of our yearly Kentucky Derby Parade. Some were built from cardboard boxes; others are converted broomsticks—all imaginatively uniting unusual found materials for the first time.

For all our parades children suggest floats, decide on instrumentation, and plan marching formations. Wonderful souvenir brochures and video footage save parade memories. There is always excitement in the preparation of a parade, enlivening the search for creative ideas.

GIFT-GIVING ARTISTS

September 11

Helplessly witnessing falling lives and towers, my daughter Ana turned to me and, in response to what she was seeing, said, "Can I give them my teddy bear?" From one kind heart speaking to many, there began an invasion of teddy bears. Within weeks a national network of art teachers was organized, and their students contributed hundreds of soft and comforting creatures, pillows, and dolls. Unlike people, the bears were not afraid to fly and made their journey on the wings of a loving donor, an airline that provided free shipment. At first, small shipments arrived, but soon large numbers of packages, outgrowing the dormitory of my daughter Ilona, who was receiving and distributing them. Ilona unpacked the weary travelers and called me after each package arrived. She was deeply moved by the stirring sculptures and the children's messages on handmade tags.

Making gifts for children affected by the terrorist attacks of September 11 deeply motivated children to create an unprecedented volume of powerful art. Unlike art assignments, these were works to which children were deeply committed. They had the feeling that their art could make a difference. An art lesson can inspire children's goodness, their desire to help and contribute to people's lives. Artworks made for a children's hospital, hospice, or for distribution by the Red Cross give a noble dimension to school art. All artists need an important commitment for great art to be made. The reasons children make art are complex, but the notion of children making art to give something of themselves to important causes and people in their lives, is a powerful motive. Children are proud to make beautiful things that are appreciated by others. They learn to value the power of the handmade and, in turn, to prize artworks made for them. An art class can be an invitation to become a gift-giving artist.

Art Gifts for Mom and Dad

It was not Valentine's Day, but I proudly walked around the school with an immense red heart hanging from my neck to my knees. On the heart, sparkling glue-gun sketches danced around family momentos under the headline "Happy Anniversary, Mom and Dad." The wearable greeting card was rooted in our family tradition of making gifts for special occasions. As children, we have felt the satisfaction of giving our art as a gift. There is nothing like it! As an adult painter, no art sale compares.

I never asked my children to make art gifts. It may have helped to see the cards and invitations I printed for family occasions. Making art gifts must have a long cultural history that artists young and old tap into. The red-painted heart was the largest art gift I received, but I saved even the small cards and other handmade gifts my children made. I value each art present and frequently show them to my art classes for inspiration. The following items are part of this collection.

Painting Gifts

After purchasing a new art book, my daughter Ilona would make unique covers as surprise presents for me. As a young art teacher, I was surprised to learn that dust jackets were routinely removed and thrown away by libraries. I cultivated library contacts to save many wonderful book jackets. Stacks of covers fill my studio and art room, and children are always welcome to browse. Book jackets became coveted in my art class, and each shipment from the library was carefully scrutinized by students looking for the "best" of a new crop.

Instead of greeting cards, our kids gave framed art, with the advantage of receiving more honored display sites than a refrigerator door. In my studio I always stocked interesting flea market picture frames, and my children eagerly made paintings as gifts to fill them. It did not take long for the idea to be exported to school and to have all types of plastic frames used in art class gift making. Children know that the "it's for you" type of art has great rewards.

Wearable Gifts

My wife Laura likes to be scattered with jewels. Fortunately her safe is constantly replenished by the jewelry fairy. Shapely cut playing card corners, nail-polished slides, and feather-decorated stamps are mounted to pin backs by our children for their trend-setting mom. The precious pin gifts led to other gifts such as earrings, bracelets, and even an old belt refurbished with hanging found-object charms. This mom's set of keys can never be mistaken, since no one has a key chain sculpted from genuine soda-can pull tabs. Our children's wearable gift production was fueled by my wife's reports of colleagues who could not wait to preview her daily walk-by gallery and wished they knew the jewelry fairy. Consequently I never have a shortage of wearable gifts to parade before my art classes in recognition of a unique kid's art.

Personalized Gifts

Adults stuck in line enviously watch the free-floating post office artists. Kids crisscross the line of people and find interesting postal forms under the pedestal tables. They ask for a pen to make me a bookmark. I happily add the new piece to my collection, which includes bookmarks made from movie tickets, business cards, and ticket stubs found at the airport. For each of these gifts I recall where the canvas was found, the art it inspired, and the circumstances of creation. Ana's bookmarks are signed and inscribed with a loving dedication.

Food always tastes better on personal place mats. I have eaten meals on puzzle pieces, drawings over TripTiks, or family photos framed by flower petals—all carefully laminated and presented as gifts. Children regularly contribute new styles to this table art. Home art production expanded when our children discovered the joys of making useful objects as gifts. Our children presented personalized name plates for Mom, and custom mouse pads and decorated mugs for my desk at work. Art for use in home or office spaces demonstrates the ability of an art gift to beautify our life and surroundings.

Gift Wrapping

Receiving a child's gift is a ceremony of unpeeling layers of art. Unwrapping begins with the painted bag, then moves to the hand-stamped gift wrap, decorated tags, handmade card, and finally the starring present. Each gift is a carefully crafted ensemble art with matching balloons, cards, bags, and wrapping supplies. For young children, it is not a gift if their art is not a part of the gift. Invitations to a birthday party lead to a decorating artist fever. Gift artists say, "I want to wrap it! I want to decorate the ribbons and the box!" The cover, the wrapping, and box become personal canvases for a child's free-flowing sticker-stamper-ribbon art. After an unwrapping ceremony at home, I painstakingly rewrap everything, so that the event can be authentically replayed in my art class. Students watch any gift opening with great interest. They appreciate the work of fellow gift artists and the tribute to their art form. All artwork heading home from our class is appropriately gift-wrapped and tagged for someone special. A popular American shopping bag and wrapping paper art display in our class is constantly open to new student finds.

Art Gifts for My Students

No one leaves my class empty-handed. There are special gifts for everyone. Recently students have left the class with such items as pressed fall leaves, beautiful postage stamps, their pick of countertop samples, miniature paintings I made to hang in playhouses, and my famous Sculpey clay action figures in custom grab bags. Kids know "good stuff," and art teachers have a feel for it too. We know that exciting collections, fun forms, and handmade presents will be appreciated and treasured by kids. The gift of art materials, an item to start a collection, and even art ideas and inspiration can be offered in sample forms. Sharing the art teacher's collections and art gifts, letting students choose the art gift and take it home, has the potential of reaching the instincts, hearts, and pockets of young artists.

Art Gifts Students Share

We know how much kids enjoy taking home artworks. We can also encourage the pleasures of sharing their art and giving art to each other in class.

Pressing hard on the carbon paper, children make copies of their drawing for everyone at their table. Using imaginary personal messaging channels, artworks, like flowers, are delivered worldwide—well, at least throughout the art room. A community chest holds art gifts such as handmade sketchbooks, printed doorknob signs, painted switchplates, decorated shoelaces, high-performance drinking straws, and customized pencils that students made and contributed to share with others. Playful channels of exchanging gifts promulgate the habit of making art as a gift for friends and classmates. Giving artworks to classmates who appreciate it can feel as good as taking artwork home.

Of Love and Art

When our children were young, my wife made pillow dolls for each of them. I am not sure if there is a direct link, but my oldest daughter Ilona, an artist, just completed a gallery show in Cincinnati of her pillow paintings displayed in a 1950s living room environment. Ilona and my wife often talk about the dolls that my daughter still has. Gifts of art are often recalled as a significant moment in life by their maker and the recipient.

Children can be encouraged to tailor an art project, to make things they know someone needs and would enjoy in class or at home. A third-grade boy lovingly painted a blanket for his sister's dolls. For an upcoming cruise, a child created hand-printed luggage tags for his parents. The habit of giving personalized and handmade things with pride tends to create powerful motivation for young artists. Unlike the adult art world with its sharp division between art and craft, children make art gifts to be both beautiful and useful. Giving art gifts to each other demonstrates art as communication and creates an awareness of an audience and the importance of a recipient for one's art.

As an officer of the National Art Education Association, I have presided over many awards ceremonies. I cannot describe how moved our members were when we started giving awards sculpted by children, instead of printed certificates. I like to think that the heart of a gift artist resided in each award and that its power was immediately felt by the award recipient. Children have a unique talent of placing great creativity and pride in every gift they make.

Remaking the World, One Object at a Time

HANDWORK ARTISTS

"Orange bumpers, flashing lights, reflectors, cream cheese in the sole—and these shoes cost more than my weekly pay." At the end of a long day at the mall, I stood before a store display of sneakers and recited the outlandish accessories, muttered about the prices. In a consoling way, 9-year-old Ana stood by and said, "Don't worry, Dad, I will make it for you." Later, while resting at home and trying to put the shopping experience behind me, I did not notice Ana busy in her room until I was called for a fitting. Nesting on a green bathroom-sponge sole was a converted shoe box, with painted laces, hooked around colored paper clips. My new shoe had everything: bagel stickers on its sides and sports card toes, rivaling the best in-store models. A child's belief that she can build a "better shoe" is a significant artistic trait and a challenge for art teachers to maintain. Young artists need to feel that they have the power to reshape the world, that everything has not been designed for them by someone else who can build it better.

Lego phones, Lego playhouses, and even a photo of a Lego spy vest decorate my office. Children can build just about anything from Legos. But how are the experiences of Lego graduates used in school? Children in our high-tech generation often don't make things at home and construct only in cyberspace. Computer games, and even the new Lego sets, come with hefty instruction manuals to construct very specific, predetermined forms. Art teachers need to consider the importance of children making things, building by hand, constructing their own objects without formulas or patterns.

One time Ana brought home a tall, slender coat rack, a neighborhood garage sale find. She immediately began to repaint the arms and tape wrap the body before thoughtfully placing it in her room. Children make art that can be placed in their rooms, or art they can wear. Important qualities of young artists are the ability to see possibilities in all kinds of objects and the confidence that they can redesign and make objects more beautiful. We need to pay attention to children's home arts, the art made without teachers or assignments. As I described in Chapter 1, in my teacher-training classes, we visit children's home studios and keep a running inventory of what kids collect, make, and alter to place in their rooms. We find exciting constructions of doorstops, storage boxes, picture frames, and shelves, along with redesigns of chairs, boom boxes, alterations of phones, planters, and lamp shades. All these are valuable clues to children's art.

Young Cabinetmakers

Ana was very excited when her brother received his new cello. Actually, he was excited about the instrument and she about the big, oddly shaped box that held magical possibilities. Ana immediately claimed the box, and to be sure of her ownership, she brought her pillow and moved inside the box for the night, claiming squatter's rights. Early the next morning she set to work sketching ideas and then suspending cardboard shelves from the sides of the container. Each of the five shelves she built into the box were draped in differently patterned wrapping paper. The exterior was treated with stickers and paste-ups of select comics. The new furniture stood proudly next to her desk, displaying collections. Cardboard is children's lumber. In Ana's room, boxes are converted to a playhouse, and a cardboard magazine rack is also resurfaced with comics. Skilled cabinetry artists live in many of the rooms we visit.

Before children are born, their rooms are designed and furnished by parents or decorators. Before children come to school, classrooms are organized by teachers and furnished by professionals. Children learn to fit into these pedetermined spaces and furnishings, instead of being invited to shape their own environment, to select or make the objects in it. Making furnishings and accessories for their room helps kids become contributors, able to change rooms and canvases, small or large. In our art class, we study the history of shelf designs and collect advertisements of the most interesting new furniture ideas. Selections from the art class lumberyard (i.e., cardboard yard) are made into bedside tables, unusual shoe racks, cardboard chairs, and collectors' display cases for class or home use.

Container Artists

Museum visits with children start at the gift shop. During a recent visit, Ana could have bought many things, and I was surprised to find her in the checkout line holding a folded cardboard trash can. "It's for my room; it's triangular with photographs, and it will look great with the others I decorated." We seldom think of children as decorative artists, yet decorating their room and carefully selecting each object for it is their art. On the way home from the museum, Ana sketched out ideas for placing her new trash can. She talked about where it would look best, what I would need to help her move in her room. Children frequently rearrange their "canvas-room," a new setup often motivated by finding, or making, a new object.

Children are inspiring company at yard sales, seeing creative uses for unusual things and describing interesting plans for placing an object. In our classes, I start by setting up classroom flea markets and invite shopping for ideas. Young designers are hired to create special containers and other accessories for the class and children's rooms. We work on the outside and inside of containers such as storage units, jewelry boxes, coin banks, and, of course, trash cans. As designed object history, we study my collection of antique clothes hangers, illustrated tin garbage cans from the 1940s, and the latest in Rubbermaid trash cans.

Portable Art

When invited to shop in town or go for a hike in the park, Ana will ask, "How big is the car, and what can I take with me?" To take along her collections and have room for what may be found, Ana outfitted a Styrofoam liner of a portable cooler with partitions and secret compartments, then decorated it with feathers, stickers, and a fancy ribbon strap. Carefully laid out on a padded lining inside the container are choice rocks, candies, a wasps' nest rolled in cotton, and her wallet, made from a postcard and small envelopes. Children are "take-along artists" who construct portable art works. Children who want to take their art home from class also want to carry it to show the world. Favorite toys have carrying cases, and kids' creations have handles, or string, for carrying and wearing. Children like garments with many pockets, bikes with big luggage racks, and all kinds of shopping bags because children want their important objects with them. As serious collectors, children need to transport their collections and create units to store and display them.

In designing an art lesson, determine if the final product is something that could be pulled, carried, or worn. Our art class designers fabricate pull-toy lunch boxes, rolling collectors' cases, backpacks, pencil cases with secret pockets, dividers, closing devices, and alarms. We hold a class patent on a variety of laptop art centers made for long car rides. Carry-along artists appreciate viewing my collection of children's wallets and vintage lunch boxes. Young artists also enjoy browsing through my trunk of important shopping-bag designs.

Figure Builders

Bread was my special sculpture media as a child. In spite of the frequent shortage of grains and my mother's disapproval of my taking out bread chunks at the dinner table, what choice did a young Hungarian sculptor have without Sculpey clay or Play-Doh? I not only made bread figures, but also trained them to perform, or pose, on my dinner plate. I never associated bread works with real sculpture, with the bronzes in the living room that I polished for my allowance. It was only after I became a parent that I became interested in children's unique ability to discover and work in many unofficial sculpture media. Walking through children's rooms we find an amazing show of magnificently dressed plastic spoons, hair curler dolls with rubber-band appendages, and fancy Q-tips wearing shiny gum-wrapper originals. Children's many handcrafted figures live between collections of dolls, posed action figures, and fast-food characters. Figurative sculptures fill children's rooms and lives, forming significant collections, which are artistically posed, animated, and directed in scenes from space adventures to Barbie aerobics classes.

Understanding the figure is a prerequisite for sculpting and painting it. Children have their own sequence of figure study. They play with toy figures in action setups and posings and recognize and create figures in all kinds of found objects. As figure players, children develop confidence and ease in forming figures out of bread ties, napkins, bottles, or just about anything. In our art class, we turn pencils, erasers, and other school supplies into figures and performance artists. We recognize children's own supply finds, from Scotch tape to foil, rocks to candies, simple combs to complex electronic surplus to form our own figurine cast. Antique dolls, teddy bears, toy robots, and toy soldiers visit our classes and are greeted as an important part of our art heritage.

Building an Ending

We call it the "the year-end roundup" in our family, and I am always glad to help. At the end of the school year, I bring the trash can and wait for the massive tossing of handouts, papers, and tests, which had incredible importance during their time. What the children save and value during this year-end ritual should interest every art teacher. The "boucherie," a detailed butcher store built for French class, and the great stained glass window on cellophane, for social studies, halted our festivities while Ana looked for a suitable place for them in her room. She treasured what was made by hand, on her own, and these would become part of her room's decor. We make our own action figures, backpack designs, and trash cans in our class so that it may become art to keep, important art for children.

PERSONAL-CONTAINER ARTISTS

I call it the "Montessori frisk." It starts during the drive up the circular driveway, as I begin asking for all things that should remain in the car and not be taken to school. Out of pockets come a stream of treasures—collections, toys, street finds—all of which seem to return each morning to refill children's most personal storage places. By the time I round the circular driveway, the front seat where my daughter Ana sat is stacked with sidewalk pieces, trading cards, butterfly wings, small figures, and her baby tooth in a pink purse. Going to school requires leaving behind the things that children play with and dream about the rest of the day.

For my birthday, my daughter Ilona, now a teaching colleague, made me an art teacher's apron with one hundred pockets. It is a big hit with children who not only like to store things in pockets, but also take inventory inside friendly pockets. Ana refuses to part with the pockets on outgrown garments, so she cuts them out to create purses and pocketbooks on her mom's sewing machine. Children never tire of looking through parents' pockets, wallets, or handbags, but as they get older they face less acceptance and cooperation from adults. My collection of vintage purses, old handbags or pocketbooks, and unusual lunch boxes are popular art room shopping sites. Being able to look through someone's pockets or pocketbooks represents a special relationship, the trust of sharing a personal space and its secrets. Purses and wallets are also places of entertainment. I love to observe serious archeologists—children on a bus, train, or in a doctor's waiting room—deeply engrossed in excavating a mother's handbag.

When children are required to leave their personal things at home, personal containers become important places of refuge. At school, lunch boxes act as private safes for objects and memories brought from home that adults cannot touch. Children have many secret places at home, in which they arrange and display their things. When children's objects are not welcome in school and few school spaces can be freely touched and explored, then lunch boxes, pencil cases, wallets, and schoolbags or backpacks become important private spaces and canvases from home, that children can decorate and set up inside. Play and art spaces, such as a drawer, a box, or a canvas, are private places one needs to feel free to explore and exercise creative control over. In the art class art teachers can admire, study, and offer opportunities to include the important "pockets" in children's lives.

Most children start with a great interest in boxes and containers, claiming any unusual box that enters a home. Parents and teachers lovingly plan and furnish children's rooms even before they arrive. Parents often buy clothing for children, leaving only a few items, such as the child's lunch box, pencil case, and schoolbag, for them to select. Children soon remodel or refurbish each official school container inside and out. Children's art is an homage to a box, which they know to be the greatest sculptural invention since the wheel. Children's love of boxes and their unique ability to see possibilities in them is an important resource for our creative studies of personal containers.

Lunch Boxes

A sign advertising my presentation in the lobby of the Dearborn Hilton inquired, "What does this lunch box have to do with Szekely?" I don't know if many of the art teacher participants were aware of my writings about children's lunch boxes, written from the viewpoint of a lunch box collector and as a frequent guest-observer of school cafeterias. Lunch duty may be dreaded words, yet the cafeteria is an extremely instructive place for an art teacher. It is often the only place were children freely talk and act like children. In the cafeteria one can view the best off-Broadway shows without tickets: animated fast-food figures, dancing apple cores, foil-dressed plastic utensils—all performing over lunch box stages. Witness here the rich stashes inside lunch boxes, illuminating the latest in kids' collections and their inventive uses. Lunch boxes become display cases for cafeteria traders. They act as game boards for toys and as toy chests, because taking one's favorite toy carrying case to school is not allowed. Vintage toy carrying cases are currently on display in our art room and discussed as a form of great American art.

In our art class we admire the lunch boxes kids bring to school, including the way they are packed and how the outsides are decorated by their owners. The art room is known to be a safe place to open a lunch box and reveal its secrets. Because of this, we are never short of unusual guest performers—objects to pose, dress, or just show and tell a great story about. Before lunch, handsomely wrapped sculptures can be found inside lunch boxes. After lunch, containers may be lighter, but no less interesting in the packing materials, empty containers, and leftover food shapes inside.

Having examined my collection of lunch boxes, everyone in our art class is proud of their firsthand knowledge of the art history of these containers. We start with turn-of-the-century tin cases and move through the different periods of metal and plastic character boxes to the many contemporary innovations in form and materials. Looking into the future and designing our own lunch boxes is always a fun part of the study. Art class lunch box designers are inspired by many sources, such as contemporary fast-food containers and materials, and by new trends in toy carrying cases and designs in portable electronics. Our Art Class Design Company's "Twenty-First-Century Lunch Box Brochure" incorporates the latest in lunch box materials and the most advanced gadgetry in each model.

Pencil Cases

I enjoy looking for old pencil cases on eBay. My fellow traders are not antique dealers, since the value of these cases is seldom measured in currency.

Recently I received an old wood foldout case, wrapped in a letter from its 74-year-old seller. In the note, every knick and inscription on the case was described along with how it got there. Each sweetheart carving held a special story in the owner's life. A lunch box, valet box, pencil case, or school bag is an important purchase of a private space and canvas, memorable to the child who decorates and sets up inside it. As a student in Vienna, each year before the start of school, I was allowed to buy a new brown pencil case. Hungarian pencil cases were brown—all of them—so as not to detract from school matters. However, inside the drab brown pencil case there was light. Each inside wall became a changing gallery, displaying a collection of pins, my Pez animal stickers, and miniature drawings. Before departing for America, fellow students presented me with a pencil case as a going-away present; it was brown, of course. America was full of surprises, and in my new school I discovered that pencil cases were not only available in different colors, but even in a choice of styles. It would have been shocking to arrive today and find Lisa Frank or Star Wars action pencil cases—or others in the shape of robots, boom boxes, or Polly Pocket complete playhouses in which pencils and play figures live. The overload of adult designs and advertising on the exterior of today's cases makes them difficult to customize, and children are still forced to move inside the cases to make the space their own.

In the art class, we build, sew, and construct the latest in pencil case ideas suggested by experts. Of course, everything is carefully set up and decorated inside. In fact, yellow pencils become canvases for paintings displayed inside pencil case galleries. The visual history of pencils—the advertising and unusual shapes of old writing tools and the incredible prints wrapped around today's samples—are a related study the children enjoy. I prefer to collect used pencil cases old and new, those which children have already had a chance to alter creatively with stickers or mark with nail polish. My youngest daughter has become an active partner in our eBay pencil case search, as she learns her pencil and pencil case art history, together with my students. She has now switched her contemporary case for a vintage model about which she proudly lectures.

Purses and Wallets

Children love to look through adults' wallets. I find children's wallets to be a great source of fun, and I became an avid collector of these fanciful sculptural forms. Fortunately, I did not have far to go, since my children have bought and taken out of circulation enough wallets to fill many drawers. Children's wallets advertise their current interests and house their most recent finds. The contents of discarded children's valets offer a wealth of information to an art teacher. Inside are paint-sample cards, a gallery of illustrated Band-Aids, trading cards, and unusual found business cards.

Elderly sewing machines came out of retirement for my art room. Children quickly pick up sewing techniques and are fascinated by the possibilities of the sewn line. They freely weave their colored threads through all kinds of contemporary materials, from films to plastics and foils, creating wonderful valets and purses. Custom-printed checks, self-portrait coins, licenses to drive or fly, unusual vehicles, and business cards for fantasy occupations are examples of what resides in an art class wallet.

Schoolbags

When I hold up a giant paint tube, a robot, or a blue whale, it is not an art supply or toy being shared in class. They are all contemporary backpacks, carried as schoolbags. Children are excited by the collection being referred to as art, but they are not surprised by these forms, or by the ones carried by students down school hallways. I proudly carried a hard leather briefcase with a big brass clasp during my early school days, just like the one my teacher had. Specially sized school bags for children did not exist, and all my classmates carried briefcases, sometimes larger than themselves.

For our Art Class Design Company, school bags represent the biggest challenge in a sculptural canvas. Some teams have remodeled and redecorated surplus bags and recycle their creations to proud new owners in the school. Other groups alter instrument cases, hat boxes, rolling suitcases, and other containers, outfitting them for school use. Student-designed bags have become a new fashion trend in many of our schools, appreciated for such conveniences as built-in pencil holders, key-chain racks, snack dispensers, and game cartridge compartments.

Final Observations

Children are the first to comment on the teacher's new hair style or neck tie and notice even the smallest change in the art room. But do art teachers show excitement when a child brings in a new lunch box or a recently renovated pencil case, or notice a backpack with signal lights turning into the room? Are we tuned into object interests that kids normally share with other kids? Is this not an essential part of teaching art? Acknowledging children's art interests, before we bombard them with adult art concerns, is a way to build artistic confidence that will last a lifetime and could expand to many other art worlds. Let's admire a display of wonderful children's umbrellas visiting on a rainy day; and when it snows, those wonderful kids' gloves and mittens can be as exciting as any handcrafted puppets. Art teaching may flourish from the resources right before us.

MAIL ARTISTS

Are you a club member? Then you must have received your special package in today's mail. We celebrated the arrival of Mr. Jelly Belly's package addressed to Ana. The Jelly Belly face on the label prompted a playful shake of the package. It had all the sounds of fun! A smell test preceded the taste test of the new flavors of jelly beans—root beer and apple cheesecake—sent to members only. On the handsome wall poster enclosed in the box, we found the entire Jelly Belly family of colors and flavors. In the package was a rotating candy dispenser, a game board for jelly bean pieces, and the secret club lapel pin and membership card. It was exciting!

Children receive the most interesting mail in the house because they send away for fun stuff, anticipating great mail finds. For children, receiving mail is a special event, a spontaneous party. As a child, I used to wait for the ice cream truck, listening for its merry bells. The mail truck moves more discreetly down our street, yet somehow the kids have a "mail sense" and run to the front door before the mail slot is even opened. Mail carriers are greeted eagerly by children, who cannot wait to take charge of the sorting act. All mail is exciting to children: "Can I sort it? Can I open it?" The town post office is also a fun place where young pockets are quickly filled with souvenirs: forms, unusual envelopes, labels, and stamps. Children observe the postal clerk with some envy. They would love to adopt the clerk's cubbies of great stuff and the carousel of stampers. Children love everything about the mail; it is fun to prepare it, decorate it, place it into a mailbox, and envision its voyage. The mail kids send to one another is often beautiful art.

Paying attention to the mail children receive and how they prepare and send mail, is an excellent lesson for teachers interested in preserving and advancing this authentic child's art. For example, what ideas were advanced from the Jelly Belly celebration? As we hear a knock on our door, Mr. Jelly Belly is sent via special delivery to class. As well as jelly beans, the latest mailings in ice cream colors and new nail polish color samples are mailed to the art class. Beyond adult color theories, we take children's color interests seriously.

Children love to receive mail even in class. I often wear my antique mailman's cap and bag to deliver the latest innovative designs in well-dressed packages for special openings with student help. Many new items for our class displays are unveiled first from art class packages, such as tiny in-line skates, electric guitars, and revolving CDs that are really candy dispensers. Besides these and the Jelly Belly dispenser, our collection includes pocket-sized key-chain dispensers as well as mechanical belt-worn and wrist-mounted dispensers. One day museums will recognize what child collectors already know, that contemporary candy dispensers are incredible works of art. Besides designing for the future by making our own versions of dispensers, we study the rich art history of an American original—the candy store dispenser. The Jelly Belly game board inspired another important survey of art history—game boards. These can serve as an introduction to every major development in contemporary art. Of course, we keep track of important innovations in contemporary game boards, including electronic games and designs by our children.

Mail Arts

To write a letter, Ana searches through her well-organized stationery trunk to find the paper that best expresses her message and mood. Stationery is the art paper of children. They look for opportunities to sift through stationery stores and catalogs, to find the latest colors, patterns, textures, and smells. Children tend to own the largest collection of writing papers in any home because, as artists, they care about the surface on which they place their marks. Children admire their friends' stationery and often save the most beautiful stationery they receive.

Children audition writing tools after the difficult decision of choosing paper. Frequently, mail artists use more than one tool and more than one color on a letter. Milky gel pens are Ana's current favorites, one of scores of writing tools with special tips that she has collected. Each letter affords the opportunity to match the most exciting papers and tools.

Decorating follows, after the letter is "sketched" out. The decorative theme often spills over to all parts of the envelope. A mail artist's palette consists of a rich assortment of stickers, photos, photo stickers, personal cutouts (clip art), and stampers. Children are natural surface decorators, beautifying every object in their possession. Artists don't do anything in ordinary ways, and so the appearance of a letter is a major consideration for children.

The envelope is an important canvas of the young mail artists. Our postmaster will tell you it is often hard to decipher information on envelopes that come to or leave our house. But children's mail is never dull. Through webs of drawings, unusual foil wraps and metallic pen poetry, children try to outdo each other's envelope decorations. We share envelopes in class shows, and I learn from kids that four-foot manila envelopes, envelopes sewn from fabrics, and envelopes constructed from hard, see-through plastic exist. Individual collectors are encouraged by our community sharing of the latest in mailing supplies.

"What stamps do you have today?" Conversations between Ana and our town postmaster is not small talk, but expressions of an artist in an art supply store. The choice of stamps is an important part of the mail's appearance. Children are avid sticker and stamp collectors, and their expertise is happily practiced in mail art. Stamps purchased are often saved in collections to go along with future works. Unusual stamp placements made by kids may not conform to postal codes, but they express the artist's vision for their envelope design. Hand stamping tends to be preferred, not only for the fun of an extra post office visit, but to supervise the stampers' placement, the final visual element of the art.

Mail from Our Class

Wherever we fly on art room magic carpets or on hot air balloons tied to chairs, we send a picture postcard of all sightings. Some cards will be sent through the art class "post office" where we are in charge of all stampers, and we may use our own "postage stamps" (drawings on blank stickers). There is a special postage discount for the most unusual pieces of mail. Samples from our International Stamp Show of student designs are exhibited in homemade albums and showcased in our favorite gallery—our class post office.

Special Deliveries

A letter from a child is not just a letter; it is a special gift of art, prepared with loving thoughts and artistic care. Children's art is not made for sale and passed on to a faceless public. Like mail art, it is a special gift, created with love for someone special. A child's mail design is a unique traveling canvas, covered with multiple art forms: personal photos, objects, cutouts, poems, and messages. In an age of computer communication, one would think that children's interest in the mail arts would diminish, but children treat e-mail and postal mail differently. Mail art gets to be filed away in a special box or basket, treasured and attended to with care, an indication that postal mail has become even more special, more personal, and more appealing as an art form to children.

PHONE ARTISTS

Between classes, I like to spend time in one of the most inspiring art laboratories in a school—the cafeteria. Here children are likely to behave freely
and creatively. While the principal is talking on his cell phone, straw antennas pop up from empty juice boxes now turned into imaginary cell
phones. Air waves are humming across the cafeteria, as children engage
in lively conversations. Leftover sandwich foil dresses up a juice-can phone
decorated with stickers. A phone user who did not have juice for lunch uses
his banana with a fruit sticker keypad to join the conversations. In a society of beepers, voice mail, and cell phones, children don't require technology to inspire their basic interest in the mysteries of distance talking. As
soon as they find out that words and descriptive ideas can be remotely
transmitted, phones become every child's magic art media.

Adults might long for silence, while children dash to answer the call,
flying over all obstacles to be the first to answer a phone. When something new is made, found, or purchased, children want to share it by
making a call. "Can I call Grandma in Florida [at long distance rates], to
tell her what I made?" asks my daughter Ana. On the phone, she gives a
beautifully detailed description of painted rocks she has glued together.
She embellishes her artwork with fantasies, told to her grandmother who
cannot actually see it. Conversations on play phones also carry lively
images that children formulate, translated from objects, visions, and experiences. Children's phones continue to be a popular toy for each new
generation.

Something to Talk About

I never saw the sculptures of my studio teacher in art school, but I "heard"
them being made: He would often disappear into the back room and one
could hear unusual phone conversations about forms with the foundry.
Children's descriptions of a substitute teacher's hair style, the incredible
sights at a circus, or their own nighttime fears sound as though children
wear magic lenses to view the world they tell about. Playing with phones
in the art class is a way to celebrate a child's ability to create pictures with
words. We listen to fantastic visions, which adults seldom find time to pay
attention to.

With pretend phones tied to our chairs, we can drive to any exciting
event. Phones on our wrists or clipped to our belts allow us to fly on magic
carpets anywhere above the class. With phones planted in our lunch boxes,
we can report on secret missions. With phones built into bicycle helmets,
we are able to drop into space and recall the experience. Phone plays con-

jure up images in our head, just like artists who see a work in their mind even before it is made. Art can be a vision to be fabricated by someone else. Of course, we always have eager fabricators on the other end of the line, ready to draw, paint, or make what is being described. Our art room calls are two-way conversations, as listeners also become active visual note takers. Depending on the nature of the mission, the distance of the flight, the description of an adventure, we may use three-way calling, operators, speakers, or video phones.

Art Surfaces for Phone Messages

An exciting variety of phone-related surfaces are available to take visual messages. A telephone book is one of the richest in contemporary sketchbooks, with an endless variety of shapes and patterns to which we can respond. As a collector of older phone books, I am happy to open the pages to phone players. The American printed surface always has a prominent place in the art room file where a portrait of our culture can be sampled through receipts, sports score sheets, computer forms, and phone-related papers such as phone message pads, Rolodex inserts, personal phone book inserts, and sample phone bills from a variety of carriers. They are all available to draw and paint on. The children are always interested in the many styles of old telephone number files, Rolodex carousels, or 1950s style pop-up phone lists, each inviting new ways to make and display art. In our joint effort to collect phone surfaces, students expand their views of surfaces that may be drafted to make art.

Phones as Sculpture and Art

In our art class, we look at new phones and old phones as art history, with a special emphasis on children's phones. On phone days, every child's phone in our home was unplugged and boxed to go to school. Jacob had a phone in the shape of a football, Ilona's phone was a large cup of soda with a straw, and Ana used a working Lego phone. After checking on what exists, children dream about what else could be created. Student dreams and fantasies are an essential part of the art class; it's where the future of art is stored. We share visions of incredible phones while sitting around a small toddler's pool filled with Legos, used to mold ideas into models. Lego sketches are further explored by working with found object treasures from our bottomless parts tub. Of the many phones I have collected, I still find phone fantasies sculpted by children the most inspiring. These space phones, pencil-top phones, and gum dispenser models with novel features can only be found in an art class fantastic phone store and its mail order catalogues, which the children publish online. Each of our phones is handsomely boxed and illustrated with instructions.

Fixing Phones

At home, our harvest gold 1960s phone sounded its final note, or so we thought, until Ana rescued it from the trash can. As she rushed by to get my toolbox, she said we should not worry, the phone would be fixed. On her floor the next morning lay a plastic hull, surrounded by a sea of unusual small parts grouped into neat piles, resulting from a careful dissection. A screwdriver is a child's chisel, their sculpture tool for looking inside things. Many flea market phones and other small appliances await dissecting in the art room fix-it shop. Some forms found inside are appreciated and saved for their own sculptural uniqueness. Others are put together into new, futuristic phone models. Disassembling, or taking things apart, is as much a part of children's art activity as building and assembling.

A Final Call

We round the curve, waiting to speak into the fast-food ordering box, and I try to steer the car into position. What makes the maneuver so difficult is the children who are ready to stampede over me, wanting to be the one to call and place the order. In our art class we use safer drive-through chairs which children build play phones for. In a society where phones are on our belts, in our elevators, and in our cars, phones have become a media that artists cannot ignore. Children tend to be at the forefront of approaching technology with an artistic eye and freshness. Phone plays have been children's way of harnessing the magic and mystery of the media. In sharing my old drive-in movie speakers while kids show me their key-chain phones, we jointly celebrate the art of the telephone.

5

Finding Art
Opportunities Everywhere

KITCHEN ARTISTS

Each time Jeremy came over to play with my daughter, I was on the guest list for dinner. After shopping around the house for ingredients, I would get the call, "Dad are you hungry?" As I headed for the porch, our inflated pink flamingo held up a restaurant sign. As a regular, I would be warmly greeted by the "hostess" at the door, and my daughter would show me to the table. While Ana explained the day's specials on the chalkboard, Jeremy, in his favorite chef's hat, would be busy in the play kitchen preparing food and waiting for the order. Everything was carefully noted on Ana's pad in carbon-paper triplicate. Ana would ask, "Would you like that on the side, sir?" She worked hard at pretending not to know me. The porch table was masterfully decorated with flowers, paper plate drawings, and stickered plastic utensils. Jeremy loved to create imaginative dishes such as stackings of colored yarns layered with rubber bands, or soap pads flavored by real paprika sprinkles. For dessert, Jeremy dipped a tennis ball in chocolate syrup and added freshly-dispensed shaving cream. After dinner I would get the bill, some freshly rolled "mints" (toothpaste in cellophane), and a gentle reminder to please pay all previous bills.

Artistic Development in the Kitchen

The kitchen is children's first art studio. Playing with food, painting and sculpting with it, begins in the high chair. As movement progresses, children take their art under the counter, exploring cookware and creating with pot covers. Children soon discover a climbing path to the top, to more action in stirring, peeling, and decorating with foods on the counter. *Homo erectus* becomes an avid observer and gets involved in everything that's cooking. Young intruders detect that they will be able to participate more freely in the kitchen by assisting, so they volunteer for all KP duty, to help peel, stir, blend, and decorate, as well as set the table. Children are attracted to the variety in kitchen ingredients and the changes in textures and colors in a blender or a pot. Children remind adults how exciting the kitchen is, as they yearn to test its many tools and create with fresh ingredients. Kids enjoy the smells and changes in foods during its preparation and get excited about the opportunities in a food display on a plate or a tray. The more kids are invited to participate in the kitchen, the better prepared they are as artists in any medium. Early art lessons about color, form, and design abound in each kitchen experience. Sensibilities with foods shape a child's artistic pursuit of beauty for a lifetime.

An Art Room Kitchen

Any art room can easily be converted into a familiar kitchen. We draw cooktops with black masking tape on tables. For refrigeration, we stack boxes decorated with "magnets." We collect colorful plastic bins for cabinetry, and stock them with collections of unusual plastic plates, napkins, utensils, and found objects that could be used to make a meal. We save cafeteria trays, and my collection of unusual place mats always builds a homelike atmosphere. When a project involves real fruits or vegetables, our art room vegetable peelers are invitingly displayed in a ceramic container. A collection of vintage or futuristic tablecloths quickly changes the art room table into a kitchen of the past or future. Small touches like a kitchen waste can or our hanger to display unusual aprons and paper chef's hats, invite kitchen artists. Dry erase boards and chalkboards are available to post menus, and of course, there is never a shortage of order pads for servers—the "good kind" with carbons.

Kitchen Stuff

It is wonderful that my grown children now collect vintage ice cream scoops, display old toasters in their homes, and call me about a great old juicer they saw at a garage sale. But the love of kitchen sculpture cannot only come from parents; it can be instilled by an art teacher. It may begin with a teddy bears' tea party, as we join the bears and look at wonderful examples of beautiful children's tea sets and vintage play dinnerware. In the art room kitchen, students can be introduced to classic kitchen gadgets, such as antique serving pieces with red handles, Bakelite utensils, folding art deco hot plates, and the whimsical tradition of flyswatters. When presented with enthusiasm, whatever the art teacher may collect, from unusual kitchen towels to Fiesta dishes, it makes an impact. Students always laugh in appreciation as I model my vintage kitchen aprons for them. A future collector's enthusiasm is stirred by participating in our placemat exchange, trading plastic children's mugs, and sharing wondrous napkin finds.

Kitchen Art

Students design and invent with foods and find counterparts for food in the environment to create poetic displays. Humor and illusion are frequent expressions of food art. The following recipes were invented by art class chefs:

SALADS

- *Nature's garden salad* made from children's seasonal collecting outdoors, tossed with pencil shavings and fish tank gravel, with dressing made from a mix of paint, beads, and glue
- *Hose dog salad* of freshly harvested fall leaves gently mixed with small "sausage" sections (color-dipped pieces of old garden hose) and lightly sprinkled with colorful feathers

SOUPS

- *Blotter soup* made by pouring rich salt and hand-creme textured colors over dish-shaped ink blotters
- *Who knows what it is soup*, a collection of from-scratch soups inspired by a collection menus in foreign languages

ENTREES

- *Yucchi plate* made from designs with lunch box leftovers and spiderwebs (old hair netting), served over a bed of colored sand
- *Dressed-up steak* made from large bones (donated by the local market), used as armatures for painted fabric wrapping held by shoelaces; side dishes made from Play-Doh with found object inserts and fillings
- *Gourmet fries* made from hand-painted pieces cut from an old foam pad and topped with mustard- and ketchup-packet drawings, served in a white carryout box
- *Taste my brick* made from bricks wrapped in sacks, glazed with shoe polish, and garnished with color-dipped marshmallows, buttons, and painted twigs (the ultimate challenge for food illusion: to make a slice of brick look appetizing!)

DESSERTS

- *Eraser chocolate* made from recycled art room gum erasers, dipped in paint, decorated with petals, pebbles, and shredded credit cards; also available boxed for gift giving
- *Sponge cake* baked from a collection of interesting household sponges, decorated with cellophane-stuffed hair curlers and nail-polished combs; served on painted plates with matching napkins
- *Rock candy* shaped from children's rock collections by hammering

and then wire-wrapping rocks, pebbles, asphalt pieces, and shells into tasty morsels, with creamy joints made from colored glue and sparkling glue sticks

- *Banana boat* made from plastic toy boats filled with "ice cream" (wrapped and painted balls) with dreamy toppings of candies, toys, and confetti

We also create with real foods. In the art class kitchen each gift of the season—a richly colored fresh fruit or incredibly shaped vegetable—is welcomed, smelled, peeled, or made into a display. Our art salad plates are known throughout the building, and some of our largest artworks are enjoyed by the entire faculty. We also work on smaller canvases, making art on toast or designing the surface of a cupcake or cookie for a creative after-school snack. With our own restyled tableware, we continue to develop home food-play favorites, such as setting the table, by designing tables for hundreds of yet-to-be-celebrated occasions. In Lego labs, we design the kitchens and appliances of the future. While kids wait for royalties as the real inventors of Mr. Potato Head, we build sculpture from auditioned foods. From vegetables, fruits, cereals, and candies, vast sculpture gardens blossom with visitors also shaped from foods.

Kitchen Homework

What happens to kitchen artists? Do they wither at an early age? I fondly tell stories about young children creating in the kitchen. Listeners of all ages respond with their favorite anecdotes, recalling joyous moments in the kitchen as young children. The number of stories decreases when we talk about school-age kids. Are they no longer considered cute playing in the kitchen? Or are adults less tolerant and responsive to children's kitchen interests? Art teachers can help avoid kitchen artists' early decline by supporting art room kitchen works and by encouraging kids to resume creative roles in home kitchens. Home kitchens, where young artists used to shine, can be the catalyst for students who are assigned creative homework. The art class consults on planning home parties, and students bring sample plates, recipes, and photos to our art class to share. We hold recipe-sharing sessions, taste home cookie sculptures, and put up great table-setting photos. In the art class we have an ongoing show-and-tell of unusual items related to the kitchen, so that students are always challenged to look and share unusual items from home.

We start by paying homage to kids' own food art, but artist name dropping is part of our kitchen play. Students are asked to look up our adult food-artist colleagues on their home computers. Children are assigned to look at the work of sculptors such as Claes Oldenburg, to research painters of foods such as Wayne Thiebaud, and to print out the creations of great Asian and French chefs from cookbooks.

The Last Course

For our anniversary, I take my wife to our favorite restaurant, one of the best in town, called the Merrick Inn. As we reminisce about years past, we are often joined by head chef Jeremy Ashby. Invariably he talks about his latest menu item, and we remind him of his first great creations served on our porch. Jeremy never forgot his artistic touch and proudly calls over servers from other tables to show us his art. I am happy to know someone who has not forgotten the fun of playing in the kitchen.

STORE-PLAY ARTISTS

"I love to work at Zany Brainy," my 15-year-old daughter Ana said. "I get a great apron, and I can make my own name tag. We get new ribbons and fun buttons to put on our apron all the time. I get to arrange toys on shelves, just like I used to do at home. Last week I was promoted to be in charge of Hello Kitty stuff, my favorite things." This was a perfect first job for Ana, who started her career playing store a long time ago.

When children play store, they are making artworks, creating items for sale and placing them into complex displays and environments. They create detailed sales areas with signs, money, shopping bags, and wrapping papers. Unlike many art media that end up in storage, a child's creations come alive in a store and can be celebrated and shared with an audience.

A store is a unique showroom. It is a means for children to show and tell about what they make. No start-up capital is required, and any object can become a store theme—whatever children create can be used to start a store. Playing store expands a child's art as store artists create a total environment to present a single object. Displaying, presenting, modeling, or even wrapping up an object a child made is a way of evaluating it, testing it in a setting and in action. Children learn from the presentation of objects in a store by lighting them, talking about them, and involving feedback from others. In our art class, stores become an expansive enterprise that combine many individually created products and present them to a large audience. Class stores become opportunities to compare many artists' views, to participate in an active exchange of art and ideas in the context of familiar and fondly remembered play.

Art Class Stores

I used to drive a chair around a table to place an order at Ana's Drive-in Restaurant. An Open sign blinking at the pickup window meant I was next, and a tray with an arrangement of fast-food containers was handed to me. Children who love to shop also love to create their own stores. We frequently unfurl plastic Grand Opening flags in our art room, celebrating a new store. There have been many kinds of stores:

- Completed paintings are delivered to our class *gallery*. As valuable objects, children dress the paintings for showing. We prepare brochures and press releases for the opening. There are plenty of customers, collectors, and critics to talk to.
- Children who worked in the class *antique store* are familiar with the art history of many children's objects. They created displays for antique tops, vintage cereal boxes, old pencil cases, and dollhouses—all from the art teacher's collection.
- Our model *auctions* provide opportunities to preview a student's family treasures, before they come up for an animated show-and-tell at a class auction.
- Art room *flea markets* are handsome displays of contemporary collectibles offered for sale. They include unusual candy wrappers, illustrated Band-Aids, and beautiful game boards. On card tables, students arrange their most interesting street finds, store finds, and pocket collections—the "antiques" of the future.
- Our *museum gift shop* is generally open before and after an art museum trip. In our gift shop, we feature handmade postcards, shopping bags, wrapping papers, hand-painted posters, and puzzles illustrating works in the museum. An art class store is a way to examine a museum's treasures by preparing our own.
- Student flyers advertise our school *art boutique*. Before holidays and during open-school nights, art class students set up a hallway kiosk, selling our customized pencils, pencil cases, book covers, shoelaces, pillows, and amazing lunch boxes.
- For the *playhouse* store, children design detailed store interiors in miniature—ice cream parlors and the latest in shoe and fashion stores. Utilizing children's model-making experiences and their love for playhouses, the art of store design is practiced in miniature and set up for sale or trade.

Store Play Props

Imagine the surprise of driving up to our home and seeing a trapeze of lines and gondolas moving from our front porch to the sidewalk. Every car slowed to look at the event Ana and her friend had created. This wasn't the ordinary lemonade stand or garage sale, but an upscale sidewalk jewelry boutique. The attractively designed setting featured props such as our discarded cardboard chest of drawers, now repainted as a counter and cash box. A large painting surveyed the special offerings and suggested pricing. A beach towel, suspended between lampposts, became an awning to shade the operation. To move stock from the more comfortable cool porch to the sunny curbside, fancy jewelry boxes were employed as cable cars. At center ring of the sidewalk store, displayed on foil-covered plates, were watches, pins, key chains, and earrings made from painted slides, coins, buttons, and stickers. Unique tags described each item. A red water gun, the price scanner, was hooked up to a toy cash register. It was an event the neighbors still talk about!

Back at school, a design team is building racks and distributing flyers for their Kiddy Slippers Company. Stores often bring together teams of artists, each contributing goods, displays, and advertising. We form art room companies with individual charters for the design and manufacturing of product samples. A clothes trolley is decorated with custom hangers and sale signs for hand-painted children's umbrellas. Our students are in the habit of asking for, or reserving, cardboard or plastic display units they spot in stores. The art room has label makers, price markers, sale tags and stickers, blank aprons, old business signs, retired stands, and mannequins available for store play rental. We print original cash and check designs that may never be approved by the Federal Reserve Bank. Exciting clothes tags, unusual wrapping papers, and shopping bag ideas are collected by everyone for the art class store. At a business meeting of a student-run custom lamp shades showroom, a "virtual branch" of the showroom was created online. We look at lighting, sounds, and every detail in contemporary store design and strive to create stores and malls as works of visual art.

Sales Talk and Art Talk

At 4:30 a.m. the neighbors were already putting up sale signs around their yards. Next to our yard sale tables, Ana set up her own. She draped her art table with a special picture she made and tried many arrangements of the hand-painted and stickered phone, the nail-polished toaster, and the old suitcase covered with a sparkling hot-glue drawing. Her old lunch box was relabeled and decorated as a cash box. During the day, Ana kept an eye on her table and greeted and talked to every customer, pointing out her "specials": preserved candle-wax droppings and foil dolls. Her descriptions used a rich array of art and design terminology we had never heard her use before. With each customer she gained confidence and offered more insight into her art.

In our art class we create make-believe stores for our art in which children describe their creations and discuss them with others. Store playing builds confidence in using art vocabulary and practicing the skill of describing art. Students use garage sale talk as they walk around the art room finding interest in someone's display or when talking to their own customers. With the affirmation that someone is interested in what one makes, there is a sense that "I can make things as good as in a real store" and "people are interested in the things I make." In a play setting, children's art talk is rich, lively, and unique.

Traditions in Playing Store

My summer studio had a secret attic. During the summer you could go upstairs to fulfill all your banking needs. Bank One, Woodstock branch, as we called it, was a full-service operation, with an antique toy cash register, play money, and a bounty of forms drawn and stamped by Ana. You had to follow the cordoned path (jump ropes tied between chairs) and stand in line even if there was no one in front of you (bank manager's rules). We were all store players once. I share the photographs and memories of the many stores my children created with my students. I tell stories of the stores I created and of visits later in life to a fascinating neighborhood store in lower Manhattan, leased by the famous sculptor Claes Oldenburg to showcase his painted plaster food creations.

Antique toy books show many fine examples of play stores and store-play items. In the modern toy store too, there is no shortage of interesting examples: talking price scanners, working ATM machines, and models of individual stores and entire shopping centers in a carrying case. Each store the children build offers opportunities for related art study. Through our greeting card store, for example, we look at the rich history of American valentines. As the designers at Fisher-Price, Playskool, Play-Doh, and Mattel learn from home players, art teachers have to do their own research of children's store dreams and learn how to welcome store players to the art class.

Closing Time

As this store closes, I hope many more will open in art classes. Creating stores is one of the unique and most interesting forms of children's art. It is an art best experienced live (or preserved on video) because it exists in temporary displays, in different media, including live, inventive playing. A child's store is filled with creative ideas, bringing together handmade and found objects in beautiful arrangements and settings. Store play is a wonderful example of how artists inspired by the environment can borrow from it and transform a site to create their own. Store-playing art may involve painting and print making, as well as performance, environmental, and even computer art. It is difficult to classify, yet this form of creating without the traditional boundaries of media may be the most useful practice for artists of the future. Store playing is seldom regarded seriously or perceived as a great contribution to art by parents or the art world (even though it has clearly influenced environmental artists), but it should not be overlooked by art teachers.

SCHOOL BUS ARTISTS

"My school bus knows the way home," says my daughter Ana. It knows my corner, my house, and the special person who meets me there," she continues. "The driver knows my name, and I make him presents for the holidays." A school bus is a child's fantasy vehicle, and the actual bus ride is a stimulating experience. The early morning bus stop is for meeting friends and a brief fling of fun before the amiable giant zooms its way to the corner.

Thomas the train, Tubby the tugboat, Scoop the steam shovel, and Dizzy the cement mixer, all have a special place in children's hearts. Although children know many powerful vehicles on a first-name basis, the school bus is the mother car. In songs and stories, pictures and models, the school bus is personified as a hero and friend. School buses wear a unique blink and say a cheery good morning. Every child's palette of toys has a friendly school bus that gets together for picnics with other buses. A teddy bear on wheels, the yellow bus is somehow comforting, a fearless protector from unfriendly elements. Because of closeness to the subject and experience, children enjoy the works of school bus artists and happily join their ranks. As a collector of vintage school bus toys I feel a powerful intersection of interests with children, as my toys get a rousing reception whenever they pull into the art class.

The Magic of a School Bus

To pick up Ana at the bus stop requires patient listening to complaints about school. As much as she appears to dislike her school day, however, Ana cannot wait to come in the house to play school. She lines up her smartest dolls and stuffed animals before the chalkboard, determines the rules, passes out assignments, and strictly proctors each exam. After school, her pupils board a school bus made from a bright yellow tent with pillows for seats. In the school bus she is also in control, blowing the horn of her Barbie steering system and waving a big red sign on the side. Daily school bus rides offer plenty of fuel for imaginative bus line art journeys.

All available boxes are on reserve in our art class, to accommodate children's favorite figures they bring in. We warm up the boxes' engines by tying brightly colored strings to the nose of each and pulling them along the hallway loaded with passengers. Students wear larger boxes with "suspenders" and power their buses with engine roars and feet along the parade route. Our preliminary test drive earns students a license for school bus driving and bus designing. When passengers are invited to reenter the bus, it is converted into such works as an amazing stretch bus, mounted on a shiny silver-wrapped skateboard and topped with tiny baseball hats. For an air-cushioned ride, a school bus carrying fast-food figures is lifted through the air by helium balloons.

Vehicles are important subjects in kids' playing and art. Art class activities need to be faithful to kids' interests and experiences. Re-creating important objects and events in one's life is an important art source. School bus artists learn that art is making changes, using one's ideas to turn the ordinary into the extraordinary. Play is the young artist's art process, and in art classes we make playthings—toys become art. All art can be thought of as the creation of playful objects from an artist's fantasy.

Cousin Bandi's House

In a seemingly faraway time and place called Lake Balaton, Hungary's oceanlike lake, I spent many happy childhood summers. My cousin Bandi's family owned a summer home on the Balaton—an old, permanently parked school bus, without wheels, but not completely stripped of its buslike character. It was a child's architectural dream, perfectly suited for playing bus rides. It had an imposing driver's seat and, most importantly, a tremendous black steering wheel. The truck inner tubes we used for swim rings fit perfectly as spare wheels, as we merrily "drove" the bus around the lake and anywhere we wanted.

As I share some old black and white photos of my bus driving days on the Balaton, the students can't wait to climb under the art room tables, the perfect home for bus ride enthusiasts. Children pull down fabric and plastic sheeting as side flaps and windshields, and cardboard panels slide to enclose the interior space. They cut shapely windows to accent the view and construct reclining seats out of pillows and phone books. A side mirror is duct-taped to the table's leg. The space-age instrumentation panel is a Lego construction outfitted with a pie-tin steering wheel. One bus features a CD player with an opening to house a CD. The engine sound effects are courtesy of a passenger chorus, some of whom double as tour guides using a play microphone.

In climbing into a playhouse or bus, there is an implied trust in the young artist, architect, and interior designer to take charge of the project and lead the renovation and remodeling. A playhouse is a child's art studio. Playing house is the source and setting for important children's designing at home—the free assembling of furnishings and environmental objects. This art can be transplanted to the art class in many forms such as playing school bus under the table. Playing house in an art class demonstrates respect for creative play as an important form of kid's art.

Reserved Window Seats for Artists

A single seat for the driver and classroom chairs are lined in rows behind it. Starting with an entrance door, a yellow plastic ribbon is wrapped around the bus. Light on the floor boards (a row of holiday lights taped around the row of seats) and a television (a fruit box with a screen-like opening) are among the bus's advanced equipment. In front of each passenger is an art kit placed into the seat pocket (plastic bags). Tables are pushed to the side, as students board a school bus in the art room. Tickets are passed out, and I put on my driver's cap, turn on the bus lights (flashlights), and take my steering wheel (a large pot cover) as I blow the horn (large pot cover knob) to pull away from class. Attention is directed to sights described outside the window. Today we drive to the winter Olympics in Utah. Weather permitting, we will move alongside major events, to sketch them from the comfort of our bus. The art room school bus is frequently used as a sightseeing bus to imaginary destinations, fantasies framed inside a window. Students receive transfer tickets for their actual school bus ride home, along with art kits and assignments for the "real" bus ride.

If you pass by a school bus with children looking out through cardboard viewers, you know they were prepared in our art class. Community surveyors from our classes wear special caps and look freshly at familiar architectural forms and details. Today children are used to observing a world passing by their car windows. We can encourage capturing the moving views as art visions. Art games can be prescribed for visual explorations, which, in turn, can be tested on the school bus. For example, on the way home from school today, everyone will have a bench partner. The person by the window describes events as they occur outside, and the descriptions will be recorded by the artist in the aisle seat. For "speed-by" recordings, students design school bus art kits from boards, fabrics, and Velcro. We display these unique works yearly in a special gallery—a parked school bus.

Each art lesson should be a demonstration of art as a journey that engages fantasies and imagination. Art is a moving experience for active children. Our teaching can demonstrate how art can be a part of any trip, taken anywhere, becoming a part of whatever children do. We can encourage making art "on the go," creating portable art kits to take along, and turning daily occasions into art trips.

Bus Play Station

Do you have a play station on your bus? We do. We also have armrests, heated seats, and cup holders. Candy and snack dispensers are onboard features on some art class buses. No, we are not a wealthy school district, but our Fischer-Price fleet was refurbished by experts who understand equipment needs. Students collected toy school buses from every thrift store and garage sale in town for artistic makeovers. The fleet was in various states of disrepair, but the old wrecks were perfect for restoration. Under the customizing hands of children, our buses sprouted wings, roared with turbo engines, and pulled mobile food courts. Modeled by bus-riding experts, these buses provided a look into school bus future. We learn that future buses will focus on safety, be able to soar in an emergency, eject snowboards in a storm, and convert to houseboats in a flood. Since school buses carry home our most precious "stuff," it is reassuring to know that well-padded compartments will be available for safe passage of personal collections and art.

When artists are viewed as inventors, art classes can become laboratories of invention. Students can picture being an artist as a visionary, able to appreciate the past and envision the future. Art assignments can call upon young artists to be futurists, empowered to create change in the world, not only create decorative backgrounds for it. In the art class we handle exciting examples of school bus art. These include examples from the art teacher's "school bus museum": vintage ticket punches, old driver's caps, badges, school bus ads, and, of course, vintage toys. Examining the past helps children envision the future, advancing the cautious evolution of school bus design, which unlike the design of passenger cars is not driven by fashion trends.

The End of the Line

Art time is travel time. To schedule trips out of the art room, just designate the children as travel agents. An art room can be a mobile home, a space station, ready to be launched anywhere. Charter a houseboat, or a magic carpet, to take kids from ordinary schoolrooms into the clouds, able to freshly breathe and inhale new art views. There may be a long line for the hot-air balloon ride on colorful balloons tied to chairs, but art teachers as tour planners and guides can insure that the most daring imaginations will ascend. Art is an adventure, and taking children to new destinations is the ticket. Every child wants a driver's license as early as possible, especially to steer a yellow submarine or a school bus.

Children are the original laptop artists who frequently make art kits designed for the family car trip. Travel art studios for drawing under water or to record images in weightless states challenge the travel artist. Kids today are in constant transit, experiencing unique views from a car, bus, or plane. Their visions from behind moving bus windows and mirrors can be converted to valuable art opportunities. Having an art focus for school bus trips can be an important way to extend school art time and to give meaning to school art by incorporating it into the children's lives.

OUTDOOR ARTISTS

Outdoor Foundations of Child Art

The outdoors is the largest art studio with the most wondrous lines and purest colors—all on the biggest canvases. Children playing outdoors discover the elements of art and formulate their own sense of beauty and personal design while handling nature's materials. Playing in the yard outside, children recognize that they have valuable interests and the ability to explore new media. For many children who skip the lessons of backyard playing, it necessarily has to become part of their art education plan.

I like to demonstrate to future art teachers that all art lessons can begin outside. While playing outdoors, adults reminisce, comparing their carefree childhood with today's children who are often overwhelmed by after-school activities and the drain of video games. I highlight this with future teachers in the hope that a significant part of their school art instruction will be spent outdoors.

Mrs. Karp's Restaurant. Mrs. Karp is a longtime friend and fellow art teacher. When I mentioned to her that I was working on a chapter about children's creative play outdoors, it started a wonderful exchange of memories. Mrs. Karp started with her childhood:

> Leaf sandwiches were a special on our menu. They were stuffed with moss and topped with whatever we found fresh on the ground. We crafted exotic utensils by breaking twigs and peeling their bark. Mulch was for garnishing, and milkweed was for melding ingredients. Fine creations were displayed on a bed of cut grass. My friend and I took turns being the chef, waiters, and customers. We found containers to use as cake molds and borrowed cookie cutters from our kitchens. All ingredients were from the outdoors; we just had to look for them. While outside I learned what creativity felt like. Nothing was off-limits, and we were clearly in charge of our backyard restaurant. I never envied children from manicured yards one could not play in.

Then I told my own story from art class:

> I came to school hungry one day, since I had skipped breakfast in order to get some blood work done. My students asked about the Band-Aid as we walked behind the school to pick up something to eat. Carrying white paper plates for food, students created my scrumptious meal from ground finds. The serious search missed few interesting ingredients. Students designed plates using roots, pebbles, and tastefully arranged petals. Time spent in the yard is a fruitful period of artistic growth. We go outside to start an art lesson because the best treats are there waiting to be found.

Pencrazi's Excavations. I spoke to Ronald Pencrazi, a well-known illustrator and designer, in his office. When our conversation turned to what I was currently working on, Pencrazi spontaneously told this childood story:

> My favorite thing to do outside was to dig. Digging always held surprises, and with my trusty plastic scoop I felt the power of a steam shovel. Without it, I would use a spoon, or find a sharp rock to dig with. I moved the earth to create gentle slopes and sudden traps for marble playing. With my friends, we also dug canal systems, testing them with Dad's old watering can. We wove rafts from twigs and sent hesitant worms on canal rides. Sometimes a trench passed through the vegetable garden and ripe tomatoes landscaped our riverbank. After Dad videotaped one of our excavations, we felt our digging art was finally recognized.

In art class we use yellow warning tape to cordon off construction sites. We take pails and shovels outside to create forts and towns—with waterways, of course. Our discussions of sculpture and architecture have a solid foundation from the experiences of building from the ground up. Children are landscape artists, but they don't necessarily sit by an easel or paint what they see—they turn up rocks, find treasures in the dirt, and arrange nature with their hands.

Mrs. Tao's Bug Zoo. Meet my neighbor and urban safari guide, Mrs. Tao. She will point out all recent births in your yard, a new bloom, or the struggling first steps of the tiniest creature. Janet Tao is just as amazed now in the complexities of nature as when she sifted through it as a child:

> Boys liked bugs. Perhaps *like* would not be the word, because I knew a boy who tortured and ate them. I remember pretending that the bugs I found were rare species for my zoo. Our garden was like a lumberyard of field stones, wood chips, and pinecones I could use to landscape bug displays. I didn't have pets, but I felt the backyard stirring with creatures to shelter and play with. On a red wagon with wood railings, I collected fallen birds' nests and carefully separated wasps' nests. I kept my best ones in boxes and in later years used them in architecture class. Our yard was my training ground for designing homes.

In art class we design homes for crawling and flying creatures. One student remodeled a discarded silver pencil sharpener case into an insect dwelling. Another child used a glue gun to craft a natural shelter from butterfly wings and pencil shavings. A fortified lamp shade made a distinctive bird house. Nest collecting inspired a bird palace, built from twigs, and a spider's nest stretched from fishing lines. Art classes can further children's interests in saving and building shelters in nature's building supply stores.

The Mandelbaum Collection. Ana Mandelbaum, a future teacher, added her thoughts about playing outdoors:

> I used to mix my own paints with uncle Jacob's old mortar and pestle. I plucked the season's most treasured flowers and added a glue mix. There were always fresh canvases like blue stones and peeling tree barks to paint. The best colors live outside. In art classes we talk about color like an abstract formula, never savoring fresh colors as I discovered them.

Our art class goes to the school yard with plastic vases. We arrange flowers, twigs, grasses, and leaves; the colors and textures of each season. The arrangements become not only a subject for paintings, but also brushes with which to paint them. How can we teach the elements of art without filling the room with them? We put up our own "preserves" of pressed leaves between contact sheets. They are useful in many artworks such as place mats or fall quilts. Students arrange their best leaf finds, taping them with wide packaging tape over wearable lawn bags. Wearing leaf fashions has become a school tradition. And when the leaves are down, we put them back: bare trees are our armatures for tree decorating. Children's art includes inventing outdoor art materials and curating important outdoor collections. Art classes can utilize children's outdoor finds.

Joe Tackett's Clubhouse. Joe and I sat in the backyard watching his daughter detailing a playhouse she had created under an old bush. The young dad was reminded of playing house in his own yard.

> Chris and I had great adventures in our clubhouse behind the Tackett home. Now I look at the small shed and am amazed at how stately it appeared to us then. It was a safe hideout, an armory. The shed had scrap wood, abandoned furniture, and just enough leftover paint to satisfy all of our remodeling ideas. It even had a roll of used painters' drop cloths for curtains. In good weather we had an outpost in a nearby hollow bush, perfectly suited for meals and a sleepover. To resettle the backyard wilderness we adapted and furnished our habitats. How can one set up a studio or permanent residence without having dreamed inside a clubhouse?

Contemporary tents are examples of visionary architecture, but not nearly as interesting as children's creations from bubble wrap, duct-taped potato sacks, and umbrellas. Bringing to school some of the materials of home shelters—like pillows and sheets—students look for places to drape, finding roofs and natural supports for their visionary architecture outside. Working in small design teams, students frame playhouses from rolled-up newspapers and nature finds. Discovering playhouses, furnishing tree houses, and building tents are important when they are part of art time, and the time investment demonstrates the value adults place on children's outdoor play.

Mr. Barnes's Stable. A collection of stories creative people shared with me about their outdoor playing would be incomplete without a tale from Mitchell Barnes, an automotive designer:

I remember visiting a friend who had it all—her backyard was a showroom of slides, swings, and playhouses, everything Little Tikes ever made. Now that I look back, I think I had more fun in our yard of grass and dirt with parents who encouraged playing and let us take our toys outside. My playground equipment consisted of toy figures and Matchbox cars. Growing around our small band of figures and all the things we could find outside, my friends and I created towns, stables, and elaborate racetracks. I never needed the giant He-Man dungeon, or the big Lego fort, because we fabricated greater palaces. I remember using the leaf piles my dad had gathered to build an elaborate floor plan with different rooms for my sister's ponies. When we needed new play ideas we just went outside.

In the art room I house shovels, watering cans, and rakes, and I invite children to bring their toy friends from home. We go outside because barn animals and action figures require a bigger studio. Our students know from previous play experiences that what they need for landscaping can be found in the landscape. For a toy train, for example, students scout the outdoors for the best site and scenery to set up their play. Small toys become participants in elaborate natural play setups, a unique landscape art.

Jill Schulz, Home Chore Assistant. Our neighbor's daughter talked about the outdoors from another perspective. Jill said:

> I liked to help my father and get all the cool stuff I could find when cleaning out gutters. I loved to rake, mow, or shovel snow, because I always found fun ways to use each tool. I loved to draw with the hose on our driveway, and create water shows by connecting all our sprinklers and timers. I could make big water marks with giant brushes and rollers. Since I was careful with Dad's tools, I was authorized free access to his toolbox. When I made a twig bed for my dolls, I used a hammer and clippers. Being Dad's helper had its privileges.

Outdoor helpers bring wonderful material samples to class, as well as ideas for using them. We construct with shingles, siding, and leftover window screening and assemble large gutter sculptures in the school yard. A quantity of bricks picked up from a job site allowed the art class to create a uniquely patterned brick path. I bring out watering cans to draw on concrete sidewalk squares. Water drawings are self-erasing, and before each picture disappears, students interpret the watermarks into quick drawings or make tracings on plastic overlays. We help the custodian rake and stuff leaf bags so that we can create monumental sculptures by attaching shiny foil tape to the filled bags. Children turn outdoor chores and tools into art.

Renee's Gardens. Renee Shaw is a highly acclaimed video artist and makes nature films with children. She listened sympathetically to me talk about children's outdoor art, and then added her memories:

> I always wanted my own garden, but I did not want to wait for seeds to grow. Instead I waited for my father to finish painting so I could use the leftover colors to make my garden, painting pretty stones, sticks, and pinecones. Coming home was a treat to see colors planted all over the yard. My winter garden consisted of brightly painted sticks hammered into the ground, surrounded by colorful clusters of surveyor's flags my father kept in the garage. I eagerly volunteered to repaint outdoor furniture. It was fun to shop for paint, to see the new color charts and exhibit my paintings on the lawn. Painting outside was fun because everything appeared brighter than in a room.

We continue the tradition of gardening with colors in the art class. We paint leaves and furry chestnut balls, and display birdhouses as paintings. In the winter, we craft snow cakes with food colors. I move art lessons outside to make paintings the size of the landscape. On a long clothesline between trees, we hang packets of fresh paints. Students draw with miles of white, pink, and yellow yarn which sticks like Velcro to fields of grass. The world's most exciting art supply store has materials and ideas to sustain an artist for a lifetime. To endorse children's landscape art, art teachers need to provide opportunities for digging, uprooting, creating earthworks, and painting and relocating rocks.

When Was the Last Time You Sat on the Ground?

Sitting on the grass and counting ants reveals how different the world looks from the ground. Lying on my back on the ground, I recall a childhood memory of sculpting clouds in the sky. Being outside always made me wonder, why does everything appear bigger out here than in my studio? The changing ground and sky made me see in ways I never did before. In childhood I learned to experience the landscape, feel the immensity of its scale, touch the minuteness of its details. If one has not played in the rain or picked up a rock to surprise a million ants, then the landscape has no meaning.

Typically, art classes look at distant landscapes to record nature only as observers. Children playing in backyards, partaking in the ground, are landscape artists without a portfolio. Young artists learn to love the landscape by handling it, and as art teachers we can put the outdoors back into children's hands. We use outdoor finds to leave our marks outside in the form of sculpture gardens and earthworks. These adult-coined terms are, in reality, art forms invented by children.

In the art class we talk about art elements such as colors and lines. But these elements are the most interesting outside. Colors stuck in paint tubes and jars become bright and alive outside. Lines are richly displayed as cracks over vast outdoor surfaces. Unattached to existing artworks or formal art materials, lines, colors, and textures wait to be touched, picked up, discovered, and played with outside. Outdoors, students have a firsthand experience with art and the sources of artistic pleasures and inspiration.

6

Learning Design by Designing at Home

SHELF ARTISTS

Individual magazines dating from the 1950s became stacks and then grew into towers. As the field aged but not the practitioner, I placed my art education magazines into playful configurations hoping to outsmart the towers from scraping the ceiling. When the magazine stacks finally outgrew our home, Ana and I hauled them to my office at school. On the way, I stopped at Kmart to purchase steel shelves to respectfully organize the collection. After building with the magazine piles on the floor of my office, Ana became very interested in assisting with the opening ceremony of the shelf box. It took one incision to free millions of exciting parts from the dark cavity of the big box. "Can I help you put it together, Dad?" she asked. She was already at the door, wearing my leather tool belt and carrying our old red toolbox.

I sat on the floor engrossed in the construction problem, unfolding the map-sized instructions and finding the right language to decipher. "You study the instructions, and I will work," she said, assigning jobs.

Perplexed with the problem of identifying the #14 screw, I hardly noticed Ana playing in the metal pile using my biggest screwdriver. Competing with my concentration were Ana's conversations with the shelf: "This could be a space station, and the top will be the tower. . . ."

After digesting the master plan, I announced that we would soon be ready to start construction. Imagine my surprise when Ana proudly announced she was already finished. I looked up to find a life-sized, Erector-set version of a shelf, with flying buttresses, bracket wings, and oddly twisted columns. This shelf obviously never read its own instruction booklet. It could not support a single journal, yet it was dramatically held together. Ana asked, "Do you like it, Dad?" "Will you take it apart?" The questions came in rapid succession. Ana clearly understood my admiration for her work when I asked her to help me move the structure from my office to center stage of the art room, waiting for Monday's art class. Over the weekend, I picked up several other boxed shelving units, not to accommodate reading materials, but to offer other young architects of the future an opportunity to test their visions in steel.

Young artists are interested in building with everything. They view all unusual objects in the environment as raw materials waiting to be put together. The opportunity to use a screwdriver and shelves, magazines or erasers, hair curlers or shoulder pads to test artistic visions is the way children formulate the future of sculpture and architecture.

Many of today's items arrive at home and school wearing the ominous warning label "assembly required." The anticipation of instructions in multiple languages with illegible diagrams sends most adults fleeing. Children, however, flock to the challenge, seeing possibilities far beyond the instructions. When children ask, "Can I fix it?" they are ready to assemble and take things apart in free and imaginative ways. Anything that needs assembly can be brought to the art class and become the basis for an unforgettable art experience. Interests in playing with tools and putting things together needs to be supported.

Children love not only assembling shelves, but also collecting them and building their own. They spend a great deal of time designing and displaying objects on shelves. The many forms of shelf art are basic to children's art. Lending children your tools is symbolic of a trust in their building and construction abilities that most art forms require. Putting children in charge of putting together a cardboard or metal shelf is an early architectural license to build and find satisfaction in creating structures with their own vision and hands. Challenged by tasks that involve building and taking-apart experiences, children's architectural models often appear with objects as ordinary as boxed shelving units.

Shelf Collectors

While I walk through the video rental store, Ana is checking out the display shelves. The best cardboard display shelves are like valuable movie posters; they are frequently on reserve, just waiting to be taken by a child who has been patient and talked to the store clerk. Less patient collectors move the last remaining items off the display shelves to help speed the rescue effort. Children are familiar with the beauty of cardboard and plastic store display shelves and, if allowed, would fill their entire room with them. Adults at home or in school are a bit slower to recognize sources for the most interesting contemporary furnishings, which are not found in furniture stores. Ana has one bed in her room, but scores of shelves. Among her recent acquisitions is a tall and slender see-through cosmetic unit with bright yellow labels and a handsome cardboard battery-display shelf. As a present to house my vintage Slinky pull-toy collection, she found a shiny black new Slinky display unit. To enhance sales appeal, manufacturers create unusual shapes, colors, materials, and illustrations to frame and house their products.

Kids know their shelves, and they value all unusual features such as authentic labels, illustrations, and price tags. Shelves are children's store windows, or museum cases, to place their most important collections. Children seldom buy furniture for their room, but they are just as interested in their environment as adults who purchase kids' furnishings. Children shop for and select store display shelves on their own.

Shelves as Canvases

Shelves are the three-dimensional version of children's bulletin boards; and like the doors to children's rooms, shelves are canvases for constantly changing displays and arrangements. A store display shelf in a child's room is his or her hand-picked furniture and canvas for a select grouping of three-dimensional collections. Just as two-dimensional design is studied in decorating the door, children learn three-dimensional design by constantly reorganizing objects on a shelf. In children's rooms, shelves and playhouses are buildings with many floors and rooms in which to design with objects. When kids say, "I am cleaning my shelf," it can be interpreted as a design work in progress, a reorganization and rearrangement of forms on the shelf. Children are just as concerned as adults with the appearance of their room and often rearrange shelves, doors, bulletin boards, and window displays to make their environment more beautiful. In a toy box, items are thrown together for a quick cleanup. On a shelf, toys and pocket finds meet on equal footing, carefully arranged by setup artists and treated like forms on a traditional canvas. A toy or a street find is not truly one's own until it has been invited to a place on one's shelf.

Some art class shelves need to be cleared and freed from storage duty so they can be used for design and display. Children can be invited to bring their own canvases—their shelves—to class. While adults view shelves as useful storage devices, we need to recognize their creative uses by experienced shelf artists in our classes. Like stretching canvases, assembling cardboard, plastic, and metal shelves and arranging objects on them can become a regular part of the art class. Incoming art supplies can be set up on shelves as art works. Toys, pocket collections, outdoor finds, and children's sculpture can not only be stored, but also designed and displayed, on a shelf.

The Shelf Exhibit

Our First Annual Children's Shelf Exhibit was held at our university art gallery. The show, curated by children, featured exciting found pieces of contemporary cardboard shelves. It also showcased children's own designs, both shelf models and actual shelves, some of which held displays of pocket finds and object treasures. Besides exhibiting the exciting shelves, the show was intended as a universal declaration of shelf art as being one of children's unique art forms. The many examples on display also suggested different ways this art form can be supported at home and by school art programs.

DRESS-UP ARTISTS

At the bus stop, two sisters shout from opposite street corners while wait-ing for the school bus. I walked slowly in between them, soaking up the conversation. "If you insist on wearing what does not match and embar-rass us, I told you I would not stand on the same corner with you. The crazy pieces you picked—Mom told you not to wear them together." Art critics are everywhere, I muttered to myself, the critics are always asking us to tone down exciting choices. Of course, I could not intervene on behalf of the young fashion innovator, but I approvingly admired her bold color sense, personal style, and refusal to blend with the crowd. But how long could a young independent dresser sustain herself without support? I wondered if the art teacher in her school would praise her bold design choices and say, "I love the unusual colors you decided to wear today."

Do we recognize budding fashion artists entering our room? Art teachers have a unique opportunity to liberate young artists from fashion dictates of what has to go with what and to encourage personal design experimentation on the primary canvas of ourselves. Without art class sup-port and exploration, bus-corner monitors quickly close in.

"Here Comes Ana"

A panel of judges—teddy bears and stuffed animals—are aligned on my daughter's bed. Ana tries on each garment she considers wearing to school the next day and asks the panel to vote. Even quarreling siblings know that children make careful choices about clothing, even if they disagree with the results. Making tough daily art choices and seeking artistic indepen-dence doesn't automatically garnish praise or support. Family and school critics, who know exactly what goes with what, what's in style, and what is appropriate for school or for the season, are always a part of a young designer's maturation. Adults and kids often clash more about clothing matters than anything else. Art teaching can provide support for original-ity and respect for children's choices. Clothing decisions are among the most serious art choices made by kids daily. Even during adolescence, kids discuss clothing decisions with friends in lengthy conversations using vivid descriptions. Every child grows up as a designer, and through clothing selection, kids develop a sense of design, taste, and style.

Although it's official on Halloween, dressing up is a year-round oc-cupation. Kids create exciting home fashion shows testing their ideas of style on pets, play figures, and themselves. They try on Mom and Dad's clothes, and each other's clothes, in many combinations before different mirrors. "Here comes Ana," announces her sister, as our designer-model walks the runway of our fireplace ledge.

Just as Ana models clothing year-round, for students in an art room, it can always be Hat Day. Each day can have a bit of the Halloween dress-up spirit. If teachers notice students' fashion choices and there is an opportunity to share and talk about new fashion finds, any art room can become the center for dress-up art. On rainy days, umbrella shows are held. On cold winter days, unusual gloves and mittens pose. Summer days let us look at children's sunglass designs and create outrageous swimwear ideas for twistable fast-food figures. We admire fashion ideas worn to class as seen in decoration with key chains, stickers, and buttons over sneakers, jackets, and backpacks. I frequently share my daughter Ilona's jean jacket which she resurfaced with medals and pins in the style of military generals.

We provide the white canvas of socks, shoelaces, tennis shoes, shirts, and painters' caps on which to create future school fashion trends. In art class we resurface found garments and also create original fashion from household objects and materials with no previous fashion lineage. To showcase new art, our art supplies include unusual fabrics and the latest in flea market clothes, fashion forms, mirrors, play microphones, and runways.

Draping and Wrapping

After a bath, children create great turbans and body wear, commandeering every bath towel in the house. Children explore draping art on many forms, from Barbies to cutout figures, pets, and stuffed animals. Children play out art ideas by dressing play figures in original and ready-to-wear outfits. Doll clothes made from scrap fabrics, foils, wrapping paper, and bubble wrap make up the most ingenious and daring dress designs. Children come to art class with vast experiences in wrapping bodies on all scales and with a genuine love for fabrics. Kids cover the world, dressing not only the human figure but all kinds of objects, from pillows to pencils.

A fabric table is a standard fixture in our art room. It wears official store signs, announcing daily sales and inviting students to touch and sample. Yards of exciting colors, textures, and patterns are always tempting opportunities to uncritically mix and match personal palettes. In art class, trunks filled with found objects also remain open and challenge students to lift fashion boundaries by showing fabrics and objects generally not considered for wearing. Down our art class runways come the parachute dress, the diaper and paper-tablecloth shirts, the Lego vest, the lampshade hat, and handbags made from pencils, jean pockets, and bubble wrap.

Our models are dolls, teddy bears, and vintage mannequins poised for draping by fashion designers who play and train here.

Clothes-Shopping Art

At birth, parents lovingly furnish their child's room and go on to appropriate many artistic decisions. A sign of artistic growing up is a child's interest in clothes shopping and a desire to have a say in what to wear. We often see the artistic exuberance of young children, touching and uninhibitedly trying on everything in a store. It is too bad that cooperative clothes shoppers are easier for parents to deal with, and kids who allow themselves to be dressed are more inclined to be rewarded than those who wander away and seek new aisles in search of their own style. Clothes shopping is serious business for kids who compare styles and colors more freely in stores than in a museum or gallery. The willingness of parents to allow kids to choose and find support for their taste and experimentation is one of the clearest signals of faith in a child artist.

Art rooms should always be set up to invite individual shopping adventures. A fabric store, clothing store, or an exciting yard sale can serve as models for the art room. I collect used store fixtures, signs, cardboard display racks, antique hangers, and old labels for store playing. In our class there are always interesting vintage bowling and Hawaiian shirts, scarves, art deco ties, and patterned vests to mix and match. We "sell" Shoe World magazine as art news and pay attention to the latest ideas on all fashion fronts. We can check you out on talking toy scanners or handsome 1950s tin toy cash registers.

Wearing Clothes History

Most parents keep scrapbooks or family photo albums of their children. I also saved my children's childhood clothing. I have Jacob's race car–driver and space-suit pajamas and his moiré-patterned slippers with changing drawings. I share with my students the tiniest shirts featuring the Fonz, Batman, and the Jetsons. Than I move the show to large teen shirts, including the Turbo Cello Rock Tour shirt Jacob painted and other concert souvenir shirts documenting his changing musical taste. These tangible souvenirs of growing up are also inventive art objects I admire. Did you ever show your own childhood clothes to an art class? Students love to view other aspects of the teacher's art, and so I share my own clothes from childhood along with photos of my boyhood Halloween costumes. From our attic, I resurrect my grandmother's old wedding dress for the class. Class dress-up artists can try on the dress, her old ballroom gloves, and funny 1920s shoes and bonnets. Students are fascinated with a personal presentation of clothing history when it is presented as art.

It is fun when my grown-up kids join in the show of their childhood clothes. They are amazed to discover what was saved. "Oh, I remember Hat Days in school. It was the only time we were allowed to wear them, and we made sure we had the most unusual hats." Kids' hat selections are an important part of shaping future interests in sculpture forms. Vintage makeup bags, red suitcases, old handbags, are used to house my collections, each labeled—kids watches, mittens, umbrellas, belts, purses, Halloween costumes. Interesting containers invite exciting opening ceremonies and future collections. Sharing art history through family clothing personalizes the art form and extends an intimate invitation for appreciation.

End of the Runway

Highlighting kids' clothing and fashion promotes a connection to other art interests. The teacher's collections are always fun to share, wrapped as they are in many layers of anecdotes. Suitcase museum items can be tried on, World's Fair souvenir scarves, and old valentine handkerchief sets are art to wear. Clothing art is unforgettably expressed through sharing sessions involving students' zany sweaters and hair ornaments, their family's scrapbooks, and the teacher's collections. Incredibly small fashion items come to class daily, and their significance would be unheralded if not for children's collecting. Wonderful designs in clothing tags, buttons, shoelace ornaments, and unusual hair notions inspire a new fashion watch, an awareness of design details that interest young collectors. When readily discarded clothing tags are saved and carefully preserved in an art class, they become a reminder to take a second look at all the unheralded aspects of fashion art around us.

HOME-CHORE ARTISTS

Dear Art Teacher,

Please list all the home chores you hate to do on the side of this paper. Do you have enough room? Let's talk about those chores with which you need help, but over which you have to bargain with your older kids, who ask, "How much do I get?"

Now relax and close your eyes to travel back in time to your childhood, when helping around the house was so much fun that you eagerly volunteered for everything. Do you remember how every chore was new and exciting, the inventions you brought to it, never doing it less than artistically? Do you remember begging your mom to let you help with a chore or asking your dad to wait until you came home because you did not want to be left out of something special? Did you find household work so exciting that you even continued playing it with your stuffed animals, creating beautiful table settings for them, ironing their clothes on your play ironing board? What happens to our common, most basic art education experience that turns it, in later years, into such an undesirable activity?

Salad Artists

Not long after being able to reach the kitchen counter, children are eager to try every tool. There is a special transforming magic in using a peeler, for example, and children wait in line to take their turn. Peeling potatoes feels very different from peeling carrots, but both are exciting to children who pocket the best strands and arrange, display, or wear other strands as instant masks. It is not KP duty because children explore peelers like scissors not to just cut, but to uncover beautiful forms and lines.

With young kids at home, you don't have to wait for help to make a gorgeous salad plate. Kids love to play with food. They already paint in the high chair, rehearsing to become great food artists. Children eagerly study form by dissecting and design by engaging in cutting, slicing, and dicing. When allowed to select their own canvas—a special serving plate, their favorite tray—the results are unforgettable examples of children's art. Students in my art class often ask, "Why do you have so many vegetable peelers in a makeup bag?" They are happy to find out that we use all of them to confirm the importance of peeling as children's home art and to build on their expertise in our class.

Table-Setting Artists

With guests coming for dinner, children know there will be a big audience and will insist on setting the table. Of course, expect settings to be original designs that will not follow Ms. Manner's prescriptions. Children will want to use your "best" items, looking patiently through every tablecloth and stack of dishes and sparing no flowers in the garden for their tableaux. Children anxiously wait for the guests and their responses to the nouveau art displayed on the table.

In our classroom, children find a good selection of background colors and patterns in the tablecloth collection. They also find unexpected colors in plastic dishes, the latest in plastic utensils, and a selection of plastic crystal vases ready to fill and use on color canvases. Parents are surprised when their children speak about Fiesta dinnerware or recognize Depression glass, but they've seen and held it in our art class. On special occasions, I also open my old trunk filled with handmade tablecloths from generations of home artists from my family.

Laundry Artists

Children are fascinated by washing machines and are eager to help load a dishwasher or prepare the wash in the laundry room. Every part of the process is exciting, from stuffing clothes through a small opening to watching changes on a spinning screen. Putting away clean clothes displays the talents of young sock-drawer designers who make art in the framed canvases of drawers.

The laundry lines in our art room make laundry days a special art celebration. Our stars from home washing arrive in a basket for students to fill the room with colors and patterns of fabrics. Art history is examined in the forms of antique clothespins, hangers, and laundry baskets from 1900 to the present.

Ironing Artists

Ironing was my favorite home chore. Although I had many toy irons and loved my toy ironing boards (a collection which I build upon as an adult), I still recall the day when I was entrusted with the big steam version. What power to bulldoze wrinkles and watch them turn into flat surfaces! I especially enjoyed making lines and folds, playfully drawing with the iron. My mother quickly recognized my talent and interests, which were clearly not in traditional ironing, so she wisely provided my own fabric for ironing art. As an adult artist, I still know my way around the ironing board, as I melt together many plastic surfaces on which to paint and through which colors can flow. My toy irons are now retired to the art class where children use them as elegant drawing tools to create pleats and fantastic line patterns and crossings.

Sewing Artists

As soon as the family pilot of our sewing machine takes the controls, a copilot quickly arrives. Our children not only patiently watch, but wait their turn at the machine. While my wife sews together her fabrics, the children collect the fallen pieces from the floor to draw on with sewing lines. While sewing, children are fascinated by turning the wheel, selecting threads, millions of stitching patterns, and testing the limits of a sewing machine's vast line-making abilities. In a memory book, I collected my daughter's first sewings. Their work showed more of an interest in the stitches and not as much for using sewing as a glue gun in fastening fabrics together. In our art class we draw by hand sewing and by using sewing machines from former home economics classes. As a living history of this art, my collection of early American samplers and traditional stitched art pieces created by my family in Europe are treasures I happily share with my students.

Polishing Artists

My son was well trained in polishing while attending Montessori school. He wanted to share his education by eagerly offering to polish our shoes, windows, and silverware. Even without school training, children are willing partners in spraying liquids on a window and squeezing polish on chrome furniture. They apply wonderful scribbling lines on the polish, and then remove it with creative moves to free the shiny surface. Polishing involves a transformation and an element of magic which children enjoy in all their art.

With large wet brushes and sponge mops, we shine the classroom floor. We paint with big round shoe polishing brushes. We draw with liquid shoe polish containers using polishing experiences and skills. As our art history lesson with a personal touch, we view my family's silver from many generations and learn about my art deco chrome bells by polishing, the best way to learn about form and details. After our silver-polishing experience, kids are fascinated to view photographic examples from the Maxwell House Silver Coffee Pot Collection now touring the United States.

Watering Artists

Children love to use the garden hose, but not just to water plants. In a child's hand a hose becomes a paint brush, which often records images on a concrete walkway. A watering can becomes a liquid marker with which kids draw large, confident images that magically dry up just in time for another. With water guns, kids create pictures in the air, on steps, and on brick walls. Now you know why I keep a suitcase filled with plastic watering cans and water guns, ready to roll outdoors and be filled for action painting over vast outdoor canvases. To save favorite images, children make tracings, chalk drawings, and videos of watering art.

Lawnmower Artists

We were all excited to buy our first lawnmower, and the children could not wait to try it. We had no grass of any color before we moved to the

Bluegrass State from New York City and had only seen pictures of lawnmowers. For safety, I walked behind Jacob, our rookie cutter, while he explained that he was cutting circles and faces. Our Kentucky neighbors cut their lawns in neat rows and watched from behind their curtains in dismay. My son could not be stopped from outlining the lush green canvas with the unique drawing tool.

In our art class we discuss all kinds of machinery and their possible adaptation as paint brushes and future drawing tools. Toy lawnmowers are also available to push into art action in class. In fact, we take imaginary drives on street sweepers and highway line stripers and push art tools such as vacuum cleaners across art surfaces.

A Public Service Announcement

With my daughter Ana as my star, I recently created a series of public service television announcements (now airing on Kentucky stations) showing a steel bookshelf kit being prepared for assembly. They were based on a true story: I had brought home just such a kit, and as I was getting ready to put it together, Ana quickly put on my tool belt and was ready to help. While I was trying to figure out which one was the #14 screw in the lengthy, multilanguage instructions, Ana was already assembling the shelf into a space station.

The announcement concludes by saying, "Let them help you." In frosting a cake, sweeping, stocking the refrigerator, creating table settings, taking apart or putting together shelves, children experience the use of a variety of yet-to-be-discovered art tools and art materials and consider art opportunities in everything. By helping at home, children envision the future of art.

7

Discovering Art in
Everyday Playing

WATER ARTISTS

Water Studio

In my long-term role as studio assistant/towel holder, I always had the best seat in the house. I file this report while sitting next to the tub, observing the creative experiments of bathtub artists. In the most private of all art studios, water play experts investigate a magical canvas with a free spirit seldom equaled. The tub is a natural space for children's experiments and water a naturally creative media. In bathtub play acts, painting, design, animation, and sculpture inventions flow together. In the tub today, sponge and cup cities ride tinted waves of bubbles. They float past plastic tub blocks, geometric pastel landscapes adhered with water to the shiny tub wall. Memories stronger than any color-wheel lecture are experienced with tub colors. Play dyes create a sea of color changes from yellow to bright orange, and then deep purple. River pilots skillfully navigate shaving cream icebergs with boats constructed over brushes with hair curlers and other tub port finds. Cartoon-shaped body wash bottles observed the action. Why children spend such a long time in the tub is best understood if we see the tub as an art studio. For kids, it is one of the last free creative spaces remaining after other rooms have long been purged of playthings.

Children collect all kinds of Styrofoam coolers and plastic storage containers for our art class, items that are reminiscent of bathtub shapes. Sitting next to these small-scale tubs, children create water plays inside the containers. Yes, we have rubber duckies and the latest in tub toys. I also curate the world's most unusual sponge collection and a vast selection of handsome shampoo bottles, interesting lids, and play figures. All are willing to get wet and act as kids' stunt doubles in the tub. In a comfortable environment, we reminisce with children about their tub art and recall scenes and events played out in the tub. For most children, this is the first time bathtub memories are referred to as something significant and talked about as art.

Cabana Swim Club

Several striped umbrellas surround the raised green and white kidney-shaped pool. Nearby on a field of Astroturf, a pink heart-shaped pool accommodates playful bathers and tiny pool toys. A yellow cabana flanks a blue pool. Inside the cabana are all kinds of bubble blowers and pouring apparatus. Welcome to the strangest pool club in the world, a layout of different kinds of Barbie pools designed during the past 25 years. Play pools for dolls, sea horses, and other play figures are favorite children's toys for water play at home. Memories of the beach and poolside can last all year as children replay them in the house. With floats, kickboards, balls, swim rings, water noodles, watering cans, fins, and goggles children improvise pool games and adventures. Many free and creative water-play moments become a great resource for small-scale pool creations.

I travel everywhere with pools of all sizes sticking out from the trunk of my car. Some are hard plastic play pools, others are inflatable, and many are doll-sized. All are ready to set up in schoolrooms, hallways, or back-yards. Just the sight of play pools, seemingly out of place in a school, has an instant attraction for children. Pools symbolically import fun and instantly transport kids into a nonschool frame of mind. When pools are set out on a school floor, they are often framed by towels from my collection of boldly patterned beach towel art. Masterpieces of contemporary beach floats are inflated creating an instant gallery of imaginative soft sculptures. Art classes sit around the pool recalling beach plays, designing their own towel classics, floats, inflatable beach chairs, and radios. Students design pools and water parks, choreograph the first-ever water circus, or prepare for the ribbon-cutting ceremony to their own boat show. Students learn to view the water as an artist's flexible canvas; and, as often the case with painting canvases, different shapes and sizes of pools inspire different artworks.

The Life of Alfonso and Underwater Studies

When Alfonso the goldfish came to live with us, his fish tank was richly furnished and decorated from the center to its glass- wall exterior. Alfonso's days were always exciting because Ana constantly fabricated new land-scapes and playgrounds for him to explore. That is probably why our gold-fish lived for centuries in fish years, enjoying an artistic nurturing. When Alfonso finally died and received a royal burial, his tank was willed to Yertle, a turtle. Yertle lived on the magnificent Riviera, a beach scene Ana lovingly constructed for him. She kept excavating new rocks and finding different ways to terrace the turtle apartment. At present, the aquarium, inhabited only by great memories and stories of its previous occupants, resides in my art class. It is still being cared for and decorated for future environments envisioned by children.

Inside our plastic aquariums made of soda bottles and storage boxes, deep underwater worlds are modeled. Our art class prepares for the dive by making cardboard scuba gear. We fish in secret waters deep below our art room, gathering only the rarest of sea creatures for their new tank home. Creating in underwater settings brings a new level of interest to experienced water players. We create model aquariums, propose underwater communities, and draw on wet sketchbooks made from reusable paper towels. Underwater studies are a new take on landscape art, a fresh look at color, texture, and the incredible sculptural forms of sea life and the design of equipment used to study it. In these explorations, children learn that art is often created in containers, that designing and furnishing environments above and below the water can be an artistic challenge.

Brighton Memories

As a child, I only saw pictures of the ocean, but it stirred my curiosity. How lucky I felt to come to America and to settle in Brooklyn, New York, near the beach. We arrived during the off-season, and my first American friend Dennis and I spent all our spare time on the beach. We met up daily with old prospectors with metal detectors, but we hunted our own treasures. Not at all like the ocean shores in my pictures, Brighton Beach was one big trash pile. But we were kids, and who else appreciates a good trash site? We built wonderful things in its praise. Each day yielded new objects to be freed from the sand, to pocket or to use in constructing our beachfront homes and seafaring rafts. We built scores of watercraft and sailed them with poetic communications to unknown shores. No writing tools were necessary; everything was there waiting to be discovered and used for some creative purpose. To this day when Dennis Chalkin, now a world-renowned photographer, and I get together, we always speak of the ocean studio we shared. The Brighton Beach sandbox and waterfront shaped our artistic lives.

If you entered our class this week, you would think the janitors were on strike. Four blue play pools in our art room are surrounded by trash, like finds blown over time from Brighton Beach. To invite children to my childhood required a dumpster to be unleashed. The water in the play pools was colored to resemble murky Atlantic water, and as the children walked in, they were as excited about the trash and the prospect of floor shopping as Dennis and I used to be. There was plenty of great stuff to walk through, to pocket and trade. There was no glue, tape, or staplers, but children proved again that they could construct fabulous structures, as we did, without them. The canvas of the water was tested by arrangements from fall leaves to complex floating gardens using outside finds. For a grand finale, the children enjoyed witnessing the art history of American toy boats from my collection, launched one by one on newly designed oceans. The children learned that the outdoors could be their best art supply store. They learned that their many creative plays outdoors are an art form, that art does not live on art paper, that it is important to go outside, travel, explore, and be part of adventures that yield art ideas and resources.

Water Play Is Basic Art

Water playing is children's earliest and often most memorable lesson in painting. In water plays children learn to move liquids freely, to see it flow, to experience its bounce, to feel the pouring. Watercolor and related painting arts depend on the freedom and skill to move water and color over a surface. Water plays are rehearsals with liquids squirting, soaking, and releasing from different containers or moving through funnels, across spoons, or in concert with different tools. Paint in the hands of an experienced water player is alive, maintaining its lively dances and playful moves. Think of all the innovations in painting in contemporary art and how they were shaped by water plays.

Some of the most important sculptural experiences also start in water playing. Children playfully test forms in water and sense their weight, balance, buoyancy, and other special qualities. In water games children learn to set up elaborate scenes and give a variety of roles and meanings to found objects. In water plays children discover their own building blocks and sculpture materials. Water players discover the sculptural contributions of nature and the use of light, air, and water in art. Through water plays, children learn to enjoy moments in a private studio and the joy of conducting their own discovery experiences.

FLASHLIGHT ARTISTS

"Dad, read it right!" said my daughter Ana. Children prefer to select their own bedtime storybook, and even though they can recite the story by heart, they love to follow along and correct any mistakes. Comforted by the familiar, children love the game of catching a reader's fanciful departures from the text.

The darkened room in which I read our bedtime stories has wonderful light sources. Unusual plug-in night lights reflect on Day-Glo shoelaces, slippers, with metallic thread, hair ornaments, and the night sky above (ceiling stickers), and of course the trusty flashlight in Ana's hand.

While I do my improvised reading, Ana provides the artistic light shows. Through the story years, children's experiences with flashlights, are one of their best-explored art tools. As I proceed with tonight's special reading, a light show accompanies me on the ceiling. Storybook monsters are fended off by shadow creatures that are projected through fingers and straws moving across the back of my white T-shirt.

In our darkened art room in school we lie on the floor, snug in our paper sleeping bags and fluffy paper pillows. It's fun to be in the dark and protected by flashlights, especially in school. As the art teacher playfully acts out a story, listeners require little introduction before flashlights become animated. Night stars in class are created courtesy of a toy projector called the Star Machine. The reader frequently stops to admire and refer to the creations of individual projectionists. Besides experimenting on the ceiling, the largest white canvas in the room, children explore light and shadow forms over pillows, socks, and each other.

Works by Flashlight Artists

If you want to know how to turn a tiny fast-food figure into a giant on the wall, just ask a young flashlight artist to show you. Most children come to class as experienced flashlight inventors. We need to recognize their practice in the media as an art form, one that can be promoted in art room settings. In children's hands, flashlights become a drawing tool, a color paintbrush, a means of sculpting with forms and light. Great contemporary light-show artists probably began their studies as children with flashlights at bed time.

- *Children use flashlights as versatile, hand-held projectors.* To allow toe monster to wiggle out of the clutches of a furry alien, children learn to animate their feet before the lens and dodge the light passing through a hairbrush. A flashlight lens can also become a slide tray for dead bugs, hair, or Slinkys, found at night near the bed.

  In our darkened art room, children shop through many drawers and compartments to test pencil shavings, nail clippings, tea bags, grapes, altered slides, and coffee cup lids, which are spread out over flashlight lenses. Long-handled objects such as flyswatters, feather dusters, and kitchen tools with handsome openings are danced in front of light beams. For example the children capture the effervescent forms of bubbles streaming from a bubble blower with paint brushes, tracing the dancing bubbles in the air and elaborating on them as they land on white paper.

- *Children insert flashlights inside things.* A large mushroom of light often hovers over children's beds when they are supposed to be asleep. Parents eager to enforce their curfew seldom stop to appreciate the hidden artist responsible for creating the light forms under blankets and sheets or inside pillows. Items around the bed such as socks, cups, gloves, and chewed gum are often used as flashlight covers.

  In our art class we set up in tents or crawl under covered tables or inside large boxes, which act as our planetarium, cave, haunted house, or a place for a night hayride—with flashlights, of course. For children, it's fun to be in the dark. They are less inhibited to play with lights inside funnels, pipes, bottles, and to further record light creations in the dark using conventional art media.

- *Children are prolific screen inventors.* The rhythmic pattern of miniblinds is illuminated by a nighttime flashlight show. Children explore the canvas of a lamp shade or a new white sneaker, or project light over white jeans resting for the next day. Some projectionists require the largest surfaces in a room, focusing light images on ceilings, the wall, doors, and door frames.

  In the art class we explore new screen ideas, test found objects, and construct unusual screens. For screens, we play with draping fabrics and see-through plastics over flashlights. We hang white laundry, such as shirts, socks, and textured towels on clotheslines. Screens are inflated from groupings of balloons, popped-up from specially covered umbrellas, stuffed from pillowcases, or stacked configurations of lamp shades. We piece together miniature screens from cotton balls, stickers, Band-Aids, and ribbons and create large, distinctly patterned or textured surfaces. Students themselves pose as screens, wearing white hats, gloves, and aprons, while others project images over them. Our most memorable screens at Disney, I-Max, sports events, and concerts are discussed.

- *Children customize and invent new flashlights.* We find flashlights decorated with tape, covered with stickers, or painted with nail polish. Children often attach flashlights to their toy robots, space guns, planes, and bikes. They have great ideas for wearing them on vests, slippers, hats, or pajamas. The shape and form of flashlights has not changed significantly from their inception, yet children have found many new forms that would be the envy of any manufacturer.

  In our art room flashlight store we feature the best children's ideas. Some models are redesigns, piggybacking on existing flashlights, while others are fanciful prototypes. In our store there are also toolboxes filled with PVC pipes and parts, unusual funnels, corrugated pipes, hoses, and many styles of cups. Only in the art class can you find remotely activated, multiheaded, rolling, motorized, color-mixing flashlights.

Flashlight Art History

A big tin box with illustrations of old Yale brand flashlights, a store fixture from the 1940s, sits on my art room counter. It is a call to fellow flashlight lovers who anxiously await the secret back door of the box to open and reveal my vintage collection. Students are interested to see flashlights originating from different periods and used by different professions. We look at old advertisements and the beautiful art on old flashlight boxes. Collectors' books help in our studies. This is flashlight history that children can hold and try out. The big neck sticking out of a child's lunchbox is a bird light, part of my contemporary fun light collection from circuses and toy stores. By wrapping up flashlights or making tracings and rubbings of them, children begin to sense the beautiful sculptural form of an everyday object.

A Final Celebration

At center stage, moving with colored spotlights from flashlights covered by orange Ping-Pong balls, the Raisin Figures dance out of a lunchbox. A soft landscape illuminates the lunchtime show, formed by lights played through a sliced tomato projected onto the white enamel inside the box. A flashlight in a child's hand is like holding a balloon; it is a cause for celebration, inviting a playful and creative state of mind. An art tool should feel as playful in a one's hand as a toy that is richly explored. A flashlight is both a toy and an art tool in a young artist's hands.

DISGUISE ARTISTS

Post-it Plays

You may not see her, but I have a busy partner at my desk watching me type this chapter. Post-it packs disappear, as Ana tries on new noses, draws new mouths, and designs new facial features. She occasionally glances toward the mirror reflecting on each new face. The tiny camera on top of the computer is turned toward her, so I can replay the scene for my students tomorrow. In the meantime, I am off to shop for more Post-its and exciting stickers—makeup for the next art class.

There has never been a better selection of interesting sticky items to cover children, the original Band-Aid and Scotch tape artists. Paid, Sale, Received, and Confidential labels are painless instant disguises, and labels are available now in many solid and glowing colors. The joy of early peekaboo plays continues to build into adventurous face-change experiments. Our art class Post-it and sticker faces encourage kids to further explore uncommon makeup. I follow the children's lead and bring in oranges for the class to peel, after recognizing a classic mask created by a child placing orange peel shapes on his face in the lunchroom.

Have You Watched Me Shave?

Judging from Ana's enthusiasm, I should sell tickets to this special event. "Can I squeeze out the soap? . . . Let me put some on my face," she says.

More exciting than covering oneself with soap or bubble bath in the tub, shaving cream forms a rich white beard and a variety of changeable thick and creamy face wrappings. Children love to watch and be invited to participate in a morning facial magic. Stayed tuned for the evening play and join us when Mom puts on her night creme.

Touching, rubbing, massaging, and feeling our faces is a basic portrait activity. The new pastel colors of shaving cream, fluorescent suntan lotions, Silly String, and other contemporary face covers contribute to the popularity of this artistic play. To learn about the richness of the face as a sculptural form, and not just a gathering of cartoon features, we play barber and become makeup artists. We invite explorers of peaks and valleys, plains and forms of faces. To build a touch of familiarity with face lines and textures, a prerequisite to informed portrait drawing or painting, we smooth fun things over faces. To follow the action, all kinds of dental, automobile, makeup, and surveillance mirrors are available.

Trying on Everything

It is not negligent parenting that requires the frequent lost-child announcements in a store. It is simply that kids easily wander away, drafted by shopping ideas and the temptation to try on everything. When secretly following young shoppers in a store, I found that not only will they try on sunglasses and clothes, but also they will model things that adults would not think of wearing. Don't tell Ana that I recently saw her trying on a lamp shade. Children will playfully get inside a pillowcase, wear a paper diaper, or mold a leftover piece of aluminum foil to their face. To learn about objects, kids "get into them," discovering as a result the most interesting headgear.

How do you prepare for an art session on disguises? By modeling your best finds, of course. In an art class you may be surprised at what you see modeled in a mask fashion show. With desks pushed to the side, the long carpeted runway becomes prominent. Children peer from behind field hockey sticks, wear plastic bins, hold up unusual flyswatters, place their nose into car cup holders and tool caddies identified as masks. Each student takes the spotlighted runway walk and provides a colorful description into the mike. The underlying theme of the parade is to see masks as something contemporary, an art made of forms that are constantly discovered and invented. Students discover that even mass-produced objects leave telling human imprints of faces stamped in them, an art waiting to be discovered. When students leave the art room feeling that anything can be auditioned as a mask, new finds continue to arrive throughout the school year. A good art project should never go away, but contribute to a permanent awareness.

Masks at Work

For some children a sticker and a lollipop are enough to conclude a dental visit. Others want it all—the plastic mirror, the floss, and the new pink dental mask. I was surprised to find a big mouth with smiling tooth drawings in my rearview mirror, as Ana retouched her souvenir dental mask. I made a quick detour on the way home to the medical supply store to get a box of paper masks, just in case Ana or my other school artists required them.

You would not believe what appeared on the heels of our discussion of contemporary masks. Students brought in a beekeeper's mask and a variety of swim and diving masks. We held a show-and-tell about masks for hockey goalies and baseball catchers, tried on a fencing mask, safety goggles, a gas mask, and a gel-filled night mask. To study these exciting forms, we traced them, played with their shadows, and wrapped each in foil and cellophane. Of course, many drawings were made on the way to designing our own originals.

A mask exhibit was held in our school entitled "American Masks in Work and Play." Unfortunately the show will never be a definitive one, since students keep bringing new mask examples to class. My favorite mask collection started in an attempt to preserve family history by saving the masks our children wore for Halloween. Today, I add to an extensive American children's mask collection by browsing on eBay, the art teacher's favorite class prop store. Under the key word *mask*, an exciting Web soup of mixed masks from all cultures and periods appears, many affordable enough to start any art class museum.

African Masks in a Kmart Culture

Children gather before Halloween in our home to share their disguises. Ana is readily accepted in the group of Kmart masks, even though this year she decided to wear an African tribal mask from my teaching prop collection. Some of the kids ask to try on other exciting tribal masks. The result is an incredible cultural summit, a timeless meeting of old and new disguises, affirming the great universal spirit of this art.

As children bring to class the masks they found most interesting in stores this year, they are surprised to be greeted by their art teacher wearing an old tribal mask. The occasion made an interesting comparison of the ceremonies and uses of masks in other time periods and cultures. Discussions covered differences in theme, manufacture, material, and design. Making totem poles from toilet paper rolls, or African masks from papier-mâché, doesn't easily forge cultural connections for students. Instead of trying to imitate examples from past cultures, we need to look for clues to universal meaning and shared experiences that are often found in children's art interests. Children maintain a culture's timeless appeal for celebrating in disguises, sensing the magical powers in wearing and discovering new forms of face coverings. Exposing students to old tribal masks is an affirmation of a living artistic path to which children continue to discover contemporary extensions.

Closing the Makeup Box

Children's sunglasses are the stars of this summer. Many new glasses join others in my old schoolbag, a dwelling for the collection. The kids trying on sunglasses in the art class feel the magic of instantly looking different. I watch Ana open her new makeup box with its palette of colors and big soft brush. She tests every color on her face, with the joy of self-transformation shared by anyone who has ever put on a mask, makeup, or shaving cream. Kids are in touch with the basic power of the artist to change, the ability to create someone else, to try on new characters on a personal canvas. Playing with disguises in the art class preserves timeless artistic mysteries and incentives for making art.

8

Home Drawing
Experiences Guiding
School Art

LINE PLAYERS

In the dirt, children dig for squiggly lines, carefully observing an unearthed worm. Finding a beautiful web, they try to relocate a spider's delicate line art. Well aware of interesting lines on the sidewalk, kids respectfully step over them. Children will bend down to pick up an unusual ribbon, twig, or phone wire, adding them to their pocket collections. Kids know all about lines. They are line collectors and innovators. Art teaching can foster children's line interests if we look to children themselves for inspiration. Art teaching needs to foster children's natural interests in real lines, their sensitive observations and harvesting. In turn, art teachers must recognize children as line artists and discover their line encounters. Lines in an art class need to be seen beyond drawing or as an abstract quality found only in adult art. We need to keep children's playful relationship to lines alive by developing art lessons in which lines move and are moved by creative explorers.

Hands are not the only part of the body involved in drawing. Children's art is inspired by action and fantasy. We play with lines by animation, listening to lines, driving, wearing, and even becoming the line. Drawing is playing with lines. Before drawing pictures we envelop ourselves in lines, playing with real lines, in real spaces. We walk the line and take lines out for a walk or a drive. We dance with lines. Our playing develops a close connection to lines, sensing them as part of us, a part of our walking, our heartbeat, our writing, or what we wear.

Moving Through Lines

In the classroom we create line environments to explore and experience how it may feel to walk through a drawing. A striped yellow snake climbs a thick wire hanging from the ceiling to the art room floor. Artists and spectators are forced to crawl through a jungle of lines. The floor and walls, covered in white paper are a background to imaginative line environments. The lines and suspended objects leave extraordinary shadows on the white papers set out to collect the shadows. We compare moving through this web of lines to the many linear elements surrounding us daily.

Animating Lines

Children come to school as free line handlers. But they become tied to long periods of intense note taking and writing, becoming mechanical line makers. Animating lines rekindles the joys of line playing and the freedom in line making.

Among Ana's favorite performers inside my red toolbox are the yellow folding ruler and the push-button tape measure. Each has had multiple performance careers in rapid succession, turned and twisted into drawings of different robots and creatures. A classroom-size supply of folding rulers and tape measures have held similar attraction for our art room performers.

Students film wonderful circuses with such guest stars as a black corrugated drain pipe, carried like a whirling Chinese dragon by a line of student handlers. And once the big box of springs is opened, there are plenty of lines with which to clown around. Animated springs are supported by a cast of twisted coat hangers and folding ruler creatures.

Driving Lines

My son Jacob always insisted he could not draw. Yet I remember his remote-controlled red Ferrari and how gracefully he drove it, tracking muddy lines across clean white papers on my studio floor. He also drew with his tiny Matchbox racers, which moved elegantly across the furniture, gathering speed to glide into complex aerial drawings. How exciting it would be if children drove their drawing tools with the freedom and imagination they exhibit in propelling toys! I tell the story of the red Ferrari in the art class to introduce drawing as a means of lending objects our playful moves. Art class drivers customize all kinds of wheeled toys with drawing tools and global positioning systems as they pass over paper roads, maps, and paper-covered globes. Tires dipped in paint or graphite or pressed into stamp pads leave tracks over a variety of surfaces. Each play invites art visionaries, as we consider universal drawing acts performed by robot cars and tracked with GPS devices.

Casting Lines

Ana recalls fishing on New York's Shokan Reservoir: "The best part was instantly casting fishing-line drawings, which I quickly named." In the art class we reminisce and recreate drawing memories that took place on water, in sand or snow, or on a foggy car window. One child described jump-rope pictures she used to make in the air, and more detailed jump-rope drawings with pinecones and rocks on the ground. With roots in children's drawing inventions, I collect jump ropes, hula hoops, and fishing rods for the art room. We run with yarn outdoors, dropping vast yarn lines, which anchor to the grass like Velcro. Drawings on indoor and outdoor surfaces multiply many times the scale of one's line dreams. Children in our class prepare line drawings made with bright surveyor's ribbons to be pulled by kites in the air. The free dispersal of lines also lifts the imagination of makers of drawings on paper.

Tying Lines

As a dot grows up, it goes for a walk and becomes a line. Seeing the world, it joins a community and becomes tied together. Parents have wonderful memories of their children tying their shoes for the first time or tying together letters of the alphabet to read or write. We refer to children's early tying creations in an art room exhibit of fanciful shoelace knotting. We tie together clothing finds, scarfs, belts, and suspenders into artistic hangings. Instead of car carriers or bike racks, we use classroom chairs and tables, to tie down objects with exciting knots and line weavings. Tying explorations create a fresh view of drawing as a means of tying and anchoring lines.

Untangling Lines

Organizing my life tends to begin with the garage. Such innovations as the garden hose reel and extension cord caddy make it more convenient for me to take these objects to school so that art students can unfurl them. A tangled anything is an annoyance to adults, but a creative twist for children. One of the largest drawings I have stepped across was made by kids untangling our garden hose. Children who are allowed to play with a phone cord, an orange extension cord, or their clipped hair, develop memorable line experiences. In the art class we get entangled in lines to creatively work our way out. Untangling illustrates the evolution of a drawing as a series of playful line changes. Keeping a drawing sheet beneath everything, allows us to trace records of each interesting line phase.

Line Construction

My favorite outdoor canvas was the laundry line. I liked the feel of the old rope and pulleys which allowed the line to move. I built cable cars along the rope for my toy figures. The laundry line was also my high wire to train clothespin performers. My art students now plan the construction of moving clotheslines across the art room. I value my early line plays as drawings I used to build. In the art room we replay children's early line constructions on the floor. My students discover nonsensical lines in assembling old train tracks and test their drawings with a brave little engine. In another play, we begin with the traditional twist of pickup sticks, but after they drop, students make the rules, using them to build skyscrapers or robots—or to spell out their names. Experiences of constructing with lines is just as important as constructing with blocks. It is a rehearsal for structuring lines in a drawing or architectural plan.

Wearing Lines

Children constantly develop fashion trends in line art to wear. What's new this year? For several years it was friendship bracelets. But now it is to weave a section of their hair with a string in friendship-braid style, which the children make from thin, colored strings. On their backpacks, children display hanging fringes made from rubber bands and paper clips. Wearing multiple belts and necklaces is also popular. Thick and thin lines, twisted or braided lines are children's wearable designs.

In the art class, we use interesting wires and unusual yarns and ribbons to create our own trends in wearable lines. We create entire garments from constructions of wall and ceiling hangings, cut down to model. Students discover the most fascinating looms, weaving lines through combs, plastic baskets, spiral notebooks, kitchen tools, and other promising openings. Weaving is a traditional way of tying lines which lends itself to wearable display.

Signing Lines

"You must be a doctor; I can tell by how you write," noted a pharmacy clerk amused by my signature. It's fun to play with lines even in ordinary acts, and I use every opportunity to scribble my name in infinite ways. While classroom teachers emphasize good penmanship and legibility, I speak of becoming a line player and line explorer. My students love to practice their special artists' signatures. Artists cannot be afraid to play with lines.

Sound of Lines

While drawing on the chalkboard, students tried to outdo each other with crazy chalk squeaks, that sounded like a jazz session. The line solos on the board inspired plays focusing on the sound of lines. I pulled out a blue fruit crate that became a conductor's podium, and called for auditioners using a chop-stick baton from my lunch. In art teaching it is important to improvise and follow the children's ideas. Conductors took their turn on the podium, while other students worked their chalks over portable chalkboards. We recorded the sound-making line event and used the tape as a soundtrack for the art display. When drawing was a live performance, there was no self-conscious line making. One student remarked, "If the sound of a drawing is exciting, it will be an incredible piece to look at." This play moved many students to listen and test other drawing tools in action.

The End of the Line

Children learn about lines as an art element, by memorizing definitions, or as a penmanship lesson with rules. But children already know about lines. Perhaps better than anyone. They are line inventors. Untying the schools' stranglehold on lines requires a steady diet of going back to line playing. When a first grader looks up and says, "I cannot draw," perhaps he or she is really saying, "I cannot play anymore; I cannot make an exact mark, and I know I am not supposed to make playful marks anymore without a line having to be something, or look like something. I cannot draw because I no longer feel how much fun it can be to just play with lines."

DRAWING INVENTORS

The children in my art class could not wait to see their gifts. They enthusiastically showed them to their friends and carefully wrapped them to take home. I explained to the students that many artists work on a "series," and that the series of drawings I was working on was inspired by drawings I observed children make at home.

I said to my students, "I love to share my art with people who appreciate it. I often say that you are my artistic inspiration and tell how much I learn from watching you make art each day. I know that you also like to make art for those you care about. To show how much I appreciate working with such wonderful artists, this weekend I made drawings for each of you." The following sections describe the drawings I made and the drawing inventors that inspired them.

Stapler Drawing

I keep my staplers loaded. I learned that students always like to borrow the stapler and return it empty. For kids, stapling doesn't always mean joining papers. Some children bring their own staplers with metallic-colored staples for jewel-like surface decoration. To decorate a birthday gift, my daughter uses metallic lines made with patterned stapler marks on long ribbons of adding machine tape. She demonstrates an understanding that a drawing tool is not necessarily a pencil.

My class drawing gifts explore stapling as a serious art form. Inspired by children, I stapled marks over Mylar ribbons and drew with another favorite hand tool of children—a hole puncher. In art class I have a stud maker, a sequin press, corporate seals, tracing wheels, and other hand tools with which to draw. Everyone is taught to sew on the art class sewing machine. Students dial up fanciful stitches to draw on papers or fabrics. Electric staplers, nail guns, and high-speed fasteners will surely alter the future of drawing.

Glue Drawing

On the back of my hot-glue gun drawing, created with colored glue sticks, I read the dedication: "To young pouring artists, who rekindled in me the fun of playing with lines." The dedication is a reminder to parents and teachers to stand by and allow children to pour glue out of newly purchased containers without admonishment—and I know the feeling of having just purchased the glue children pour with dancelike abandon. What appears like a complete waste is in fact, one of the freest drawings our young Jackson Pollock will drip. This scene, frequently replayed in homes and classrooms, should not result in punishment, even when children sprinkle cocoa, paprika, or the contents of a tea bag on their lines. The student receiving the hot-glue gun drawing appreciated the swirling free marks. She happily joined the class celebration by breaking out ketchup and mustard packets we had collected all week. So we can have fun pouring yet preserve drawings, we lined with soft napkin canvases the protective shell of styrofoam fast food containers.

Makeup Drawing

I found my daughter in my wife's makeup drawer, eyeliner pencil in hand. It was hard to explain why a pencil that looked like a pencil was not a pencil and should not be used for art. Fortunately, she did not listen and secretly used the eyeliner pencil to draw wonderful pictures on tissues she found on the bathroom counter. Ana also worked on lipstick drawings and nail polish sketches, preferring unusual makeup tools to her crayon box.

Showing my next drawing gift to my class, I explained that I share the thrill of finding and introducing tools in drawings that were not intended for art. I drew this gift with wood markers, meat markers, and shoe polish dispensers, sharing children's inclination to search for drawing tools in all places. In our art class show-and-tell, we try to outdo each other with new drawing tool discoveries.

Melted-Crayon Drawing

When Ana noticed her new crayons, which she had left outside, melting together in the summer sun, she decided to do more baking. I had no objection to her idea, even though I was not sure how the color crayon globs would come off my wife's baking pans. By late afternoon her handsome color chunks were cool and ready for drawing. Ana enjoyed making her own art tool and the power of drawing with many colors at once.

I continued to distribute drawing gifts to my class, and in a drawing I was about to give to one of the children, I demonstrated how I fused crayon shavings with an iron. I made color blobs, attaching them to the tip and top of a pencil before the blobs cooled. Students were fascinated with the tool, which I used "kayak style," rowing back and forth on my paper. I shared a collection of old crayon chunks, slabs, and other multicolor drawing tools that fascinated me as a child. The students created crayon bundles and bouquets, tied together with rubber bands, and tested them in multicolor drawings.

Broken-Pencil-Point Drawing

In my drawing class as a child in Vienna, we used Herr Manfreda's text, *Wie Ich Zeichnen Lehrne*. I show students the text and the three-page introduction on the correct way to sharpen a pencil. When I started teaching, students constantly asked to go to the pencil sharpener—I thought they were all Manfreda students. I soon discovered they were interested in the contents of the sharpener, in separating the shavings from the pencil points. I was impressed by how students skillfully drilled and inserted broken pencil points into soft objects like erasers, inventing multipoint drawing tools. Students also used the curled pencil shavings to make jewelry.

Inspired by pencil-point drawings, I used a gardening glove and covered each finger with double-faced tape to arrange broken points. Everyone was impressed with my drawing glove and could not wait to create their own multipointed tool. Students found perforated kitchen tools, watering can heads, and pieces of window screen—all used to organize pencil points. We created and dreamt about drawing tools of the future, from pencils as plotters inside computers to mechanical pencils inspired by cordless screwdrivers.

Foggy Finger Drawing

It's a rainy day and I can just barely see the road to school. The car pool crew doesn't seem to share my anxious moments. In fact, they laugh while sketching on the foggy windows. The finger drawings range from portraits to fanciful line patterns. In the rain and behind schedule, I surprise the girls when I pull off the road to take pictures of their drawings.

I recount my story to the class and give away a drawing entitled "Finger-Drawing Car Crew." My finger-cruising paint lines inspired by the originals on the car window are sandwiched between two sheets of overhead transparencies framed by black tape. My students ask if they could draw on the classroom window and window-lined lobby during the next rainy day. I am ready with Saran Wrap to cover any window and use markers and paints.

Antenna Drawing

We got cable television this weekend and the discarded wire antenna it replaced had many bidders. Holding it like a divining rod, Ana attached drawing tools to the antenna and "remote-controlled" it in swaying and collapsible modes. Children know that drawing tools can "ride with" any object. For new tool-handling scripts, I consult children who draw with crayons attached to rackets, umbrella tips, and baseball gloves.

I used clear tubing from our discarded aquarium to squeeze different colored pencils into both ends. I demonstrated to my students how the pretzel lines in my picture were twisted by independent drawing moves steering the plastic tubing. Drawing Tool Inventors, Inc. collected handles all week. Now the collectors have spread out bike handles, clamps, and gooseneck lamp parts flea-market style for other student shoppers and traders. Students select parts for new drawing tool inventions. They proudly demonstrate their tool ideas and trace them into a class-sponsored drawing-tool catalogue.

Drawing Straight Lines

From my days in architecture, I saved many types of compasses, triangles, and T squares. My wife, the fashion designer, also kept many unusual rulers that yielded endless drawing pleasures for our children. They played with the rulers, taping them together into linear constructions used for drawings. In recognition of children's inventive drawings with rulers, my next drawing gift explored drawing with a collection of templates. From our science and engineering departments, I have been collecting the rulers and templates with which they work. Children in class were also anxious to try drawing with my many antique lettering rulers and templates. Debunking the notion that only freehand drawing is art, we explore the beauty of ruled lines. We look at the work of contemporary artists who rule and tape lines, and children discover new rules—and tools—for drawing.

Tracing and Drawing

Some of my children's most inspired drawings started as tracings. Ilona's tracing of her teddy bear depicts an important friend in her life. Many tracings accompanied Ana's excitement about her first violin. She fancifully transformed her violin drawings into dream creatures, conjured up while practicing. When I read Ana a story at night, she traced the story's characters on my back or traced shadows on the wall while I read. Tracing is children's way of inspecting and fantasizing about objects.

My next gift was a tracing of souvenirs of a day. I traced parts of the many doors I pass through, the floors I walk on, and the objects I encounter. In the art class we trace movements, shadows of ourselves, our art works, or favorite toys and collections. We trace our bodies in unusual settings, in exciting moments, or from reflections in mirrors, then turn them into action figures or moving Lego constructions. Tracings are not silent children standing in Egyptian poses. Children's best tracings are active and animated; they are playful photocopies and instant snapshots of people and objects.

Graffiti Drawing

My newspaper always has amusing editorial additions. My children draw mustaches on the clean shaven and sketch a trapeze under an unsuspecting politician. Fashion ads in our mail are transformed by expert stylists. Lacking the anger of street graffiti, children's adventurous markings over print worlds tend to be gentle, decorative, and humorous. Improvised masks, altered backgrounds, or unexpected details provide kids with a voice in the world.

Finally, I show my drawing gift—a weaving of doodles photocopied from children's school notebooks. I tell students that artists doodle constantly, and I see their informal drawings as elegant art. Pocketed receipts, junk mail, appointment-book pages, and flyers frequently become my canvases. Students bring in charts, manuals, tests, handouts, and school papers to magically mark over with permanent markers. The ability to draw over any surface is a powerful use of drawing. The Magnum is the "big" marker of markers, allowing the smallest child to append a powerful mark and artistic comment to any surface.

The Gift of Invention

Children are drawing inventors. Their drawing is certainly not what most adults think of as drawing. Kids know almost instinctively that drawing is everywhere, anything can be used to draw with, and any tool or surface can be converted for art use. Teaching drawing is showing interest and enthusiasm for kids' drawing inventions, instead of drawing lessons that talk about drawing as something adults invented, skills to master, and steps to follow. A drawing lesson should open doors for young drawing artists to look for drawing opportunities everywhere, starting with their own drawing inventions.

SCISSOR ARTISTS

The Joys of Cutting

After finishing a drawing, kids often ask for scissors. "Can I cut it out?" With a cut, the art is freed to dance, to become a doll, to form a strand of play jewelry. "Now can I have some string? I'm going to wear this to show everyone what I made." Cutting takes a picture and makes it a toy. Children's pockets are homes for pictures, dolls, and creatures they cut out. Young children love cutting, and a pair of scissors is a magical tool.

With the power of scissors in hand, children freely scribble and cut through papers. If paper is unavailable they will start on their hair. With scissors, children make selections and take slices from the visual world. Kids use scissors like a vegetable peeler, trimming edges and encircling images. Kids cut peepholes inside pictures to make places to stick their noses through. Scissor holes through the eyes awaken portraits. Kids value scissors as a fine chisel, drill, and drawing tool.

In school, children are required to follow lines, to cut on the line, to color inside the line, and write between lines. A school "genius" is able to demonstrate mechanical cutting skills at an early age. The only place where playful scissor use is valued is in the art room.

Cutting Play

Funny things happen when scissors are set out on art room tables. Waiting for the art teacher to finish a lecture, a student cuts grasslike fringes on every page of his notebook. When students officially begin the lesson, one child takes two pairs of scissors to cut paper from opposite sides. I watch children in order to learn about their scissor art and begin art lessons with scissor plays.

Scissors travel in children's hands as they cut new roads. Do you have a scissors driver's license? We drive scissors across detailed maps and cut around curved mountain roads. We follow the "tire marks," or dotted lines of tracing wheels, with spiral cuttings. In night driving, fast-paced scissors try to keep up with moving flashlight beams. Take along your canteen for cutting adventures across desert surfaces.

What is the name of your favorite scissors? Scissors can be dressed, cast in parts, and called by name. With bright noses, creative costuming, and a clown-college education, scissors become clowns who leave funny and unexpected marks. Scissors can have more than nine lives, cast as musicians for rhythmic cutting or transforming into fierce creatures tearing and devouring a surface. Playing the part of a paring tool, scissors can peel away at a large rectangle, cutting corners, edges, loosening the rectangle's geometry to create new forms.

Hug a big piece of wrapping paper and squeeze it into a giant snowball. Open to inspect it and you'll harvest gorgeous found lines. Fanciful folds, unusual pleats, and playful tearing provide inspirations for cutting—not regular old school cutting, not cutting mechanically on a line. We cut with fire and invention, rediscovering the beauty of a cut line and the way we felt about scissors as young children.

Cutting Piles

My wife and I ponder over each receipt at tax time, while creating tempting mounds of paper for our enthusiastic scissor shredder. My daughter Ana patiently waits with her scissors in hand for the piles to swell, so she can playfully cut several layers at a time, reshaping the unusual papers. In the art class, playfully cutting multiple layers involves students shopping for stacks of unusual papers, then scissoring through the stacks to fill a bucket. Uncensored, fast, and free, cutting through paper pads and piles creates beautiful lines that can be held in our hands. We trade, cut duplicates, and tie together scissors for multiscissor cuts. Laundry lines with clothespins await the bucket brigade who hang and arrange the most unusual cuts.

My art classes shop for unusual receipts, envelopes, printed forms, and charts to staple into cutting pads. To feel our different cutting moves, we stand up to cut. An elegant fallout of lines sails from paper pads onto large outline drawings of wide-screen TVs, billboards, and giant picture frames. Scissor plays produce beautiful cut lines and shapes.

Editorial Cuts

"Were you all 'photographed out' by the time I came along?" Ana asked. She had been admiring her sister's photo album and then leafing through her brother's album. "Where is mine?" It's because I was the youngest!"

After a thorough search for all her photos, Ana set out to reconstruct her childhood with her trusty scissors. She playfully reshaped the edges of photographs, reframing them. She freely cut around scenes to focus on what she considered important or to scissor-edit sights and people she did not want in her album.

No wonder Operation is my students' favorite scissor play. Wearing surgical masks, groups of students stand around a patient, a body tracing on a white paper sheet on their operating tables (their desks). With playful scissor actions students remove imaginary organs, cutting beautiful lines and forms from the patient. We also operate on well-known artworks, using scissors for art appreciation. We cut into a masterpiece's reproduction and dissect the work's lines, shapes, and structure. Cutting up one's own art can also tell us a great deal about its construction and provide evidence of its design and details.

Fast Cuts

The hungry green monster roared through its first road test, swallowing up my studio table cover and spitting out long white paper lines. Ana found the green, battery-operated electric scissors at a garage sale and could not wait to use it. With power and adjustable speeds, the electric scissors cut long flowing lines. The world's longest scissor lines became an art class challenge.

To simulate power scissors in class, we attached fuel lines and power packs to civilian models. We unfurled long papers along the school hallway to extend our drag strip. After countdown, each scissor handler added sound effects and took their scissors for a speed run. Jet Ski Scissors made sharp turns and used small round stickers for speed control. The Fastest Scissors in the West galloped while making legendary cuts, leaving a trail of dust. In speed-testing scissors, students try new scissor holds, lightening up their grip, laying knuckles low on turns. We draw cutting tracks and raceways and dream up gears, remote controls, and new scissor attachments. Students turn their scissors into figure skaters to mix speed and grace while performing on ice. Using scissors as dancers, students cut with twists and power, moving all over a surface.

Delicate Cuts

Brides of past generations turned their hopes into lace doilies they made for their future households. As future guardians of the doilies of our family, our girls loved playing with these intricate artworks. Applying the most delicate scissors to the task, they cut paper versions for their rooms and playhouse. I proudly share their self-inspired art with my classes as examples of intricate scissor drawings.

To drill and cut into papers, students survey the art room for trash cans and backs of chairs on which to stretch paper canvases. Students drill test holes, tiny openings, which can spread in all directions when cut into lacy place mats, delicate doilies, or stencils. The droppings from the canvases are fine lines reminiscent of Ana's nail clippings collection. From the clipped lines, one student assembled an imaginary computer chip. We also play with readymade paper stencils and doilies, cutting new openings and connections. In each cutting play, students are encouraged to collect and use what they cut and also what they cut away from, which would usually be discarded.

Art Appreciation for Scissor Artists

To appreciate the beauty of cut lines, students try to lift and animate my enormous 1895 iron shears. We also imagine what it may have been like to have a door-to-door salesman come to our home in the 1940s with a case of shiny new scissors. From this vintage scissor salesman's case, students test sewing and cosmetic scissors. Students love my antique children's scissors collection. Scissors have a fingerprint, a unique cut, made by their weight, shape, and blade construction. Scissors have a wide range of marking ability depending on the speed, direction, and handling style of each user.

To feel the beauty of cut lines, we study the art of shadow artists who cut fine paper profiles in the early 1900s. Wonderful scissor artistry can be found in old postcards, especially my antique valentines collection. Paper dolls also cut an illustrious piece of American art history. We also look at the ailing Matisse's cut works. Some children lie down to cut elegant shapes from Matisse's famous bed, while others stand and act as his trusted assistants waiting for detailed instructions for pasting the cutouts onto large papers on the wall.

The Final Cut

Dads have interesting toolboxes to explore, but moms have the coolest scissors. When Ana, at age 8, began cutting my hair, I had to make an appointment. After all, it took time for her to gather all the mirrors and combs—and to look through Mom's sewing box for the best scissors. Ana's hair salon bills and receipt pads are used to inspire many art class hair styling appointments for happy and hairy pumpkin heads. To be trusted with scissors is part of growing up and enjoying new creative challenges. Perhaps we take a step back in school where kids use safety scissors that make cutting safe but not much fun. Cutting, like scribbling, is among a child's first loves and artistic explorations. The art class can again be the place where children have fun with scissors. Let joyous cutting begin!

FROM COPYIST TO ARTIST

Henri Rousseau's Small Disciples

Walking down the school corridor, I glance at the art work posted along the hallway. I am surprised to see each first grader has drawn the same Henri Rousseau painting. While waiting outside the art teacher's classroom, I hear her say, "If you draw the lion's eyebrows as dots, it will look like a cat. Draw them as dashes, if you want to do it accurately." "What is accurately?" asked a first grader. "It means you want to do it correctly," the teacher explained. The art room walls displayed museum posters including a number of Rousseau's.

A lesson led by adult art ideas, rubrics, and formulas, conducted in a shrine dedicated to adult artists, demonstrates that children's art does not carry much weight in the art room. During the time I visited this school, I was teaching a series of drawing lessons to children in a different way—recognizing my students as artists and emphasizing the uniqueness of children's art.

What Did You Bring to Class?

Bouquets of Drawings. At the start of each art class I receive gifts. "I brought some drawings to show you," said a little girl. Children look forward to sharing drawings with me that they have made at home. The girl unfurls a wonderful drawing of a pony in a field of rainbows and hearts. I thank another artist for the picture list of guests she has made for her birthday party, especially the scary portraits of the uninvited. Young artists are interested in my response to the pictures, but eagerly fill in a pause with their own explanations. I try to make sure that many great drawings are brought to class, as many as will be made here to take home. Our classroom walls are constantly refurbished with drawing gifts, an indication of what is valued here. Art teaching is not just about the upcoming lesson; it is also about making time to encourage a child to draw.

I hold a daily bouquet of drawings reminding me how beautiful children's visions and interests can be. Instruction in adult invented drawing techniques separates children from their art. Drawing needs to stay connected to children's hopes and dreams, to have meaning for its makers.

Authentic children's drawings are not exercises; they have reasons for making them. During drawing time children should have the feeling of being free to draw, of reconnecting to their art. What we call free drawing time in an art class often yields genuine drawings. Starting with the children's contribution to the drawing class confirms that we are working with artists who have ideas and the ability to express them. In order to keep children's art the focus of our teaching, we need to be constant observers and collectors of home art, and a fan of the art children show us.

Sketchbooks and Idea Books. "I brought my summer sketchbook to show you!" As a final act of the school year, children create sketchbooks, to be filled during the summer. Summer drawings are reminders how artists work all the time on their own. Coming to school with drawings underscores the idea of student preparation for each art class. Most art classes require that you come as you are because the art teacher prepares everything. I teach students to come to class with drawing ideas, to keep visual diaries, to doodle all the time, and take visual notes.

In the fall, when children search for new notebooks, binders, and notepads to take notes (on others' ideas), I ask them to find and make their own special books in which to file their ideas. Our drawing books are places where students look through their own ideas for self-assigned drawing tasks. The drawings, observations, and plans students bring to class are their preparation. To teach artistic independence is the point of every art lesson. Students come to my class to make art; they bring their idea books, and I ask them, "What do you want to draw?"

Art Supplies. "I brought in stuff to draw with . . . my mom's eyeliner pencil, a Liquid Paper stick, and a black tailor's chalk," says one student. Another says, "I made a box for my collection. I call it 'drawing tools of the future.'" Children coming to the art class are eager to share found supplies and feel they are testing them for the first time in drawings. "Look at this old vacuum cleaner bag—and I found my Dad's old Rolodex to draw on." "I will put my drawings into this CD case with these plastic name-tag holders." Before drawing class begins, children show and trade objects and ideas.

I encourage students to look for tools, surfaces, and drawing opportunities in everything. Instead of being handed essential drawing ingredients, young artists welcome the opportunity to search on their own, to discover new drawing sources and contribute their ideas to the future of the media. The mission of every future artist in my class is to invent drawing. My role is to insure that everyone comes to class with many finds accompanied by ideas.

Lunch Box Collections. "I brought my lunch box." After lunch, children carry their lunch boxes to class like safes filled with precious items to use in our drawing class. Inside are Legos, fast-food figures, plastic utensils, and foil pieces fresh from animated lunch box performances. In addition to making the perfect stage for performing apple cores and dressed-up utensils, lunch boxes also act as magician's cases, toy carrying cases, doctor's bags, salesman's sample cases, picnic baskets, and garages. In class, a bite-carved apple makes the transition from lunch room to art class and shares an animated story that is subsequently recorded in drawings. Welcoming lunch box–toting youngsters helps to assure a safe passage for their ideas, for the unpacking of collections and art dreams to be opened in the art room. Allowing kids to bring their favorite stuff to class helps to put them in charge of drawing.

Pocket Collections. "In my pocket is a toy wheel, this plug, and my tooth that fell out yesterday." Personal and unusual collections end up in children's pockets. For parents, pocket contents are a laundry-time nightmare. But for kids, the contents of their pockets are a fertile crescent for stories and ideas. In the art class, we inventory, sort, set up, and display the contents of pockets for still lifes and action scenes, souvenirs of special visits and occasions to relate and draw. Pocket debriefings become preliminary play rehearsals and idea sources for drawings. Children's drawings based on their unique collecting instincts generate wonderful drawing ideas. Drawings that begin with children's objects are entered into playfully and with confidence.

Toys as Models. "I brought my teddy bear," said a little girl. She created a wonderful hat for her bear, outfitting him for a tea party designed under the art room table, to which we all received wonderfully drawn invitations. When it's okay to bring the ones you love to art class, children bring their favorite figures to dress, celebrate with, and pose. When children bring a teddy bear to class, it is just what artists do, working with their favorite models. Telling kids how to draw a teddy bear is like telling children how to love their stuffed friends. Sitting at an art table with kids, I learn a lot about teddy bears—their names and what they like. I even find out that bears can draw. Drawing is having something to say, and kids have a lot to say about their favorite things.

As a form of personal notation, children search for personal and playful ways to draw their beloved toys. Every art lesson needs to speak of why and how artists do what they do. Why do artists use still lifes? It is because of their relationships to the objects of their choice. A preliminary artwork is created by posing a subject to be further shaped in a drawing. Each art lesson also needs to express these freedoms in drawing, instead of being lost in the search for the "proper way."

What We All Need to Bring to an Art Class

Our students should bring themselves to art class, filling their pockets, lunch boxes, and shopping bags with personal finds and collections. Art teaching is preparing students to prepare themselves for each class with items that speak about their dreams and interests. My colleagues look into my art class and cannot believe that students are playing under their desks with teddy bears. What does that have to do with drawing? Art teachers sometimes forget what inspires children to draw.

Children's drawings should look like children's art. Take a step back in a school hallway to tell the difference. Are the drawings driven by adult ideas, adult notions of art, and adult art models, or are they representative of the active hands and voices of children? Are the children in this display studying some technical issues in drawing that were proposed and solved by adult artists a long time ago? Would these drawings ever be made by children at home, on their own? Art teaching needs to connect children to their rich drawing roots, their own reasons for drawing, which in turn have inspired so much of modern adult art.

Painting at Home
and
Painting in School

BRUSH ARTISTS

Kids paint with everything before we put art brushes in their hands. High-chair painters use their fingers. Bathroom artists squeeze striped colors from a toothpaste tube and test makeup brushes. Children's painting explorations are furthered in our painting class. Visitors to our art room may be surprised to see someone holding a fishing pole. Attached to the artist's fishing line are bobbers and sinkers that he dips into colors and uses as customized painting heads. Another student looks like a nurse removing a patient's splinter. She carefully paints with tweezers, changing tiny makeup sponges and dipping cotton swabs into paint.

Students understand the inside joke when I start a painting class by saying, "I am sorry I forgot to bring paint brushes." My students find and create exciting tools for pouring, smearing, rubbing, scrubbing, spreading, mopping, dripping, soaking, or spraying colors. Students eagerly join a brush search, auditioning all objects from fine grass, a feather duster, a watering can, rocks, and pickup sticks. Bottles with spray tops, eyedroppers, and pour tops become viable painting tools just like at home.

Brush Views

What is a paint brush? How do you think it was invented? Children's creative views suggest different courses the future of painting may take: "A brush is something to take paint from a jar to put it on a paper." "It is like a spoon that can scoop up paint and take it somewhere else." "Brushes suck up paint and take it to where you are painting." "It's like a knife, something to spread paint with." "A brush came from a broom, to sweep colors around a canvas."

Ideas for what a brush is also touch on ideas of what it could be. If the brush is a transporter of paint, students envision other things to load with color for transportation to a job site. We take ideas even further as students describe how ice cream scoops and construction equipment could be used as a paint brush. If brushes are siphons of paint, we discuss using basters and eyedroppers, or building special vacuum cleaners for painting. Inspired by the idea of the broom being the source for all paint brushes, we gather other cleaning and polishing tools with which to paint. We brainstorm about retrofitting sanders and using scrapers, rolling pins, and seed spreaders in creating art.

Brush Dreams

When our friends the Barnes family adopted a Hungarian sheep dog, they invited my daughter Ilona and me for a visit so he could meet other

Hungarians. We were greeted by a giant shag carpet with eyes, as Shmutzig brushed his long white hair against the floor. "He looks like a supersize mop," Ilona said, while I took a picture. In our art class, I shared a dream of dipping Shmutzig into paint and training him as my brush. We renamed our class mop Shmutzig, and the students were eager to try painting with it. Dreaming is a mode of artistic travel beyond the ordinary, an important part of an art class. A sheep dog opened up visionary painting sessions for students wearing fur gloves, using the collar of an old coat, and dipping carpet fringes into paints. Dreams about painting can point us toward undiscovered brushes. When we paint with our dreams, we also recognize practical stand-ins for even the most fantastic brush ideas—like a mop for a dog. Dipping into real paint, students are encouraged to power their painting tools with the spirit of fantasies. Part of painting is the experience of it: We look for new and innovative ways of having that experience in order to create heightened moments of awareness and excitement.

Imaginary Brushing

Our playful moves before painting are calisthenics to free the mind, the body, our hands, and the brush within our hand. The air itself represents a free brushing zone, where brushes are played with as a toy. Before painting, we rev up our Hot Wheels cars, circling the table and launching cars into playful flight. We stand up to move freely, letting our hands fly imaginary stunts in the air. A student holds the hand of a Barbie doll and moves it freely through paint globs, crossing tire marks painted by speeding Hot Wheels car tires. Children are freer toy handlers than brush handlers.

Before a painting adventure, we pretend that our brushes are equipped with magic powers. We twirl them as batons, balance them as magic wands, hire them to conduct an orchestra, or clown with them in our imaginary circus. Bowing, we ask a brush to dance, inventing new moves for it on the ice, or the dance floor. In a dark theater for brushes, our flashlights spotlight brush performances, and we listen for exciting brushing sounds. School brushes get stuck in students' hands when they are engaged in limited, mechanical, and permitted moves. They need to be freed from a tight and controlled grip, rehearsed in nonpainting moves.

Action Brushing

I was painting on a ladder when my son, bouncing his basketball, dropped it into the paint bucket. Impressed with the black marks on the white tarp, he kept dribbling. Knowing that Dad, the art teacher, would appreciate his brush marks, Jacob asked if I wanted to take a picture of it. Kids as action players need active brushes that can keep up with their active moves. School brushes usually are used like school writing tools—with tight control.

After a good paintball fight I can't recognize which of my kids is decked under the layers of color. I remember taking a picture at a paintball parlor to share with my students the energy of applying color in battle. In class, students invent fascinating ideas for action brushes, painting with moving jump ropes, rolling marbles, and bouncing tennis balls. Away from sitting, away from tables and chairs, we paint with moving bodies. One such student invention was a Twister-style action tracing of bodies moving with brushes over a paper gameboard. When squirted with water the action targets loosened a flood of flowing colors. Students from a joystick generation also can invent a variety of remote painting devices, such as remote-controlled toys to command in action painting.

Brush Styling

I have frequented my daughter Ana's bathroom beauty parlor and barbershop since she was 7 years old. As she puts a towel around my neck and gathers the best scissors in the house for my haircut, I'll remind you that Ana has an impressive resume. At 5, she practiced on her own hair and styled hair for countless dolls. When Ana ran out of clients, she practiced cutting and braiding the hair of my old house-painting brushes.

I share with my students her makeovers—brushes with parted hair, brushes with curlers and bows. Our students practice reshaping bristles, redesigning handles, and inventing extensions for retired house-painting brushes. Each new look suggests a new brush handling technique when a restyled brush is paint tested. Old brushes with paper-clip spacers, tangled bristles, red bicycle-grip handles and retractable antenna extensions are moved in ways that no one before has held a brush. Long-haired paint rollers occasionally visit our salon to have their coats trimmed, retied, or repatterned with strings, rubber bands, and insulation strips. The new paint rollers roll out new patterned paths, and the student customers have an understanding that brushes and rollers can be creatively customized by the artist.

Big Brushes

After painting the house, I can hardly recognize Ana under the paint drips. She holds a giant brush in one hand, a big roller in another. As Dad's summer helper, she demonstrates her house-painting tools. Big painting jobs require big tools, and kids love to load color on the biggest possible painting tool. Home painting chores are important painting experiences for children. In home painting, children can explore new tools and a variety of interesting surfaces. They can change the color of surfaces on a monumental scale. I show photos of Ana spray painting outdoor furniture and painting the railings with a painting mitt. Involving kids in choosing colors by looking at color charts and in sorting through the incredible painting tools available in a paint store is an important inspiration for young artists. Home painting chores are important art starts and models for school painting. In our classes, we search for the biggest canvases and opportunities to work with the biggest painting tools.

Collecting Brushes

When children paint in school, they expect to find paint brushes. But in our classes children empty their pockets to find them. Today's assignment was to fill pockets with objects that have never been tried as a brush. As we empty our pockets, we celebrate the places each object was found—"a kitchen brush," "a paint brush from outdoors." Each room in the home, every street and store aisle reveals itself as a brush source, and children cannot wait to look for others.

Who collects gold strands with a silver handle? No, not an aristocrat, but my daughter, the grand collector of scrubbing tools. To honor children's collections, we are currently displaying the spoils of brush detectives and the painting tools they uncovered. Sharing a collection of unusual toothbrushes leads to a lively sharing of sources for brushing tools. To shop for painting tools, we visit the hardware store and beauty shop. We look at kitchen stores to expand our understanding of where brushes reside. Collecting unofficial paint brushes leads to new ideas for brushing moves and new canvases on which to perform. We look for painting moves in scrubbing the sink or brushing our teeth. We try out any unusual found brush and display many as a work of art. My antique Chinese calligraphy brushes hang from their brightly colored loop crowns on my studio wall. They have never been immersed in black and only leave their places to visit my painting class. Selecting beautiful painting tools needs to be a part of the joy of painting. To collect brushes and admire masterpieces of brush construction elevates young artists to a lifelong love of brushes.

The Final Stroke

I know a lesson was successful when my students continue to show me new painting tools. When a student is excited about a spark-plug cleaner he found at the auto parts store, he is verifying that all objects have hidden painting talent. Being constantly challenged to look for brushes everywhere is fun. The artist who discovers a folding barbecue brush with which to paint is a painter with an open mind, a painter who is an inventor, always searching for new ways to paint.

COLOR ARTISTS

Our family album has many pictures of our children making art. I bring the albums to class to show children their roots as young painters. The photos speak volumes about growing up as color artists, artists who love to experiment with colors and paints. My students are color artists who see beauty in color unattached to objects or themes. Their painting acts are fresh as they intuitively search for exciting new colors and ways of displaying them.

Making a Mess

I always had fresh paint on tap in the studio where my children came to play with colors. Photos in my album show how the leftover colors were moved from container to container and energetically laid out in handsome blobs on the paper covering my art table. No adult artist mixes and applies colors with such gusto. Before painting, children are inspired by color and a pure love of paint. Before they brush colors into pictures, children's color experiments are called a "mess" by adults.

Children applaud when I open my paint closet at school. They love everything about painting—the feel of paint in their hands or on their noses. They stir, mix, and pour every color they can think of. The theme of my painting lessons is supporting the joys of color inventing, the magic of colors and water mixing into a lively substance.

Uncluttered by adult painting rules and color formulas, painting for children is a discovery, filled with surprises. They find new ways to transport colors they make, auditioning all tools and surfaces as possible brushes and canvases. Painting is too often taught as something that is known, something that has been perfected by adult masters, a legacy to be studied and appreciated. Art teaching can announce that painting is yet to be invented. We host the future of painting, the children who will untie painting from its past. Experiences in our art rooms help to advance painting.

Color Inventors

In another of my photos, the children are sitting on the kitchen counter, mesmerized by the colors born in the swirling blender. There is anticipation in their expressions—and the surprise of finding new colors. Young painters' spirits are awakened in the kitchen: They are eager to stir and blend. Experimenting with funny "milk shake" colors in our kitchen or mixing colors in my studio were Kodak moments for my children. My daughter had a vast bottle collection in which she poured and saved the colors she made with my studio mixers. Finding a magic and mystery in playing with colors can insure a lifelong interest in painting and in the colors of nature, food, or fabrics. Art teachers can value children's excitement about color or replace their excitement with color facts and formulas.

My art room is a color laboratory housing the most unusual collection of funnels and hoses. Students in lab coats stir colors in kitchen pots or white photo trays. They mix colors in flea market mixers and blenders. Color discoveries are celebrated like fine wine; they are shared and swirled in tiny cups and premiered on clotheslines in self-sealing clear plastic bags. The best color finds are poured into clear gel caps, arranged to create dazzling displays. We pour, drip, and channel colors onto sponges, watch colors soaking and merging on a blotter or settling into the folds and layers of white dinner napkins. Before brushing paint into pictures, children experience paint as an active substance, alive and capable of expressive flowing, spreading, and soaking—over, under, and in between surfaces.

Arrangements and Collections

In another photo, the paper chef's hat completes the picture. Ana is pointing to the colorful salad she assembled from the reddest tomato, the brightest yellow peppers, and the orangest orange she could find in the kitchen. For her color creation, she selected a yellow Fiesta-platter background. Children know the colors they want. Their color loves are an important element of their painting world.

Students can be encouraged to save their best color finds to bring to art class, where we celebrate the colors in our lives. For art class meals, we set tables with the latest colors in paper plates and tableware, preparing the boldest platters of color. In plastic crystal vases we arrange flowers, colorful leaves, or forms crafted from the most interesting napkin colors. We create many "dry" or "paintless" paintings by arranging and displaying color finds inside drawers, over trays, platters, place mats, or in a vase.

Sometimes kids save street finds simply because they like the colors of something. We show an appreciation for the importance of color collecting with ongoing exhibits of student finds. Over one hundred fantastic nail polish colors are currently in a classroom show, curated by a dedicated group of colorists. Every day is a color day welcoming students to dress in beautiful colors and load their favorite color finds in every pocket. Teaching painting is about supporting young painters' color interests—the colors they notice, the paint samples they pocket, the carpet samples they save, the color mixes they find in stirring yogurt or when slipping unusual food colors into cookie dough.

A Final Image

Our nation looked with amazement at how exciting red can be as we received the first close-up images from Mars. To commemorate, I took photographs to class, not from NASA, but of our pet Yertle's aquarium. Several years before, Ana had not only showered her turtle with affection but also created a bright red landscape to light up his life. She painted rocks, dyed plants with food colors, and designed red waterscapes. In the art class we constantly redefine the color scheme of the room with carpets from colorful fabric finds and redyed bathroom rugs. Flowering among the room's ordinary furnishings are painted chairs, trash cans, and an orphaned coatrack that became an upright study in colors. Art lessons in painting can open up possibilities for observing and altering the colors of spaces and the environment. Today I will be taking pictures of our school yard where we punctuated the landscape with red Mars rocks.

My students find new ways to transport colors from paint containers to a variety of unusual surfaces. We share in the discovery of new colors, making the wonder of color a primary ingredient of every painting session. Our paintings venture from tables to floors; they float on water, adorn rocks, and levitate on air as flags and magic carpet paintings. My students embark on a lifetime of searching for unusual color experiences. They collect colors and explore color arrangements with all kinds of everyday objects. Keeping our childhood excitement about colors, paint, and paintings alive during the school years is our venture. If you photograph the children leaving my art room with their paintings, you can see this excitement. Instead of carrying their paintings rolled up in shopping bags, the paintings *are* the bags. You can see this connection to color in the wise use of leftover paints and the ways with which children feel free to experiment with colors and paints. They leave my room with painted rulers, colored sticker displays on their lunch boxes, and oops! . . . someone painted designs on his shoelaces. All artists have been moved by great color experiences in their lives. As art teachers, we design experiences for students so they can experiment and discover colors as if encountering them for the first time. Our color searches and collections provide students with opportunities to redefine the bounds of color and find new references to design color wheels depicting freshly invented ice cream flavors.

CANVAS ARTISTS

As a symbolic leap into the future, I decided to remove my old paintings from the wall and separate them from their stretchers. My daughter Ana assisted in the ceremony of freeing the canvases from their frames. She was in charge of rolling them up; but instead of rolling, my trusted assistant placed the paintings all over the room. "Look dad, this one could be a nice tablecloth!" She moved one painting to the floor and asked if we could use it as a carpet. "Or if you don't want me to walk on it, it would look great as my bedspread." Ana reenacted the history of contemporary art, by allowing paintings hanging on a wall to enter all parts of the room. She held canvas in her hands as a piece of fabric that could be placed or displayed anywhere. The canvas removal ceremony can be adapted to many class plays used to question what a canvas is.

Canvas Draping

In the middle of a school day students enter the art room, surprised to find their chairs up on the tables. After shopping through drop cloths, bubble wrap, white sheets, and paper tablecloths, students arrange chairs draped and posing in fabric held in place by clothespins and rubber bands. Following the preliminary play, students paint their canvases with hair brushes and other unusual painting tools. Each draping idea encourages new ways to paint. Paintings that are dry are tried on other art room surfaces or worn by the artist. The art room can become one large canvas, covered in white paper from floor to ceiling: Doors, windows, and even the sink can play a role as a canvas. Painting sessions may begin by dressing everything in white. We set tables with white tablecloths, white plates, napkins, placemats, and utensils, all posing as canvases. When students themselves get dressed in white paper clothing, watch out—they have become walking canvases ready for painting. Beyond the art room, we imagine draping streets, buildings, trees, and country roads in white—all to create new artists' canvases.

Object Canvases

I take many pictures of my own children's studios—their rooms. One of my favorite photos is of my son repainting the uniforms on his toy soldiers.

Children not only paint their toys, but everything else in the room. In a photo of Ana's room, one can see her beige pencil sharpener wearing nail polish colors. Children's painting careers often start as object painters and not easel painters. In a photo of Ilona's room, one can see she used similar brush marks to paint the visor of her cap, as well as her phone and clock radio. I share these photos with young students to validate their own painting experiences, which seldom receive the same appreciation as traditional canvas art.

School painting sessions begin with students sharing their most interesting canvas finds. We paint chairs, trash cans, lamp shades, staplers, and other canvases that children bring to class. I ask that they return with photos of the painted object set up at home. Students look for canvases no other artists have explored. Each discovery suggests new places to find canvases. Camping suggests sleeping bags, tents, blankets, and picnic baskets on which to paint. Legos, dollhouse furnishings, cars, and other toys wait to be painted in our class. A painted tent is set out in our school lobby, announcing that any place and any object can become a canvas. Students walking by the tent are asked to vote for unusual canvases on which they aspire to paint.

Personal Canvases

I show photos of Ana's personal gallery—her fingers and toes painted using toothpicks. Pictures of the children in our bathroom mirror reflect improvised painting sessions on children's lips, cheeks, and hair. In their closets I document the girls' painted jeans, shirts, shoes, and shoelaces. In art class we paint on white gloves, socks, shoes, shirts, hats, sunglasses, and umbrellas. Students pose for fashion photos of each other, wearing the canvases they painted.

We don't do Seurat in our art class. To appreciate adult art in a painting class is fine, but students need to see themselves as artists and be initiated into an art world that still welcomes innovators. We dream of new canvases, new ways and places to display colors. Central to a painting session is the opportunity for invention and discovery.

Moving Canvases

I was ready to part with my rocking 45s and my old record player, but my daughter saw the pile of music history and transformed it all. First, she boldly painted the record player's top cover. Then she used the record player like a potter's wheel to spin and paint records. Active children often find moving canvases.

In the art class, we look for canvases to sail, float, fly, pull, or move by remote control. Students customize skateboards, add wheels to make a canvas into a pull toy, and create paintings on rolling suitcases. Students take canvases off the wall for a walk, turning them into shopping bags. Students still recall the time I brought my old VW bus to school as a guest. Kids painted the car's nose, hubcaps, and windows, and mixed colors with the windshield wipers. They loved seeing their moving canvas on the open road and witnessing mechanical brushes "repainting" their art in the car wash. Painting experiences should be memorable journeys over unclaimed surfaces and a passionate altering of life's canvases.

Miniature Canvases

Children enter the art room with bulging pockets. This special day every-one cannot wait to share the secret canvases brought to class. To empha-size that canvases are yet to be invented, our art lessons often involve students in outside research. Each student reveals special painting surfaces such as slides, plastic spoons, Ping-Pong balls, floppy disks, buttons, and name tags.

In our home, caps on every bottle in the refrigerator are hand painted. Ana's canvas search extended to the caps of shampoo bottles, which soon displayed her distinctive, sparkly palette.

While watching a disappointing movie rental, Ana took out her nail polishes to paint the leftover popcorn kernels in the bowl. Her miniature portraits were as intricate as Fabergé eggs. The glowing little paintings came to rest in jewelry box displays. As American painting grew to room size, children maintained the tradition of painting miniatures.

Canvas as a Container

Can paint live inside a canvas instead of on top of it? Leftover colors are always brewing in my studio. Ana opened up several gel-cap vitamins she found on my art table and refilled them with mixes of my leftover colors. She arranged the tiny capsules over a white food tray. In playing with my leftover colors, Ana has created paintings by arranging colors poured into see-through bottles and Ziploc bags.

In our classes students import collections of plastic bags and bottles to fill with paint. We arrange color packets with clothespins on wall-mounted plastic sheeting or on clotheslines where they look like flags for a grand opening. We've also created a recipe for paint sandwiches: (1) pour colors over a large plastic sheet on the floor; (2) fold the plastic over the paint; (3) mix the colors by pressing and walking over the folded layers of paint and plastic. Our clear color-mixing containers are not abandoned after painting, but rather displayed as paintings all by themselves. By allowing paint to be seen from behind or inside a canvas, plastic sheets, bags, pockets, and containers redefine what a canvas can be.

Canvas Assembly

An art exhibit on the cereal box is a typical work by our instant breakfast artists, who use stickers as instant canvases. Sticky canvases like Post-its, Band-Aids, and stamps are used to stake out art space over a milk jug or vitamin container. But wait—it's not over. Ana, the breakfast artist, uses extra ketchup packets to paint white napkins that will go into her lunch box. Children often assemble paintings like a puzzle. Instead of painting on a single sheet, children test paint marks on smaller canvases and arrange them in different canvas groupings. Finding modular canvases to paint, students bring dominos, file cards, and old credit cards to class, setting them up in different configurations and dealing them out like playing cards.

Outdoor Canvases

If you visited my summer studio in Woodstock, New York, you would know that children lived there. The painted bluestone slabs around the house, the driftwood gallery, and our multicolored lawn furniture give our artists away. A hike in the woods or a walk along the river results in souvenirs. What children carry home is a clue to their outdoor canvas ideas. Beyond nature's canvases, summer fix-up projects provide canvases, such as shingles, wood scraps, bricks, gutter pieces, or an old door.

When students return to school in the fall, we build on their outdoor painting experiences. Shopping baskets accompany us outdoors as we search for the best in fall canvases—the most colorful leaves to paint. A play pool becomes an outdoor gallery to float painted leaf canvases. Snow in the winter offers the whitest of white canvases for our students to test new color mixes. In the spring, when everything starts to grow, we roll out rice-paper carpets over fresh grass and steer lively, flowing colors over the paper carpets. A backyard or school yard is not only a canvas for flowers, but also a place to discover vast canvas possibilities and to display children's paintings.

Canvas Dreams

In a gallery show, I am often asked why I don't frame my paintings. My response is that framing is a language of the past, when paintings were about illusions created to be viewed through a magic window, or picture frame. Since my paintings were removed from the wall, from their frames and stretchers, they cannot be returned to their confinement. In my art and in my teaching, I want paintings to fly as freely as a flag. My students and I actively search for canvas ideas that allow our painting dreams to take imaginary flights. Art teaching is freeing students to question and invent, to see art in everything, and to rethink the idea of a painting surface.

10

Experienced Printmakers Wanted in School

POCKET PRINTERS

I teach printmaking to young printers. Children are hands-on observers of the environment who use printing to save and share collections of unusual objects they pocket. The prints we do in school are child tested, child invented, and are always accessible to texture and pattern collectors. Our printing starts with objects children find, what they decide to keep, and what they declare as treasures. The following thoughts are based on observing what children find valuable to save and the printmaking processes used to "lift" images from their finds.

Found Surfaces

"Can you take me to school before the carpool, Dad?" Two round trips, the first one starting at 6:00 a.m. was an unusual request, but instinctively I felt it must be important. The freezing temperature in the car limited conversation, but my thoughts of what prompted this ride in the dark included studying for a possible test, tutoring, or another early morning orchestra rehearsal. As we neared the school, sunlight started to peep up and shed light on our early morning affair. "I wanted to be here before the janitor starts sweeping," Ana said, "so I can look around and get all the cool stuff from the floor."

As an art teacher, how could I quarrel with my young artist's dedication? I am not even upset by her many attempts to dismantle our driveway, picking out loose asphalt pieces for her rock and shell collection. If Ana gets off the school bus with a drooping jacket pocket, it means she had a good collecting day. Admiring something in her collection will prompt Ana to take out soft papers, wrap it up, then share its gentle rubbing. We frequently take rides to fill her bike basket and my extra pockets with crushed street finds, unusual leaves, or part of a comb. We sort out collections after each trip and informally print playful rubbings with the "rolling pin" side of a crayon.

From old clothes I cut off big pockets for students to pin on their own clothing. The new additions celebrate the importance of pocket finds. Outdoor safaris include wearing our special pockets to fill with surface finds. We close our eyes to make trades based on what we feel. Students are also welcomed to art class after they have filled specially marked collector bags with precious buttons, caps, chips, keys, or door knobs. Printmaking is about all the objects we gather, objects students can use to stamp, wrap, and take rubbings as printed impressions.

Coin Printers

To fill in the blanks in her coin collection book, Ana makes rubbings of other coins. Children have interesting art collections, like coins, that can be supported and explored in the art class. Rubbing is a universal form of play and a fundamental printmaking technique. Most printmaking techniques start as a memorable childhood play. I teach printmaking to experienced printers, children who happily recall their own coin rubbing days.

In class I teach my students different coin-flipping games I played as a child. We fill the concrete squares behind the school with a sprinkling of copper and many unusual foreign coins our students contribute. Students feel free to adjust the accidental coin patterns on the ground to compose their print. The background for our rubbing activities are outdoor grounds, with ample cracks, interesting trash, and nature finds. We roll soft paper carpets over outdoor grounds selected for printing. The rubbing of coins further inspires expansions to concrete cracks, fallen leaves, and even an insect passing under the paper. Rubbing is an act of feeling surfaces by extending our fingertips with graphic tools. Rubbing can be mechanical, or it can be playfully choreographed to explore all sides of a tool, all pressures and movements of the hand. Students can be challenged to invent rubbing, to rub like no one has done before, to stretch the possibilities of this art form.

If a child is lucky enough to find money on the street, they keep looking down. Yet while some children hope to find their fortune on the ground, others seek it in coin collecting. Children will sort through everyone's change, hoping to find a rare treasure. Knowledgeable young collectors showcase their coins in handsome albums. Rubbing is also a way to gather, collect, and share collections with friends. In our art class, coin collectors make their own coins. We use rubbings to draw over existing coins. Students rub and join parts of different coins, merge redesigned fronts and backs. Like chocolate coins, students wrap unusual coin finds in foil or soft papers before rubbing. Children search for circular objects—buttons, checkers, bingo pieces, poker chips, round stickers—as new coin candidates. See-through cardboard coin holders and slide mounts become our frames used to build our own albums of art-minted coins.

And then there are children like my daughter who collect crushed coins. My students show their appreciation of Ana's collection by rubbing their favorite pieces in it. We discuss making and preparing our own printing surfaces by hammering, carving, drilling, and wrapping objects. We look for other objects such as foil pans, soda cans, and vintage license plates to crush and print from. In printmaking sessions the students have nicknamed "the wrap," we use soft paper to wrap crushed objects and other found textures like tree barks, phonograph records, circuit-board sections. Students then rub the soft paper packages to create unique impressions.

To promote the richness of looking for textures beyond one art lesson, we made home rubbing kits. Students filled "porta-pouches" with stripped crayons, graphite sticks, tailor's chalk (a great rubbing tool), and interesting papers. In the next art class we welcomed students' home rubbing adventures, which yielded such gems as coin wheel covers for a miniature bicycle built for two elephants, a sea monster with scary "foreign coin" eyes, and beach-ball nickels and pennies being juggled at a circus. A sensitive rubbing of a woven place mat became the background for rubbings of a child's coin collection. As an example that any place can be represented in a rubbing, one child re-created his room by stapling together rubbings of different parts of the room. A printer's eye learns to notice everything.

Pocket Stampers

The stamp pad on my desk has always been a favorite toy in our home. Piano-playing fingers have passed over it, leaving fingerprints on many things. Matchbox cars have raced across stamp pad inks, tires recording turns and skid marks. Erasers, washers, and Lego parts, emptied from pockets, became animated by the stamp-pad spirit, giving pocket finds new activity in playful image making.

My daughter Ana looked upon the postal clerk's stamper carousel with envy. As a child, she declared her intentions to become an artist and a postman. She took her dreams seriously, and during our garage sale outings, she collected many fine old date and business stampers and stamper carousels. Ana's extensive collection of toy stampers from fast-food places is often enlisted in decorating mail. She opened a branch of the U.S. Post Office in her room, inspiring the eager young employees in our art class postal plays. In preparation for class, my art students collect unusual envelopes, postal forms, blank stickers, and file cards with which they design postage stamps and post cards, ready for stampings. Children take turns as customers bringing in mail, packages, passports, pet licenses, and driver's licenses. Each item can be stamped or notarized with antique notary seals.

Unofficial Printers

When they see me enter class with plungers and toolboxes in hand, my students suspect a major repair job. "What needs fixing?" they ask, and "Can we help?" I explain how much I love collecting old stampers, especially those forms that are not thought of as stampers. I post an Open sign over the red toolbox prepared for stamper shoppers. The many compartments of a toolbox house interesting washers, tire repair parts, furniture leg protectors, and a rubber-ribbed glove. In the old tackle box, also in service, students find squiggly plastic baits for printing. Inside the makeup case, students discover lipsticks used for lip prints on soft tissues. Mile-long paper towels and adding machine tapes are unfurled as stamping freeways in the hallway. The art class takes on a printed look, as test prints in the hallway are cut to wallpaper the room. Students are fascinated by my collection of old wallpaper rollers. We list all the possible home art projects for our printmaking, including wallpapering a play house, printing our own fabrics for rugs and umbrellas, and making hand-printed door signs to our rooms. The best stampers are still waiting to be discovered and used for playful printing.

Rubbing Symphony

Rubbing is a symphony of subtle pressures resulting in changing impressions. To contemplate rubbing and sounds, we hum, buzz, zoom, and sing as we rub. Sweet and gentle sounds, to outright loud noises inspire different surface contacts with each surface being printed. We rock and rub, dancing and moving the rolling pin side of wax crayons or the tips of a lithography crayon. We dance like elephants or move like lizards, pressing down on objects being printed, exploring different pressures, altering our moves and speed of contact with each surface. In street prints, we bend down to celebrate what is under us. Rubbings help to focus on what is usually ignored so that the ordinary can be looked at with care.

In silence we listen to rubbings, allowing the sounds of the process to influence our moves. Changing the sounds of crayons brushing over a surface is a way to vary the impressions lifted from it. Children not only find beauty in the surface of objects by rubbing, but they feel free to use the object in interpretations, overlapping printed layers, creating new patterns and connections with the lifted impressions. Paper rubbings are cut apart, reassembled, drawn over, and used to construct new prints.

Stamping Jazz

I look forward to rehearsals with the "Jazz Cats." We improvise sounds with stampers over music sheets set up on metal music stands. The children play their own invented scores or follow a conductor on a fruit crate podium who listens to a secret tune on an old Walkman. Everyone sets up with pads and found stampers on individual music stands. Stamping beats are amplified by the vibration of the metal stands. Children and stampers make swinging musicians, as they explore the various sounds and moods of stamping. Stamping is an art of movement and sound resulting in a printed pattern. I feel a long way from the harsh sounds of stampers during my childhood under Communism in Hungary, when an official's stamper controlled life, work, and where we could go. Stamping in my American classroom is a celebration of artistic and personal freedom. It is an art of playful sounds and rhythmic moves. I vitalize, therefore, lots of noise in stamping, resulting in a rich variety of stamped impressions.

Where It All Begins

I am sitting with my 6-month-old grandaughter, Emilie, who amuses herself by reaching behind me, gently rubbing her hands along the texture of the chair. I offer her an alarm clock, a shampoo bottle, and a baby-wipe box to play with. Even though the clock and pink bottle are alluring, she keeps returning to the baby-wipe box, rubbing her tiny hands against the raised letters on its top. She smiles and keeps returning to the textured box top after exploring other things.

We print in our art class to rekindle the joyous moments of textural awareness and its pleasures in our world. We explore printmaking to stay in touch with patterns and textures—to stay close to collecting samples, building scrapbooks, and playing texture games. One cannot be a designer in art media without harboring some of Emilie's pure joys for the felt and visible textures and patterns in our life. Art teaching too often gets caught up in the adult processes and terminologies of printmaking, and we forget to tap into what children already know about it.

LIFE PRINTERS

Early Printers

High-chair printers enjoy the texture of each new food. Few printing acts are more exciting than watching a young child feeling his cereal and experiencing ways of spreading it on his hands and extending impressions over his chair, face, hair, and clothing. Adults ascribe these early forms of printing to a desire to be messy and receive them with a washcloth. Children's first prints are heeded as unfortunate growing pains and accidents and not something to take note of or encourage.

As children learn to walk, printing acts become more mobile and reach further onto home surfaces. Handprints are unappreciated on clean floors and walls, and learning to walk also means messy footprints. When reaching countertop status, children use forks and cookie cutters for printing. Early printing impressions are messy but significant in forming a child's initial interests in physically connecting with interesting surfaces and in manipulating textures. When printing moves to paper and tables, with neatly prescribed materials, monitored by parents, printing acts and surface explorations become less daring. In the art room, we look back to boundless body printers for a second chance to shake up our printing world.

Body Printers

As a little girl, my daughter Ana loved to test my wife's brightest lipsticks by kissing everyone. She composed a thousand other kisses on tissues, mirrors, and a white-wigged mannequin she found. Our body has many unheralded printers—knees, ears, and elbows—that seldom get starring roles. In surveying our personal printer, students think of unusual ways of using their bodies—and of new surfaces on which to stamp. Water-based stamp pad colors make good substitutes for makeup for safe body prints.

Containers of grape jelly, strawberry peanut butter, and tar-black "salad dressing" (a mixture of sand, salts, and paints in baby food jars) are fun for dipping fingers and hands. I coat all class surfaces in white paper for the children, who cannot wait to get into the food jars to begin printing.

In the freest form of printing in any art class, kids get dirty hands and press their fingerprints over paper-covered chairs, tables, and walls. This coming-out party is for those who love to print and dip their fingers into textures, then test them over everything. Caught up in the essential fun of printing and inventing patterned impressions, children dip, squeeze, press, and dance their fingers and hands. Students who know that parts of their bodies can perform as printing tools will remember the excitement of printing.

When great designers work to create fashion beneath our feet, how can we ignore such printing opportunities? In our art class we look for the best contemporary shoe soles, and welcome children with dirty shoes on our paper carpets. Stepping in shoe boxes with a small layer of graphite powder helps to detail printing walks and dances. When the ground is soft in the school yard, we spread paper carpets by the entrance door and later use the printed foot patterns collected in artworks. Printed walks are also rehearsed over concrete after a rain or in the snow. Children like to take their shoes off and dress them in sticky Dr. Scholl's foot care products. Printing with fingers and toes is fun, and we also learn about the use of printing to record the world around us.

Environmental Printers

While melting crayons into big chunks, Ana watches the cooking process through the glass screen of our microwave. Big crayons spark big rubbing ideas. "Let's make rubbings of the whole city," she says. Ana knows the penalty of stepping on a sidewalk crack, yet she is not adverse to making rubbings of them. She makes detailed prints around our house by starting with the sidewalk, then moves her rubbings to the brick walkway and up the steps.

Kids look down more than adults do and are more aware of the many interesting surfaces we cross during the day. My students valued the ceramic floor designs in our old school lobby and voiced their disapproval when it was scheduled for demolition. And when demolition began, sections of the old tile were constantly disappearing from the job site. Students can be encouraged to use printing at home and feel that any place can be recorded and captured by printing. Children can be challenged to describe home spaces by recording its surfaces, piecing together prints from lamps, furniture patterns, and samples of floor and wall textures. One student pieced together her room from rubbings from its caned chairs, wicker baskets, and the place mat on her desk. Postcards from home are student projects, showing rubbings of the surfaces that make each home a unique place.

Tire marks demonstrate a familiar form of printing in a city. Our art class studies interesting tires and tire marks. We visit a tire store to look at a showroom of those big printers. Back in the classroom, students rev up and roll Matchbox cars over stamp pads, then steer the cars over adding machine–tape highways. Roller skates, pull toys, and riding and remote-controlled toys can also be used as printers. Water puddles become inkwells for bike-tire printing after a rain.

We build roads in the art room from tar paper, window screening, bubble wrap, and coasters, using textures and patterns contributed by students. First bare feet, then crayons, are used to test our roads. Tires and other rolling printers represent a state of active, moving, printing action.

Printing Dreams

Has anyone ever printed a pyramid? How could we print the bottom of the ocean? Wouldn't it be fun to have a road-striping machine to print with? It would be interesting to print a country road and contrast it with a city street. We could print a phone booth! Many things we cannot print in school, but these are great printing dreams for the future that are beyond budgets or other limitations. It is exciting to share children's wonderful printing visions of places, equipment, and new printing tools and possibilities.

Sometimes out of our young printer's dreams incredible real prints materialize. For example, trees stand in our school yard wearing tourniquets of paper, looking like Vermont during maple syrup season. The fall leaves around the trees are gathered and arranged in kaleidoscopic patterns to be rubbed and printed into natural doilies. Children were inspired to wrap and drape the trees, grasses, and boulders of the great outdoors for printed impressions. Students prepare tool belts for outdoor printing safaris and discuss the yucky prints of worms and other city wildlife that could be saved through prints.

A Lasting Impression

We buy texture books for young children who reach out to taste and feel every texture around them, but a child's early life is already a texture book with active surface files. Children are aware of their busy printing lives, leaving a trail of hand- and footprints on countless surfaces during the day. In the art class, we create with lip prints, fingerprints, footprints, and tire prints, all to emphasize awareness of the wealth of art possibilities in daily printing acts. Children are rewarded for slowing down and paying attention to interesting surfaces accessible to everyone. We keep printing diaries—pattern books and collectors' cases for texture collections. Printing is a medium able to keep pace with active children. It is a portrait of a child's growing body, impressions of movement and play. Printing can be used by children to describe their increasing awareness of their environments, indoor rooms, outdoor "floors," and buildings. For children, prints are their souvenirs of places through which they pass each day.

PRINT-STORE ARTISTS

Ana's Stores

How many stores did you own in your life, including those played as a child? In our house, children always played store. Ana started her print boutique by looking for raised letters to print from our old appliance knobs. To make store signs, she rubbed the numbers from our street sign and license plates, all of which she expertly combined into handsome display art. The store's signature wrapping paper was printed over the Peg-Board and corkboard in the garage. I was invited to browse through samples of leaf rubbings on paper aprons and bookmarks displayed on her bulletin board. Hand-colored rubbings of objects from my wife's jewelry box were framed on her carpet/sales floor. Ana's establishments combined an interest in collecting, displaying, printing, and playing store.

Ana was never hampered by having to use a proper printing technique. From her basic understanding of printing, she invented printmaking as required by the item she created. I admired her practical and playful reliance on printmaking in creative endeavors. I recall when she wanted the rubber floor mats from the leased car we had to return. Print impressions from the old floor mats spawned an elegant line of place mats. In turn, Ana detailed the place mats with other print impressions from sink liners and doormats. To fill her store's play cash register with play money, Ana rubbed the raised surfaces of lamp bases and coin portraits, making intricate backgrounds to which she added raised impressions from corporate seals.

With minor changes, I enthusiastically imported many of the objects and images from Ana's home store to our print store at school. My students could not wait to become franchisees and start their own printing operations.

Art Class Printing Stores

A student customer brought an egg to the class store, and asked for it to be printed. People come into our printing store, and you would not believe some of the things they want. I can just imagine what the associates would say if they went to Kinko's. A customer asked for a color print of a phonograph record, and someone wanted to have an album of prints made from the shells she found on her vacation. Art class printers always say yes; our motto is "We can print anything." To create incredible images, we emphasize inventiveness in printing. Students in our class take turns as clients and printers. Finding ways to print any unusual texture or pattern is the students' challenge to each other.

Students in a print store learn to practice many forms of printmaking to create a variety of stock. From behind the counter, one quickly learns that there is no correct way to print anything. Students tailor ways of printing in response to customer requests, freely inventing and combining methods. With a brief introduction to printing, and an emphasis that all printing techniques can be modified, students witness playful demonstrations of inventive rubbing, stamping, and altering found objects.

Opening the Store. When children open a store, they start by making money. In our art room, we fill toy cash registers and ATM machines with the money children create from rubbing the front, back, or underside of objects like phones or boom boxes. Some bills are stamped from playful denominations carved into insulation boards. We offer gift cards, imprinted from old credit card rubbings, for those who want to make future purchases.

Custom store signs are printed from the raised surfaces of tape, string, and dried glue sketches. Students also print signs by recutting and customizing vintage stencils. Small store signs are laminated to receive pin backings and are worn by the staff.

To create a catalogue, students decide on the store's name, what the store's specialty will be, and the stock of items to be printed. Students collect surfaces such as cardboard, foam, home siding, insulation board, and drywall to be carved as illustrated plates and reproduced in the catalogue.

Shopping Bags. With any purchase from our in-class store, you get a specially printed shopping bag and matching wrapping paper. Rubbing surfaces from a vintage shopping cart stored in our art class provides an interesting background for shopping bags. For printing over that, our shopkeepers have gathered a vast selection of keys and key chains. Hanging from the handles of the shopping bags, are the inked key chains used to imprint each individual bag. We frequently display printing accessories such as blocks, brayer trays, and tissues, all ink marked, and a beautiful consequence of printing.

Greeting Cards and Stationery. Student prints fill a revolving wire card stand from an old Woolworth store. Our boutique cards are printed from designs made with self-adhering weather stripping applied to interesting backgrounds like doormats, CDs, and work gloves. Of course, children's card prints are often decorated with stickers. To appreciate printing in everyday items, students look at my collection of antique valentines and share each other's budding collections of beautiful greeting cards.

One group of students prints machine-age stationary from car elements including grills, hubcaps, lights, and chrome features. Another group uses textures from nature including tree trunks, rocks, and pinecones. This outdoors-inspired stationery is printed on handmade papers crafted from autumn leaves and grasses, the natural textures and colors of the season.

Wallpapers. Customers in our class can choose from samples of custom-printed wallpapers ready to hang in a playhouse. Students create sensitive rubbings of old walls: historic bricks, decorative woodwork, stucco, and stone. Wallpaper studies foster a love of wall surfaces in general. I share my collection of Victorian wallpapers with raised patterns and encourage sampling by rubbing. Print artists become more aware of looking for interesting surfaces in all kinds of building materials and save samples and discards from all home repair jobs for our printing store.

Table Dressings. Our place mat collection pays homage to potato prints, without discriminating against other vegetables and fruits that can be used for printing. Starting with teary onion prints, then moving to joyful cucumber and radish stampings, students add their own drawings to turn the fruit and vegetable prints into portraits and caricatures. We are constantly on the lookout for unusually textured place mats to inspire interpretive place mat prints.

Students decide to include ready-made prints in their store display to inspire others to look with more interest and respect for the printed arts in daily life. Over a period of a week, everyone collects the best examples of illustrated paper napkins and plates they can find for a group show.

Maps. Fanciful maps were the largest prints made in our shop. To print maps, students started saving the old plastic fluorescent light covers our school custodian discarded, then tied them to tables with jump ropes, tape measures, and strings. The textured covers, wrapped in line weavings, made striking prints that looked oddly like mysterious maps. To label and illustrate their maps, students carved eraser stampers. One student made a printed map using an old rolling pin, which she carved and crisscrossed with wide rubber bands, ribbons, and wires.

Unlimited Options

If children only learn potato printing, what happens to squash, carrots, and the rest of the texture world? Printing lessons can limit children's printing options. When printmaking is presented as something adults have already invented, requiring a mastery of handouts and naming of tools and their proper use, it doesn't encourage open minds toward printing's unlimited possibilities and it doesn't relate to children's interests. For example, printing will attract their interest if presented as something useful for saving collections and for sharing finds with others.

Store plays challenge students to find a printing technique for any found object and surface. In creating store goods, children customize rubbings, mix stamping and carving techniques with found object prints, and custom-wrap objects to print all sides. If they only learned potato printing, could they print a circuit board?

When I came to America as a child, I was fascinated by wallpaper and started a lifelong collection of samples. It was obvious even to a child that exciting printed art lived everywhere, not just in traditional frames. Store playing is an opportunity to focus on surfaces and printing in all areas of life. As an art teacher, I borrow from the rich traditions of children playing store and their ingenuity in finding ways to make impressions of the objects they are interested in showcasing in their stores. A lifelong view of printing is creating art lessons that don't depend on specific tools or processes, but instead reveals that printmaking is something students can do any time and on their own.

11

Discovering a Third Dimension: Children's School Sculpture

BLOCK-PLAYING ARTISTS

Before Legos there were Oreos. Building with everything around them—from foods, pillows, and pots and pans—is a part of children's art history. This instinct to build with all forms of things is neglected as kids get older and enter a conceptual and less physically oriented world. Block playing is basic to art experimenting, as children personally test many art and design principles. A block set is a basic art supply. Blocks are visible in early childhood classrooms, and art teachers have an obligation to save the vanishing blocks for later grades. As you enter my art class, Lego tables in each corner of the room welcome block players.

After Legos there are Lock-Blocks, Magnasticks, Bristle Blocks, Link-Its, and Pringles. We collect and test most new and vintage block sets in our art room, but we also continue to support children's interests in playing with potato chips and found objects. In fact, in one of the students' favorite trunks rest pots and pot covers, funnels, strainers, and other kitchen utensils. Even though adults lock the cabinet doors, kids don't cease to be interested in under-the-counter-style building. Art classes can extend the life of block players, who sketch out ideas and visions with blocks, until architecture school, where students regain respect for building with their hands.

Block Lessons

Let the blocks stay in the art class as an essential art supply for self-discovering art. Equilibrium can be felt by balancing blocks. Soaring is experienced by building sky-high towers and skyscrapers. Construction and destruction in art is seen when a block structure falls in a storm and student archeologists reconstruct its past. Adventurous spanning of spaces are pushed to the limit in ruler constructions over art room canyons created between tables. Building walls and fences explores the sensation of enclosing space and forms. The solidity of a block is clear to designers filling playhouses and spaces with blocks as furniture. Laying out a sidewalk with bricks is an experience of pattern and sequencing with blocks. Blocks make the experiencing of objects in the environment more tangible. They are also a tool to examine abstraction. Head constructions reduce the forms of a head to blocks. Our cubist life—living in block houses, driving block cars around block buildings, carrying block packages—is best expressed in block layouts.

A bit envious of her brother's new electric cello, Ana creates her own solution to a futuristic instrument. She brings a music stand to perform with her unplugged Lego sound machine. Children test and showcase their ideas in block prototypes. They set out blocks to furnish forts and playhouses and plan future stadiums for competing action figures. Block playing starts our art classes as students fearlessly explore ideas without erasing. Blocks become our models, our still lifes, our stories, our props, to be further explored in drawings, paintings, or videos. After an art lesson, blocks are a memorable means of summing up, evaluating, and fantasizing beyond the lesson.

All Kinds of Blocks

Pocket Block Sets. As I have said before, children's pockets are important object collection containers. A request to empty pockets reveals the beginnings of such building sets as magnetic marbles, bread ties, paper clips, and bottle caps. My pockets are emptied into a red parts box with many inviting little drawers; it seems to endlessly refill itself with unusual washers, magnets, bolts, and transistors. Our students designed official Pocket Block Sets, in small decorated containers, carried in pockets and lunch boxes. Miniature building sets serve as reminders that block playing can happen anywhere and anytime.

Big Blocks. I share my summer videos with art students. They are surprised to see an homage to cabana architecture built with inflatable swim rings and air mattresses. Children often turn to life-sized constructions, inflating the scale of traditional block plays. I videotaped kids who rolled up newspapers to make bricks, which were difficult to blow down once they were configured into a large-scale playhouse. In class we turn chairs, umbrellas, and trash cans into play blocks, attached with ribbons of Velcro. I've also contributed worn tires and a load of firewood to large-scale building experiments.

Soft Blocks. A gathering of pillows in a home is akin to a lumberyard delivery for a builder. From my art room pillow collection one can build a small mountain or improvise any other soft dream construction. Children who treasure soft stuffed animals also build with cotton balls, socks, shoulder pads, diapers, hats, and other soft forms they find around the house. Tub blocks adhere to each other when wet and gracefully flow in the gentle breeze of art class play pools. By stuffing all kinds of plastic bags, students manufacture other soft blocks. Reupholstering projects at home always mean a bounty of custom building blocks made from foam rubber pieces.

Edible Blocks. A chopping block was one of Ana's earliest block forming devices. Our abundant apple harvest led to all kinds of edible blocks, original fruit plates, and fruit construction over peanut butter sandwiches at home and edible building projects in school. Building with bananas made wonderful sculptural forms. When I notice a child successfully building with cereal, candy, or crackers, the item becomes a play block joining Pringles, Wheat Thins, or Cheerios, stocked on the art room shelf. How fortunate that crackers are packed in ready-made block sets. My cereal and snacks shopping is not based on nutritional information, or taste, but how well they perform in tabletop constructions.

Block Rolls. Children celebrate each new purchase of toilet paper packages by freeing all the rolls. Rather than worry, I bring in a pantry full of supplies to inspire a schoolwide building celebration. Suggested by builders at home, paper towel rolls are added to toilet paper rolls, and juice, fruit, and soup cans come along as solid bases on which to structure the paper roll monuments sprouting from the art room floor.

Interlocking Blocks. Although most block plays produce temporary structures, children like Legos and Bristle Block plays because the locking pieces secure their constructions. As an avid observer of children turning home chores into art, I find clues to art room supply needs. Currently available interlocking pieces for my classroom builders include a thousand different clothes pins, over a hundred electric plug converters, a huge gathering of different combs, and a basket filled with PVC sprinkler system parts.

Mixed Blocks. In my son Jacob's hall of fame built from blocks with a baseball cap dome, his oldest baseball cards are on display. Children's block playing often combines play blocks and found objects. Children's outdoor building projects use a combination of nature's blocks—slate, pinecones, twigs—along with play blocks and figures from indoors. When we play with blocks in the art class, shopping sites are left open for students who want to incorporate constructions with revolving plates, trays, phone books, retired phone receivers, or bike helmets.

Collecting Blocks

Children find blocks to build with even if they are unrecognized by adults. The coal pile was one of my favorite childhood playgrounds, where I secretly selected the best pieces to build with and carefully washed my hands so that the unapproved artistry would go undetected. In the art room, we pool our finds of erasers, rulers, books, pencils, or lunch boxes for building. A large trunk is opened up for collecting interesting sponges. Expert collectors have netted such impressive building sets as plastic storage baskets, classy perfume boxes, and take-out food containers. Participants in collecting unusual blocks appreciate the maiden trial, and help develop new building categories for future collectors. We encourage the search for vintage block sets at yard sales and antique stores, in collectors books, and on the Internet. Examining early Legos (which used to be cylindrical shapes) and other rarities from the art teacher's collection builds an interest in the rich visual history of play blocks.

Creating Blocks

In my own past, I remember the secret block project of painting my plain square wood blocks as soldiers in parade uniforms. Each block had four painted soldiers that could be arranged in different parade formations. Children often create their own play blocks by redesigning existing block shapes or by shaping raw materials into blocks. We sand wood pieces, paint them, and place them into hand-decorated boxes. Other student inventions include a handsome building set of painted twigs, custom cut with pruning shears. Another student painted tennis and Ping-Pong balls and outfitted them with Velcro for easy assembly. One student's play block creations were modeled from oven-baked Sculpey clay.

Real Estate for Block Playing

My children preferred sculpture gardens to art museums. At Storm King, in upstate New York, Ana admired the art by climbing on it or crawling inside. Inspired by the visit, and once again at home, she moved stuff outdoors, setting up our monumental mouthwash bottle on a high earthy mound. Ana built natural bases and excavated sites for a twisted toothpaste tube and lifted a row of shaving cream cans onto a slate pedestal. The young curator was in trouble the next morning when the family searched for the missing items. I offered to help with the retrieval, guiltily remembering the days I used to borrow combs, hair curlers, and all the brushes I could stick together to build with. While the dark earth behind the school is our students' favorite spot for block plays, we meet as sculptors and architects over a variety of surfaces. We build on shelves, stairs, inside hatboxes and instrument cases, and under water in an aquarium. Students learn how each site influences their choice of materials and style of construction.

Cornerstones

Pickles, carrots, forks, and soap pad constructions in our art class celebrate the unquiet hands of children. No one is afraid of building with our play blocks or, indeed, building with any object. No one says, "I cannot think of anything to do," or "I have no ideas." Quick block sketches warm up the art spirit and open up possibilities for the rest of the art day.

DOLL ARTISTS

Figures and Memories

Soldiers. We all have interesting sculptural histories we fondly recall from childhood. Mine had to do with the plaster general and his troops, for which I designed parade formations. I selected each soldier with care, looking carefully at faces, inspecting uniforms, and adding to the kindly general my own painted decorations. My fragile soldiers stood in still Egyptian poses; action had to be provided by a choreographer's imagination. Sculptures were very important to me as a child. When I had to decide what to take with me for our frightening border escape from Hungary, the soldiers in my pocket protected me against the Soviet border guards. Now that I think of it, it is not surprising that my senior sculpture exhibit at Cooper Union was a display of plaster figurative works.

Dolls. Ana opened her doll factory by placing her doll factory sign over a folded cardboard screen into which she inserted shelves and pockets to hold colored glue sticks, yarns, and a fabric collection. With the rich resource of her mom's scrap fabric trunk and plenty of interested customers, Ana figured out how to cut basic patterns and give each construction its own clothes, lipstick, buttons, shoes, and unique identity. Despite the most amazing dolls bought for children, there will always be a special love for the ones they make themselves. Very often a child's doll is their first major independent sculpture project. Children dress, feed, and cover up their dolls. They tell them stories and take them for walks. Playing with and caring for a favorite doll becomes a memorable relationship with a figurative sculpture.

Stuffed Animals. My parents were certain that their son would be a doctor—probably a surgeon. All signs pointed to it: Just consider how seriously and frequently I cut up my teddy bear to look inside. My mother could hardly keep up with sewing incisions and keeping the bear from being completely emptied of its stuffing.

Everyone remembers the loving features of her first teddy bear. Soft stuffed figures are children's introduction to fantasy figure sculptures. We hold stuffed animal parties in our art class and invite the children's favorite figures to meet my collection of vintage bears. The many soft figures that live in our class are frequently invited to pose, perform, and generally inspire our art works. Some even take art lessons from the children.

Fast-Food Figures. Grandma had the biggest recliner in our house. The green chair's cushy arms resembled fresh grass, acting as a perfect clearing for my son Jacob's many fast-food figure setups. Unfriendly villagers would post themselves under the lamp shade across the way, but they could not be seen until the lamp was on and shadows gave away their secret hiding place. Similar tiny figures ride in children's pockets or dangle as key chains from backpacks. One need only open the stage door of a lunch box to free fast-food figures ready to perform. Polly Pocketdolls, the tiniest of figure families, come with many miniature environments, while other figures are bred in Happy Meal boxes. From these tiny sculptures, children learn about scale and develop a unique art of fast-figure sketches by grouping and performing small figures inside of, or on top of, unlikely stages.

Action Figures. My first plastic, flexible figures arrived in a Care package from America. The cowboys and Indians were neatly tucked as prizes inside chewing-gum packs. It was the first time I had seen figures that could be freely posed, and I was excited at how they could show the actions I wanted in my play scenarios. They opened up a whole new chapter in my figure playing. Today's action figures have serious joints and bendable qualities allowing incredible posing to match the figure with the active expressions of the owner. Children create Barbie aerobics classes or space battles as exciting sculpture sequences ready for videotaping in the art room.

Figure Studies

Children explore the future of figurative sculpture today by handling figures in virtual reality, by voice activation, and with remote controls. Toy figures are now able to talk and walk with children, changing conceptions of sculptural relationships between a figure and its audience and advancing children's views of sculptural possibilities. In our art class, we view the history of toy robots and become a first testing ground for new figurative innovations. In these classes we cover all the basic components of figure studies.

Posing Figures. Posing figures is children's art, explored over many canvases in their room. Under a domed stadium of one child's bed, the manager of a baseball team directs his club of GI Joe players. Dolls set up on another bed wait for tea to be served. For the tea party, Raisin Figure band members are displayed for a musical performance on top of a boom box. In play, dance, and sports, children experience being sculptures, feeling sculptural balance, movement, and forms. Children's growing movement experiences are lent to toys, moving toy bodies into creative poses. When figurative toys regularly reside in your art room, children naturally call upon them as models.

Talking Through Figures. In expeditions over Bean Bag Mountain, the yellow art class beanbag chair, children move play figures and invent stories to accompany these movements. As children narrate the action, stories set the scene and pave the way for moving figures. Children talk to their toys and speak for them. Voices and action are almost inseparable. No subtitles are needed since figurative pieces are considered alive and able to talk. An important teaching tool I call "silly talk" promotes play acts, but be careful not to interrupt young sculptors in a special "trance" as they converse with play figures. Play microphones also encourage voice and figure performances.

Silly Talk. Silly talk is a useful part of an art teacher's palette, liberating students to perform unreservedly in an art class. Were it not for the art teacher's silly, exaggerated, humorous words and stories, students would censor their silly, humorous, and uncommon art ideas. Being silly, saying funny things in class, can be the most direct path to open thoughts and ideas that would otherwise be dismissed by children afraid to explore the unusual and unfamiliar in school. Implausible imagery, funny descriptions, unlikely scenarios, word play, unusual sound effects, can all model creative behavior. Silly talk takes the air of seriousness out of art for a moment, long enough for the unimagined and unheard of, to be seen, and enter into children's art.

Grouping Figures. In a fish tank on my art room counter reside scores of stuffed figures. Sorted in old lunch boxes are bendables, wind-ups, Transformers, and new fast-food figures. Our cast is large enough for a film studio's lot. We design adventures, fashion shows, races, television shows, sports spectaculars, and talent shows that involve creating groupings of figures. Art class casting directors set up events with figures of all sizes and combine setups of ready-made figures, which kids costume and make up with original creations.

Placing Figures into Settings. I often come home to find my shoe rack missing, borrowed for a hotel, with dolls driving inside my best shoes. Children create rooms, furnishings, vehicles, and landscapes for their figures.

In our art class, a variety of what kids call setups or action scenes are created with figures and found objects. Children set up over a choice of canvases such as carpet samples, pillows, shelves, hat boxes, or instrument
cases. They create scenes under tents and blankets, similar to props kids
would use in home plays. These extensions to figurative plays used at home
call upon young designers to cast figures into interesting interiors and landscapes.

Recognizing Figures in Objects. Hello, backhoe! Children have an incredible ability to spot human qualities in objects, even large construction
machines. Children will inspect the kitchen drawer to find play figures in
measuring spoons, ice cream scoops, and strainers. Supermarket trips are
opportunities to animate shapely bottles or find play friends in the vegetable aisle. A hairbrush, a mop, or a kernel of popcorn is given a name
and kids play with it as their doll. Art classes can build on children's ability to free the hidden figure from objects.

Transforming Objects Into Figures. A child's favorite doll may have been a
slipper or a feather duster in a previous life. Children invented pencil toppers in the same way they will dress clothespins, shoes, or hair curlers,
detail dust pans, and lend sticker eyes to a flyswatter. Children's playful
sculptural seeing frees objects from their everyday use and provides them
with new meaning. The ability to see the essential forms of an object and
to change it into a playable figure is an artistic trait worth fostering. In our
classes we audition to see how a collection of folding rulers could be turned
into a troupe of performing figures and use screens and shadows to highlight performance details. In the art class, we provide a constant challenge
to transform objects into figures.

Shaping Figures. While adults free a figure out of stone, a child's best figure work may be shaped from bread dough on the side of mom's bread-
baking tray. As candle wax melts, children instantly form play pals. In
children's hands, household materials that don't have great sculptural
distinction are squeezed into extraordinary shapes. On an airline food
tray, a napkin, tissue, foil, or candy wrap can be turned into inventive
figures on a playground. Young hands seek out the cold snow, the fresh-
est mud, the messiest contemporary play substances, such as Yak, Gak,
or Slime, to shape. Kids dismantle pens for spring people and open paper
clips leaving behind a chain of little persons. To further the appetite to
shape figures, our art room shopping sites are filled with unusual candy
wraps, foils, and fine jewelry boxes where small figures can rest as valuable sculptures.

Building Figures. Children's figures are not carved, but constructed. Children make soft figures out of their pillows, construct amazing figures by stacking erasers or Legos, and build rock, twig, and pinecone people outdoors. In the art class, we simply extend soft figure plays, geometric figure building, and outside doll making. Our art class uses pillows, balloons, beach toys, and leaf-filled lawn bags to create large talking figures to trace, light, perform, and most important, to treat as serious sculpture.

Figures Come to Life

While adult sculptors have fabricated figurative images from stone, metals, and wood, kids create figures from plastic spoons, foil wrap, and crackers. Children's dolls, and figurative sculptures are born as a result of playing and are made to be played with. Adult figures are stuck to pedestals, while kids' figures are as lively as their makers. Children's figures are puppets at heart, made for moving, and prepared to perform. Children sleep and eat with their favorite sculptures, and like Gepetto's they are dressed and brought to life.

HANGING ARTISTS

When I was a child, doing the laundry was a momentous family occasion. Between the warm and fresh-smelling lines of hanging clothes, I used to set up the best hiding places and clubhouse. After the folding ceremony, I became commander of the lines, stretched between wood pulleys and punctuated by wood clothespins. On the line, I tested the sail of my Young Pioneer scarves and souvenir handkerchiefs and composed music by hanging pot covers to clang in the wind. The best lesson ideas often derive from childhood recollections. When brought to class, play memories and art mementos from the teacher's childhood paint a powerful homage to children's art.

Calder's Birthplace

Enter a child's room by the glow of a night-light to experience a hanging artist's works coming to life in exaggerated wall shadows. A dragon sleeps, suspended from Ana's ceiling fan. The ornate giraffe is really a shadow of her painted clothes tree, on which she is constantly hanging new items. The dancing umbrellas are drink stirrers she collects and hangs from the blind cord. A tiny head hanging on the doorknob is transformed into a masked giant in shadow life. A survey of a child's room with the lights on discloses interesting hanging sites, means of attachment, and unusual items drafted for hanging, all useful clues for the advancement of the hanging arts in school. Every child's room is a hanging artist's birthplace, ready to be noticed and promoted by school art activities. Art teaching addresses hanging art by doing a mobile and showing the works of Alexander Calder. Children practice a broader view of hanging art and explore beyond mobiles.

Mr. Vidor's Hangers

I discovered my love of hangers in old man Vidor's closet. As Hungarian refugees, my parents sublet a room in Mr. Vidor's modest apartment in Vienna. The West had a special meaning when we opened the hallway closet and found a line of dark, rosewood-sculpted hangers with shiny hardware. I must confess that I still have one of the old Viennese clothes hangers; it formed the basis for my favorite collection. I proudly carry clothes hanger and clothespin sculpture history in a vintage suitcase to show every class.

For a hanging art lesson, students looked for their own "Vidor specials" in family closets and stores, exploring what is beautiful and old, exciting and new, in hanger art. Students in the art room are greeted by a white paper wall screen, illuminated by light sources to provide sharp shadows. Students trace and share their hanger finds, taking artistic liberties by customizing hangers already altered by their shadows. The art teacher should not be the only one who prepares for an art class; daily art homework is a means for students to shop for objects and ideas.

Art Rooms Prepared for Hanging Artists

Next to the classroom entrance, an old restaurant stand displays the daily art menu. In spirit at least, students daily leave their school to enter a special place—their art class. The Welcome to the Hanging Art Lab sign has a miniature illustration as a clue to what the new setting inside will be like. Small details in art room design can have a large impact. Enter and notice the crossing of colorful clotheslines at various heights and inclines. Unusual hangers and hard to find clothespins are perched on each line. In a flea market–style setting that encourages artistic browsing, unusual containers are open to shoppers. A tackle box offers sinkers to test hanging weights and balances—and colors in the form of lures and lines. My dad's old green toolbox is still fun to browse through for wire rolls, clips, springs, and all kinds of hooks and connecting devices. A camp trunk is labeled World's Largest Clothespin Mine. This lab setting is inviting for kids who love to hang things as an art.

Eye hooks and C-hooks in different sizes are set into all four classroom walls for easy hanging and coupling with pulleys and strings. I am always searching for unusual hooks and hangers to mount. Interesting places to hang stuff encourages hanging. The class Peg-Board sports the latest hardware. Lines and a red net suspended from the ceiling allow performance artists to consider the space above. Light stands and tripods are used to modify the path, angles, and connection of "trapeze" lines. Students who hang art can also survey many outdoor armatures. We create hanging works on playground equipment and trees, and we run lines through school-yard fences.

The National Hanging Arts Laboratory: Report on Recent Innovations

Personal Hangers. In the 1980s, children's fashion dictated charms. Everyone collected and traded plastic bikes, TVs, and dolls for hanging displays worn on belts, bracelets, and necklaces. Showing the items today still stirs interest, because children will always appreciate interesting hanging forms. Our body is a principle armature for kids' experiments with advertising buttons, jewelry, and key chains. My tool belt was always a popular item to borrow and furnish. A large collection of silver and gold safety pins in all sizes awaits the art class. We collect and create hanging forms made from wires, paper clips, beads, and found objects, and we curate exhibits on moving galleries—student jackets, hats, belts, and backpacks.

Figure Hangers. Crib toys and people moving around the crib are children's first interest in hanging forms and motion. Children eagerly reach for hanging forms, but it takes time to finally connect and be hooked on the excitement of making one's own hanging statement. I created a hanging sculpture over the crib for each of my children. For travel, I made a miniature hanging, suspended from the car's rear view mirror. Students enjoy seeing my crib creations and a personal side of hanging art history.

The school gym and its many hanging apparatuses, is an exciting place to introduce the hanging arts. While hanging from ropes, bars, and rings, we learn about shifting weights and balances in artistic hanging. Students compare graceful gymnasts to the playfully hanging monkeys on our zoo trip. With items from the marionette collection, we practice moving figures suspended from lines. Remain standing and imitate hanging art experiments to feel balance and the performing capabilities of different objects.

Hanger Designers. Not all hangers are welcome in a child's closet. A hanger is a miracle of modern design that kids instinctively appreciate. With such a hanger-wise audience, hanging sculpture in schools should not begin with

just ordinary wire hangers. Our class designers make their own by shaping wires or connecting twigs, bones, or springs, and then accessorizing
with beads and clothespin attachments. We open existing hangers for
modification and combine parts and wholes from different hangers into
new designs. In hanging art, the hanger, too, can be the art.

Hanging Sequences. We go to our school's circular multipurpose room to
experience being surrounded by kids' freestyle hangings of hundreds of
jackets, lunch boxes, and backpacks on hooks. Many interesting chance
hangings in our environment are revealed to students after the multipur-
pose-room study. I wait for permission to clear the hooks for an art session, using the same space for planned hangings. Our still lifes, colorful
hangings of scarves, caps, ribbons, hoops, and potato and plant netting,
become unique visual symphonies. Inside the classroom, hooks with
suction-cup backs can be freely placed on tile walls and windows for
innovatively hung passages of small collections such as business cards,
repainted paint-sample cards, folded wrapping papers, candy, or blazing
fall leaves.

Outdoor Hanging. Sometimes we bring the outdoors into the art room.
Nearby ski lifts were the most exciting of all hanging objects for me as a
child in Austria. I show and tell about my collection of toy ski lifts and plan
a day to design a cable car system in the school yard. The tall chain link
fence has a great advantage—there is no shortage of attachment points for
overhead cable lines. Winter tree-decorating projects have no religious significance; all children love to hang items such as their creations of painted
CDs, decorated playing cards, and potato chip bags.

We use every available doorknob for hanging outdoor pocket finds,
but also set aside a wall in class. A large sheet of plastic covers this wall,
with rows of little slits for clothespin inserts. The plastic wall is a backdrop
for hanging finds in see-through bags or for object displays. Kids are invited to hang items into the open plastic "scrapbook."

Beyond the Mobile

Children's many interests in hanging forms can be found in their room
and in their play. The typical school mobile is not the best example of
children's hanging art. It is an art based on kids' earliest fascination with
hangers, moving forms, and hanging things in the house and outside. As
artists of hanging forms, kids inventions have yet to be named and clas-
sified. Art media should be approached, not as school art, not as adult
art, not as known art, but as something new to be discovered. Artists who

hang finds and creations need studios, places to shop for materials and ideas, recognition, and reminders of their many related play experiences. Then they can be set free to discover what hanging art of still and moving forms can be.

ART ON WHEELS

Ana's purple 1950s Schwinn bicycle was so big and heavy, that I had to walk it for her. She wanted the wide-tired "tank" (found at a flea market) because of its imposing color and because it had not one, but two baskets—a wicker basket in the front and a wire one in the back. While I pushed the bike, she picked up street treasures to fill both baskets and placed the overflow in my pockets. During autumn, leaves were woven through the baskets, and during the summer fresh wild flowers filled it like a vase. I proudly wheeled Ana's living displays of forms and colors around. I also learned to admire other children's bikes in the neighborhood and often asked to photograph their bike artistry. Children's bikes undergo remarkable alterations by owners who dress up handle bars, decorate the frame with stickers and flags, and weave noise making beads through wheel spokes.

Children enjoy seeing my early bike works, and it is fun to share photos of my first bike. Its frame was basic black, since color choices were limited in Europe after the war, but the bike looked anything but basic. Among its exciting attachments was a sculptural fitting of found, bright chrome pipes, my make-believe motor and dream of a motorized bike. With future art teachers, I often visit the bike accessory aisles in stores to learn about the latest items available to the bicycle decorator's palette. In these aisles reside the most interesting striping tapes, self-adhesive reflector shapes, and camouflage seat covers. Many other children's play creations move on wheels, glide on skateboards, piggyback behind pull toys, or could be entered in custom car shows.

Collecting Wheels

Wheels move children's toys and help them to keep up with active players. Creative dreams are mobilized by spinning wheels. Every child discovers the excitement of the wheel and the vast possibilities it offers. Tiny Lego wheels acquire large fantasies constructed over them. As a child in Hungary when most things were scarce, I collected ball bearings that flew out from the wheels of army trucks. I admired these tough forms and their delicate movements and converted them into play scooters, racers, and other things the metal wheels suggested.

After our neighborhood bike shop closes on Monday evenings, fabulous deposits are left on the sidewalk for the next day's trash. In the twilight my children and I start to prepare the haul to school. Like a true ball-bearing hunter, Ana finds fabulous ideas in each discarded spoke, training wheel, and used tire. Future Ferris wheels, rolling printers, or moon explorers all start as ideas on the sidewalk. We can encourage children to develop their own wheel sources, to share their best wheels, casters, or tire finds, and to complete plans for their use with the art class.

Decorating Objects with Wheels

In the art room, eager students, who love to assist with setting up my childhood train set, help to move all furniture aside. But why all the stickers on the railroad cars, and why was the locomotive painted with nail polish? I was not a destructive child, but I repainted the tracks to simply make my favorite rolling toys more attractive. In the art class, we expand the modest layout into an elaborate imaginary track system with new cars, tunnels, and bridges. We add rail yards, stations, and scenery. Of course, the children sticker and decorate all their railroad creations on wheels.

Ana's childhood doll carriage makes regular appearances in our art class. She decorated the ragtop pink carriage with pillow creations and pictures advertising her favorite dolls on the sides. She constructed additional storage compartments from boxes wrapped in fabrics and ribbons. The boxes hang from the carriage handle and sit over the main frame. Jingling on a chain attached to the carriage is a select display of unusual key chains. Children frequently decorate their carriages and carts, customizing what is important to share with other vehicle artists.

From the art class toy chest different wheeled objects can be rounded up for conversion. Plastic toy trucks, red Radio Flyer wagons, and Matchbox cars are overhauled with new colors, foil armor, paper and plastic wraps, fringes, and banners to be proudly paraded down school hallways.

Building on Platforms with Wheels

Twenty-five brightly painted skateboards line the center of the art room, ready to roll. Our theme is the Macy's Thanksgiving Day Parade. Children designed floats to ride on top of the rolling skateboard platforms. Using fancy woven and dyed cords, the children guide their floats like pull toys. The floats transport children's characters and settings. Each float is highly detailed, down to its decorative new hubcaps. Wanted are old, clip-on–style, four-wheeled roller skates, which no child would want to be seen wearing today, to serve as future platforms for art room pull-toy designers.

Unusual fast-food trays, revolving Rubbermaid platforms, and exciting box tops are some of our best chassis to mount over wheels.

The love of pull toys stays with most of us for a lifetime. We mount lunch boxes on rolling platforms and convert them into circus trains. We also study the incredible art history of the Fisher-Price, Gong Bell, and Slinky pull toys and other lesser known works of American pull-toy sculptors. Children at home like to push, pull, and carry their stuff wherever they go. We learn from children pulling or pushing their wheeled toy phones, banks, or toy carrying cases. We learn to question whether each art lesson could be moved, carried, or placed on wheels. When we notice how children like to steer suitcases on wheels at the airport, a used suitcase collection for art class designers naturally follows. After we talk about how children love to be pushed inside shopping carts and later to command and steer their own shopping carts, we find play carts and historic examples of vintage shopping carts for our art class. Our plays and art explorations simply extend kids' interests in contemporary wheeled platforms and containers, which we redesign, refill, and redecorate.

Putting the World on Wheels

Several years ago our art class walked down to the shopping center to meet the visiting giant Hershey's Kissmobile. Children were excited to see one of their favorite treats on wheels. They were inspired on our walk back with ideas of other forms in our world that are already on wheels—and of what else could be mobilized. Could we mount personal wheels to get around more efficiently in the city? How could our pets be put on wheels? Could our entire lunch, not just a piece of chocolate, be on wheels? And so the conversation flowed, with many plans for adding wheels to school backpacks and lunch boxes. Children are inventors, it is one of their great art forms. For mechanical inventors, we need to have available as a basic supply in an art room, a large trunk of assorted wheels with which artists can experiment.

A Final Spin

It was a momentous occasion in our home that marked a long distance of memories from pushing our child in her carriage, then walking with her and her own play carriage up and down our street. Ana took her driving test, and for her the romance with the wheel continued. As we walked up the ramp toward the drivers' test site, she said, "After this test, I will be free, Dad, you will never see me again." I was a little shaken by her comment and would have been quite willing to cancel the road test, if it meant losing my daughter. There was no turning back, however, and even if I secretly wished she would not get her license this day, I had to smile as she waved, driving by with the examiner. Perhaps young wheel artists are preparing to move by us from the start. Maybe they decorate their trikes, roller skates, and skateboards to celebrate each step in their freedom and independence in life through their art. We need to pay attention to important occasions on wheels as parents and art teachers and learn from how children place their stuff, their collections, their art, and themselves on wheels, just moving toward the day they will drive away.

SMALL-SCALE ARTISTS

Between children and adults, there is no contest as to who keeps the most unusual collections. In a black film canister, my daughter Ana keeps nail clippings. She can give you a guided tour of her most interesting ones. In another container, she keeps broken pencil points; in still another she houses her baby tooth collection. When she finds unusual washers in my toolbox, they move into her plastic slide pocket "showcase." In binders, Ana curates collections of unusual matchbooks, unopened cereal box prizes, and illustrated Band-Aids. Inspired by her small stuff, Ana also makes tiny art. Thumbnail-sized bugs and ballerinas fill our fanciest living room containers and Model Magic figures even line up inside our medicine cabinet. In my eagerness to clean the tub, I sometimes wipe off finely detailed hair drawings before I can photograph them. One hundred or more nail polish colors stand in readiness, Ana's artistic palette for painted nail miniatures. There is something about little things—small toys, insects, play pals, and street finds—that attract young collectors.

Children's Small Art

American art has grown from framed art on a wall to wall-sized art. While adult artists think in terms of room sizes, children dream of tiny forms they can pocket, carry, and hide from adult inspection. Children's art scale is palm-sized, toy-sized, yet abundant with big ideas, adventures, settings, and fantasies. Children plan big things in a small scale. Giants and dinosaurs are fun and scary, while little things are controllable and appeal for protection. It is interesting that, of all the living things in the world, children are so interested in insects and dinosaurs, creatures of such vastly different sizes. The saga of tiny things abounds in children's rhymes, songs, storybooks and protected collections.

Using toys as scale models of their world, children taste, examine, and set up their visions of larger worlds. Children's small-scale dreams are molded into tangible forms in play setups and small artworks. Small art allows kids to be in charge of private explorations, "vacations" from school and adult worlds, ready to take off with transportable things in a pocket.

The sizes of books, notebooks, school folders, and art paper defines school-scale art. But children dream of giants and love to listen to stories about elves and tiny creatures. Just remember the importance that Smurfs, Matchbox cars, Cracker Jack prizes, magnets, and key chains held in your young life. Tiny hands forming tiny people out of cereal, foil wrap, or paper clips illustrate the size of children's personally improvised art. Children provide the clues for rethinking the scale of school art. To respect this interest, we make an art of collecting nail-sized canvases (or use fingernails as canvases) and explore working with tiny art tools on projects admired with a magnifying glass. For portrait busts, we fire up the popcorn popper in class to discover the most interesting people on the many sides of each hot and delicious-smelling kernel. We search the pavement, nature's floors, and school hallways to find small canvases, art tools, and inspirations for art.

Leprechauns and Smurfs

For little people living in a big world, it is comforting to have objects they can control and tower over. Matchbox cars can be driven without a learner's permit. Polly Pocket leases may be signed without a realtor and furnished without Mom or her decorator. Kids easily enter the worlds of Smurfs and Raisin Figures, setting them up in imaginative places and providing the script and inventive accessories for instant adventures. Plays with tiny figures and creating settings is an important aspect of children's art. Fast-food figures can be disciplined for a bad grade or lined up in a parade to perform circus acts. Tiny books and tiny cars are taken along on a drive in the family car. During a period when everyone else seems to be in charge of every action and detail in one's life, it is nice to have a small world with which to have fun.

Small Excavations

Recently we purchased a wholesale-sized container of Cracker Jack boxes for the children's lunches. Imagine our surprise when we opened Ana's door to find Cracker Jack heaven—piles of prizes among dozens of opened containers, with Ana feeling her way to the bottom of things. Children love prizes. They are skillful excavators of full cereal boxes and are willing to eat any Happy Meal just to free the arrested little figures inside. The ceremonious opening of prizes is repeatedly replayed in our art class, as everyone breathtakingly awaits the signs of pay dirt in magical containers. We study prize history from a new collector's book on Cracker Jack prizes and rummage through the teacher's historic collection. Of course, we create our own prizes hidden inside dream boxes.

Pocketing Art

If you shop for clothes with kids, you know the standards: a nice outfit has two pockets, a great outfit has a million pockets of all sizes, preferably with zippers, buttons, and locking devices. Children's pockets are safes for collections of pocket-sized stuff. In the cement mixer of a pocket, all kinds of seemingly unrelated items are affiliated by the curator's tastes and interests. Kids' shopping often focuses on small items which do not require bagging, but which can just be pocketed. There is a richness to having sidewalk pieces, unusual candy wrappers, buttons, and fast-food figures all scrambling for space in a single pocket. With no concern for use or value, a beautiful pebble, an unusual bag tie, or a paint-sample card may land in a pocket for the highest artistic motive—just because it is beautiful. In our art class, we collect pocket-sized containers to organize and display pocket finds. We also make pockets and save pockets from old garments to broaden our collecting capacity. Kids exhibit finds in different types of clear pockets including plastic bags displayed with clothespins on clotheslines. Clear fast-food containers are used for more formal displays of small treasures.

Children's small collections are uncensored by adults. They are individual choices and paint a fine self-portrait of the young artist. What is kept inside children's pockets is a valuable starting point to set up personal still lifes. A still life that represents children would include a portrait of the tiny things that reside at the bottom of a child's pocket.

A Portable Art

If you look for children's art, it may not be work in frames, permanently installed on walls, or in collectors' cases. When children make art objects they are often items that can be carried, easily moved, and taken with the artist everywhere. Different ways to carry and store tiny objects are a child's artistic concern. Children love carrying cases for small cars and figures. Containers with many different compartments, drawers, and dividers are preferred. Kids have an affinity for small boxes to keep small things. My historic collection of Barbie, Matchbox, and Star Wars carrying cases stay in our art class. We constantly share examples of all kinds of new tool and parts boxes, exciting tackle boxes, unusual makeup cases, and new ideas in jewelry boxes. We talk about the use of these cases for art and collecting and above all look at contemporary storage units filled by children as artworks.

A Small Ending

To find genuine children's collections and art interests, look deeply into their small containers, lunch boxes, and pockets. Check the items kids use to decorate their rooms, schoolbags, and clothes, such as stickers, pins, key chains, and magnets. In kids' special fascination with small things, art teachers can find new scales, themes, and ways to store and even display kids' art. The many tiny figures that represent their owners are only a small part of a larger family of objects with which children design, create stories, and make their own creative settings. Children's first still lifes are often the arrangement of small finds. First interiors, architectures, and landscapes often involve the creation of settings and shelters for small object collections. The beginnings of children's interests in sculpture and careful selection of objects center around collections of pocket-sized items. School art needs to expand the child's imaginative travels in small-object worlds and celebrate the uniqueness of small-scale art.

12

Children Invent the Future Art World

IDEA ARTISTS

When my daughter Ana was 8 years old, she wrote and illustrated her first book. A response to a school assignment, she wrote about her favorite collection—paper bags. I share the text to demonstrate that children have wonderful ideas, often inspired by ordinary objects.

HOW TO PLAY WITH A PAPER BAG

Paper bags are the most fun to play with.
I collect long and tall ones, short and fat bags.
Some bags hiss when you pull them to be long snakes.
Others are fun to crunch, to see the folds they create.

I wear bags as my crown, with a fancy bag as a glove.
Bags with silver linings are my magic slippers.
Plain bags I dress up for gifts.
And bags make the best barking pets.

I have bags big enough to climb into.
Did you ever drive a bag that had cellophane windows?
Just roar to start the engine and blast a bag into space.
I add pockets to a bag to carry more passengers.

My soft pink pillow is really a vacuum cleaner bag.
Put on a doctor's mask to operate on a bag.
Bags are the best toys to play with.
They can be built higher than Legos, and be more things than my
    brother's Transformers.

Art teachers know that children will have a zillion great ideas for every art project, if their ideas are solicited. An art class should be a special place in school where children rediscover that they have great ideas, worthy of talking about and showing. A valuable use of art time is finding out about the immense wealth of ideas kids bring to an art room. In my art room I use a variety of objects to help children discover ideas.

Getting Inside Objects

Inside a blue play pool, a motor boat makes fancy passes. The skipper, in a sailor's cap, navigates the waters by turning a pot cover steering wheel. In a nearby carriage, the queen waves to a crowd, pulled by a team of white play ponies. A hot-air balloon's gondola is occupied by brave teddy bear explorers with binoculars. To find creative ideas, children climb on board containers converted for adventure. Travelers get into the latest laundry baskets. Sitting inside boxes, suitcases, and giant paper bags, students uncover the possibilities of turning containers into forts, race cars, or dump trucks. With stuffed animals, dolls, and action figures used as stand-ins, it is possible to travel the galaxy in a Frisbee, race inside a soap tray, or steer a dustpan. Art class students discover great ideas by getting inside an object and making the necessary conversions.

Wearing Objects

During a recent flight I took the movie was terrible, but fortunately there was better entertainment on the other side of the aisle. A little boy eagerly unwrapped the headphones inside a plastic bag. Carefully adjusting them to his ears, he listened to his mother's heartbeat. After the patient lost patience, he tuned his "ears" to the window checking on the health of engine sounds. As night set in, the headphones became night vision binoculars trained on the heavens. On a break, this fast-paced idea artist twisted the headphones into a ponytail. As the food tray arrived, he traded utensils for the trusty headphones, and explored their use as an elephant's-trunk food shovel. This exceeded the parents' patience and concluded the show.

   We often begin the art class by trying on bath towels, net potato sacks, or earphones. Children discover ideas by putting things on, especially things that are not supposed to be worn. At home and in our art class, kids shop and search for interesting things to wear and explore new ways to wear them.

Lending Sounds and Noises to Objects

Children's morning routines often include warming up the engine of objects. Bedtime slippers drive away roaring. Before sandwiches are fastened into a lunchbox, they zoom around the kitchen as foil racers. Selecting pencils and pens for school means launching them first, after a tense countdown and test for space worthiness. With a rich variety of sound effects, children fuel Matchbox cars and bring to life the cast of Happy Meal boxes. Children discover new ideas for objects by adding their own soundtracks.

   In the art class, our tools roar and dance to the beat kids provide. We attach a variety of mechanical, electronic, and creature sounds to our art tools as they move over art surfaces. Brushes are swished, stampers are amplified by drum roars, and crayons are moved by grunting dinosaurs.

Children cast new sounds and noises to move art tools with new moves, crossings, and rhythms.

Stories About Objects

After a recent ice storm, our neighbor was busy chopping fallen branches and moving them to the sidewalk. His daughter collected branches and carried them to the garage, "a warm place for nursing them." Her idea was to wrap up the poor branches and to offer cheerful decorations. As she handled the fallen branches, I took notes on her stories and dreams about them. In handling objects that children find interesting, they also spread seeds of ideas by talking about them.

In schools kids are usually quieted. Children never stop talking—they are always too noisy for adults. Perhaps it is because they have so much to say that children are so valuable to listen to. In the art room children can get their voices back. Art teachers can encourage updates on what children notice and feel, and students can report on their latest finds and ideas. "I found a bird who could not fly south with his family and I think he needs an underground tree house for the winter." Talking about what children see and dream about as they handle and collect objects leads to unique art ideas.

Remaking Existing Objects

Kids have a better idea about any adult design or invention. Their designs for homes, furnishings, cell phones, backpacks, cameras, or pencil cases are more daring and inventive than any adult's ideas. "We can make our own" is the theme of our art classes. Children design their own objects for their rooms, for personal use and for school, and present ideas about them. By creating their own version of things, children learn that all artists gather ideas from the environment and improve on them. "Making our own" creates confidence in one's ideas and ability to go beyond the art and design world adults set up for children. By remaking objects, children rethink possibilities and take charge of the future.

Object Shopping and Collecting

My students receive weekly shopping assignments that focus on broad categories of found objects. During the past weeks, children shopped for unusual containers, extraordinary papers, and beautiful product brochures. After shopping, students come to class with great ideas. Before offering the teacher's assignment, I listen to what the children thought about, the ideas they gathered from their finds. To start art making with one's own find is how artists work; it is starting with the artist's ideas. Traditional school supplies are neutral objects and surfaces, devoid of ideas in themselves. Children who discover and collect special items at home, in backyards, in stores, and in art room shopping sites have great ideas for using them. Students are encouraged to continue idea shopping if an art room is set up as a rich self-service shopping site.

Playing with Objects

Play with everything in our art class! Explore the most unusual ideas you can find in any material, tool, or object. Playing is children's way of discovering ideas. Before portraits, landscapes, or still lifes, there needs to be a play with tools, surfaces, and objects in order to discover the possibilities. Borrowed from the child artist, the following are some of the plays used in our art class:

- We build with clothespins, plastic forks, pillows, erasers, dominos, and shoulder pads, treating everything as play blocks, assembled in endless configurations, while paying attention to the builders' stories and ideas.
- We take everything apart, looking inside an appliance or a computer mouse. Wearing surgical masks, we operate with screwdrivers, opening interior worlds and ideas.
- We inflate or stuff gloves, sacks, or bags and turn things into soft blocks that generate additional ideas.
- We accessorize by adding wings to slippers, handles to boxes, wheels to handbags, antennas to pencils. Each accessory suggests new ideas for playing with an object.
- We beautify with stickers and ribbons, and paint over cereal boxes, luggage, toasters, lamp shades. Each new layer suggests many new uses and new appreciations for a form and its possibilities.
- We wrap up shoes, chairs, and hands in all kinds of papers, stickers, fabrics, and foil, and in their abstract form, we find new ideas for their use.

Preliminary object plays are the start of each art lesson so that children can start artworks with experience and their own ideas.

Active Hands and Perceptive Minds

Kids with a big box of Legos sitting before them don't wait for an assignment or ask the art teacher what to do. Like artists, they start playful and active investigations. When active hands and perceptive minds take over, children don't need permission to have great ideas. All art classes can be presented as figuratively laying out a set of interesting blocks before children, who can then start playing and gathering ideas. Art teaching is about making children feel that they (and not the teacher) are the idea people in class. Children should not feel constantly like students and see the art teacher as the only one who knows art. In every art class, children need opportunities to shop, gather, and discuss their ideas and plans.

INVENTOR ARTISTS

A runny nose and a persistent dash for tissues prompted Ana's invention. Her newly invented allergy wear featured a pink tissue box hanging from her mom's gold necklace and the bathroom wastebasket wired to my tool belt. When everything is at hand, tissue runs are unnecessary. Children's art is about new ideas. And teaching art is about preparing kids to invent their own art, to discover ideas on paper and in real-life situations.

Pillow Doll

My daughter Ilona's special pillow and her favorite doll were bedtime necessities. But in a contest of dreams the pillow and doll always got separated, and she frantically searched for them the next morning. Then she had an idea! Using her mom's sewing kit, Ilona stitched the doll to the pillow. As it often happens to children who invent the new, 20 years later pillow dolls were commonly sold in stores, and Ilona never received credit or royalties. Consider many major trends attributed to contemporary artists, and you will discover their roots in children's inventions. Christo extended the wrapping arts, but who were the initial pioneers of this form? Oldenburg made food from nonfood materials, like children who create amazing play foods for make-believe stores and restaurants. Earthworks, table settings, and household chores, when treated as art, all have their roots in children's inventing.

An art class should be a place for kids to exchange ideas, a place where they can regularly share inventions with others. In turn, art teachers should take children's inventions seriously and discuss children's unique contributions to art.

Inflatable Clubhouse

Vacuum cleaners used to be equipped with a reverse switch. Like finely tuned jet engines they could be switched from "inhaling" to powerfully "exhaling." I remember my neighbor's son duct-taping all of my vinyl drop cloths together and using the vacuum to breathe life into a gigantic space bubble. It became a playhouse, requiring a password for other kids to enter. Now for old times' sake I inflate a similar model in the art room and tell the story of its inventor.

If you teach students that an artist is an inventor, how would you set up your art class for inventors? The sign on our art room door changes, for example, from Wizards' Lab to Test Kitchen, according to the mission inside. Wearing white lab coats (a hospital donation) with adjustable name tags, inventors may be carrying portable toolboxes to take something apart or sorting through the many little surprise drawers and cubbies in the art room. A stamper kit with a copyright symbol is available to classroom inventors. Laboratory record books are used to diagram student ideas.

Ice-Cream-Cone Rocket Ship

After the ice cream is licked away, the fun continues. From a front row seat in the ice cream parlor, I watch members of a winning soccer team celebrate by animating cones, launching them into space, taking them for test drives, dressing them up with napkin capes, and carving out ice cream cone spyglasses. Fortunately, I remembered that I saw packs of 100 ice cream cones in the discount store, just waiting for my art room inventors' playful hands. Quick inventions with ordinary objects such as Styrofoam lids, paper clips, or ice cream cones can warm up the art spirit.

When an art project is assigned, it has already been invented. Instead, art could be taught as a search. We could say, "What we are doing in class today has never been tried; no one in the art world has done this." Students are motivated to learn when they are the first to try a material, explore a new medium, or invent with a form. Young inventors can be constantly challenged to identify objects useful for inventions. Art teachers can demonstrate a sense of trust in the judgment and ability of young inventors to create new and better things out of all kinds of forms.

A Glove in Hungary

In the CARE packages my family received in Hungary, there was always something fun for a child. In one package I was disappointed to find only a leather glove. Nevertheless, I proudly wore my large, pairless American glove to school. In the snow I demonstrated how the glove was designed for scooping and shaping perfect snowballs. My friends argued that the funny glove was really a winter face mask or something used in street fighting. Years later in America, when I was learning to play a popular American sport—baseball—I finally learned what kind of glove it was.

Artistic recycling is inventing new uses for everything. Inventors' minds are challenged by unfamiliar objects, such as a vintage oil filter wrench, antique kitchen tools, or a baseball glove from America. We think of new uses for old things and unknown objects. An inventor's gift needs to be exercised in an art class. In our classes each student receives an "artistic license" on a card, and CARE packages from imaginary places provide our raw materials to pick apart and discover what could be invented with an object.

The Lego Vest

There is no prize for the winner of our most-unusual-fashion show, yet there are many enthusiastic participants. Entries have included jackets woven from gum wrappers, aprons hinged together from slices of plastic water bottles, and belts from CDs. One of the most memorable fashions was a Lego vest, with pockets for extra parts, and tires for buttons. Fashion inventions by children are unencumbered by the baggage of fashion history or trends.

Adults design tract housing, while kids invent dream homes. Kids are the futurists in design, with an innate sense of excitement about the new. Students in our art class are constantly charged with bringing back examples and descriptions of interesting new inventions in any object category. We follow the latest from European shoe magazines to Japanese electronics. We build lists of what we consider the world's great inventions, such as paper clips, Post-its, or the screw. We learn by examining design trends, then look for things that still need our inventing touch.

The Gift of Inventing

Observing the difficulties of a fellow student struggling to draw because of a shaking hand, Ron came to me after class declaring diplomatically, "I could make a drawing pencil for Josh that would make it easier for him to draw." I was touched by the observation and the confidence in my young inventor to solve the problem. A fine gift of a handsome looking drawing tool arrived the next day. The pencil had a red Velcro attachment for easy handling and a decorated spongy pad wrapped with colorful rubber bands for a thick, soft grip. Josh was delighted to test the new, distinguished-looking art tool and worked with the inventor to make adjustments.

Practical inventions for others, as well as for one's home and community help students view art as a means to improve life. Children as art inventors have a natural curiosity to explore, to beautify, to question the designs of the adult world. Art class inventions can be focused on practical concerns with tangible results.

"I Can Invent Anything!"

An art class has to build self-confidence in students to go out into the world with a sense of optimism as an artist. After the latest magnets, key chains, and pencil toppers have been collected and traded, what else is there? Young artists need to feel they can invent their own, create something as good as any object found or bought. If we teach our students to see themselves as inventors, they will look at their art ability more openly, not only as involving skills and techniques. With the belief that creative ideas will take you a long way in art, fewer children will express the sad notion, "I am not good in art." Students will proclaim, "I am good in art because I have great ideas and I can invent anything!"

CHILDREN AS ART TEACHERS

When my daughter Ana was very young, she loved to play teacher. She used to line up her teddy bears on her bed to take attendance. Then she would demonstrate to her class of bears how to build with phone books and pillows. When she gave a drawing lesson, she taped crayons to her dolls' hands. I was so impressed by the art emphasis in Ana's teddy bear school, that I invited her to teach an art lesson to my class. She prepared for days and came in with props and examples. After Ana's lesson I had no shortage of student volunteers ready to give an art lesson. She verified for children that they can also teach art. A goal of art learning is always independence, for everyone to become his or her own art teacher. Teaching for artistic independence can never start too early. As art teachers, children acquire confidence in their art and in coming to school as artists.

The Art Lesson

"Do you want me to bring this to your class?" Ana points to her case of tiny computer parts.

> Do you want me to show my parts box and how I take things apart
> for art supplies? I can show your students how I decorated my
> bathroom tiles with stickers and drew on the shampoo bottles.
> Maybe they would like to see the ugly picture frames I buy at

garage sales, so I can repaint and hot-glue things on them. I can
show how I dress up pencils or bring in my pushpin collection and
the bulletin board I decorated.

Young art teachers want to share their personal art forms.

Ana finally decided that she was most interested in presenting rubbings of her turtle figure collection made into charm bracelets. The turtles
wore sunglasses and had purses on their illustrated shells. I urged Ana to
show facets of art she did at home, things she thought most adults don't
consider art. Ana freely shared her art sources, the places she looked for
supplies, and even some thoughts about how she finds time to make art.
Ana's art presentation was very different from the typical school art lesson. Her examples struck a familiar chord with students, who suddenly
found many of their own creative activities and collections important
enough to talk about.

My students were impressed by Ana's turtle rubbings and how she
made them into wearable objects. Ana showed how she likes to make things
for herself, decorate her room, and make art gifts. Ana told the class that
rubbing, tracing, and stamping is her camera to take pictures of everything.
She said art was changing objects she likes into things to wear, like the
rubbings of house keys dangling from her backpack. She modeled rubbings
of her seashell collection in her hair and tracings of our red kitchen tools
worn as a long necklace. As a sign of appreciation for Ana's art lesson, my
students made her a pin from their fingerprints, pressed on a bouquet of
layered stickers.

"Let's Make Something!"

To get me into her room, my daughter Ilona's favorite line was "Dad, you
never play with me!" Now, do I sound like a dad who never plays with his
children? "OK, Ilona," I said, "what do you want to play?" With the sneaky
smile of victory, Ilona waved me to her studio, to be seated on the floor.
"Let's make something!" she said. Usually the "let's make something" was
followed by a pause while Ilona went shopping, dipping into Mom's
makeup case for hair curlers and cotton balls, selecting choice washers from
my toolbox, and inspecting trash cans. With supplies in place, she signaled
that we could start. Ilona did not count on an art lesson from me, nor did
she announce what I should do. We completely respected each other as
artists and understood that we could proceed on our own. During the construction phase we talked art and admired each other's work. "Let's make
something" brings an essential concept of home art to school—the notion
that young artists can and do make art without an art teacher.

"Lets make something" has become one of my favorite propositions in the art class. It is a stirring start for a new group of students, directly suggesting, let's work from *your* ideas. When students lead the art lesson, it engenders respect for young artists, a trust in their ability to shop, come up with valuable ideas, and work independently. When students find a great art idea, they are eager to teach it to others.

Children Are Art Teachers

I always admired my children as artists. They knew it from the excitement of my response to their creative play setups and the hundreds of photographs I took of their inventions. There was always a pad in my pocket to write down fantastic ideas the children shared with me. If it involved an object, I wanted to borrow it to show my class.

Children should be artists-in-residence and visiting artists-in-schools. It makes sense for children to come to an art class to talk about children's art. I am not sure I should tell fellow teachers, but I had my children come to my art class as often as they could. Ilona came to present the phone and matching trash can she painted for her room. When she visited my art class, she was greeted as a celebrity. Having seen and heard about Ilona's art and art classes, kids were already familiar with her. When Ilona could not come to school, she wanted to hear about how her idea played out in class and how her home art was received.

I admired my children's object finds and the collections they built from them. I took notes on plays associated with dressing up, playing house, planning a store, decorating a door, or designing corkboard displays. I never started an art class without mentioning my children's home art. Ana and Ilona knew that I loved hanging around their rooms, which were their studios. I frequented children's studios to talk about art, to learn, and to listen carefully. When my children came to class, they saw how we played on the floor and took hayrides under the table. They saw their influence in the shopping sites around the art room—setups in the children's old fish tank, in a hatbox, or in a parts drawer. Ana said that she really taught me well. Our school art room was the only classroom that had fun stuff on display and had its doors decorated by children.

I was not one to nag about cleaning up or throwing things out at home, nor did I refer to even the most unusual find as "junk." I encouraged shopping everywhere and enjoyed the children's unique collections. Recounting my son Jacob's many finds inspired my students to come to class with full pockets. My children always felt in charge of the content and displays in their rooms, and I learned to run my art room the same way. An art room can be a place were kids' ideas rule, where their collections, observations, plays, and inventions are not overshadowed by the art lesson. When children are called on to share their art ideas and teach art, it is recognized that they are the artists in the art room.

Talking to Children About Art Teaching

A child preparing an art lesson suggested that we use a play pool and fill it with interesting objects for an art room treasure hunt. Another child playing teacher talked about pockets as a portfolio and a lunch box as a child's shopping place. In planning art lessons with children, you find that they understand the pleasures of unwrapping, sorting, and digging, and they envision shopping adventures in junkyards, flea markets, or a classroom set up as an attic. Instead of working on desks, children set up the art lesson as a picnic, a magic carpet ride, or an ocean on the classroom floor. Kids use the space under desks as caves, tents, and forts, with an instinctual knowledge of where kids like to play and what is fun. As we prepare for art lessons, the students and I share favorite shopping stories of interesting crushed-object, yard-sale, and trash-can rescues. I remember one of my students jokingly saying to me, "If you want to talk about art teaching, or how an art lesson will turn out, just talk to the experts" (meaning the kids).

Having children be art teachers presents an opportunity for significant talks about art. Inherent in preparing for classes with the children are discussions of where art lesson ideas come from, and that they can come from children and home art. Preparing together, we teach children that an art teacher is not an inspired wizard of ideas, but art lessons and art-making ideas are accessible to everyone. Children encouraged to teach art know that the art teacher is not the only one who knows about art in an art class. Teaching is a way of underscoring children's wonderful experiences in art, a recognition that they come to class with important art experiences. Children as teachers learn what to expect from the art teacher and what they need to bring. Children learn to look to themselves for art. They learn that in an art class everyone has to come prepared, everyone has to restock the room with materials, collections, and ideas.

Creating Opportunities to Share Great Thoughts

My first day in art school I was handed a list of supplies. Not only was the teacher kind enough to draft the list, but also he said everything was already ordered at the school store. I was amazed that someone who had never talked to me or looked at my art already knew what I wanted to make. I wasn't sure what I wanted to do, but I had many ideas. Maybe my art teachers had better ideas. Perhaps he did not care about what I wanted to do at all.

In teacher training I was taught about lesson plans. I learned how to plan for all age groups and every possible student population even before I met with children. I was licensed to deliver a curriculum and manage a class. It was not a question of my student's art. After all, don't parents and teachers know what is best? When I finally started in the elementary art room, I was amazed how often my students said they could not think of anything to do.

As a parent, I finally became the art teacher I wanted to be. I was amazed how little of what I was doing in school had to do with children—the way they approached art, the materials they used, the places their art was evident, their home art interests. I felt the difference between my young children, who created the most amazing things at home and who were always willing to share their great plans with me, and my student's responses to the best lesson plan. I began to see an art lesson not as a skillful presentation of my ideas, but as creating the time and opportunities for children to feel they have great thoughts to share and present, as in the sample lesson plan in the Appendix. If children would see a relationship between their creativity at home and the events in an art class, perhaps they would not claim to be without ideas. When art classes feature only adult art ideas and artists, children conclude that they have little to contribute.

I occasionally start a class, or even stop in the middle of my talk, and say, "So what do you want to do now?" When children freely respond with an outpouring of great ideas, I know they are confident in being the artists in the class.

13

A Lifelong Appreciation of Beautiful Objects

ART HISTORY AND APPRECIATION
AT HOME AND IN SCHOOL

The Expert

When my 7-year-old son started collecting turn-of-the-century tobacco baseball cards, we followed every flea market lead, and I went to every sale. Jacob knew his facts and prices. He could point out every imperfection and admire all the details in the drawings on the small cards.

We began to talk of portraits as art and discussed the early printing processes used to produce the color lithographs. I was so impressed with Jacob's knowledge and enthusiasm for his art collection that I partnered with him in giving a presentation at a National Art Education Association convention. He must have been the youngest speaker at a major convention, but this was his subject, and Jacob delivered a wonderful presentation before several hundred art teachers. Describing baseball cards as portrait history, Jacob's words were layered with thoughtful appreciation for the beauty inherent in this form.

Art appreciation comes from supporting children who develop their expertise in a field of art they collect. Becoming a youthful expert and knowledgeable curator in an area of art develops taste, confidence, and independence in deciding what is beautiful. Child collectors form a keen eye and develop the maturity to find significant ways to display, preserve, and share their finds with anyone interested. If young collectors are recognized, an art class becomes a gathering place for enthusiastic experts, sharing their appreciation for beautiful things. Yes, collecting baseball cards has a place in the art class. Children benefit from teaching each other the art history and beauty within their collections. In our art classes, we display stamps, old greeting cards, and illustrated shopping bags to celebrate young art lovers and embrace their interests.

To appreciate art is learning to love art. It is the most personally demanding kind of teaching in which an art teacher can engage. Appreciation goes beyond looking at art, beyond learning art facts and information about artists. It is showing examples of what the students and the teacher are attached to, care about, and what they daily appreciate and dedicate themselves to.

Our *Vitrin*

Home chores are often the first contact with great art, the art objects a family values. Appreciation for me started at home, with my parents' attitude toward beautiful things and what they considered important to preserve.

In old photos I share with my art class, you can see me cleaning and polishing. To comb the fringes of our oriental carpets I used to get a *forint*, a Hungarian coin. But nothing was worth more than the chance to dream about the carpet's magical patterned mazes or to imagine myself battling the mythical creatures within those patterns. I remember the feeling of responsibility in being allowed to dust our fine china in the *vitrin* (china closet) while listening to the family history of the Herendi sugar bowl. In each object held, each intricate silver surface polished, laid the seeds for my future as a collector. My love of carpets and porcelain began as the keeper and preserver of our family's art. As a teacher, my carpet collection from all over the world frequently lands in the art class, ready to comb and to inspire fresh dreams.

Art classes can display items from home, complete with the stories children associate with the objects. For those who may not have a rich array of experiences with home treasures, the art teacher's passion for collecting provides an important opportunity for children to experience and be in daily contact with beautiful things. Appreciation is a subtle aspect of art teaching. An art teacher who is also an enthusiastic lover of beautiful things makes a difference.

When my children were born, they became the keepers of Bakelite pocketbooks and caretakers for my growing antique toy collection. Soon each child had their own *vitrin*—a Double Kay peanut vendor's case, a revolving Timex watch display, housing old head vases and salt and pepper shakers the children chose to collect. By taking care of family collections, the children learned to find their own. Their collections—case and all—frequently appear in my art class. I also have many empty old showcases in class and a legion of students interested in filling those cases. My students love to assist in unwrapping the things I bring from our attic: my grandmother's old beaded gloves and straw bonnets. They try on each hat and playfully wear her gloves. Framed pictures of Grandma wearing the items form a connection with the past.

Appreciating Asphalt

One spring morning my daughter Ana left for school wearing a light jacket. Nothing was unusual when I met her at the bus after school. Ana always asked me to hold her stuff during the walk home. But I noticed that her light jacket now weighed a ton. Back home at the kitchen table, Ana started to empty her load, pulling large black forms of tar from pockets I never knew existed. She explained that the best pieces had to be saved because the school's driveway was being redone. Not to break the spell of her enthusiasm, I just emptied the donut box with cellophane windows on the table, so she could arrange and save the black display. After all, young artists need our help. Let it be a lesson for parents and teachers, that if a light jacket goes to school and a heavy one comes back, it is just an occupational oddity of living with young art appreciators and their imports.

Supporters of art appreciation need to stay in the background, accepting and showing uncensored support for the objects in which children delight. It is important to appreciate the appreciator—their collections and art views about them—regardless of the form in which the collections arrive home. In the art class, we need to notice what kids prize, accepting their views and choices, instead of rushing to replace them with what we consider beautiful, valuable to collect, or special to look at as art. Collectors have to be appreciated if they are to venture further, make daring choices, show us their interests, and make their collections public. Art teaching is welcoming the things that children admire and bring to class and offering an unfailing forum of support. When young artists feel that their choices are respected and their art observations are valued by someone, they continue to confidently speak out about what is beautiful, showing us what they really appreciate.

Living in a 1950s Ranch

Actually, I didn't live in a 1950s ranch-style home, but I have spent many hours playing in a model of one. And after logging countless hours of redecorating, there was plenty of interest left in the old house for my children to play in it. Nowadays the beautifully illustrated tin ranch, with period wallpaper and curtains, whimsical linoleum and mid-century furniture, is housed in my art room. It stands beside a stately Greek Revival mansion, neighboring a wood Victorian home complete with a wraparound porch and proper gingerbread moldings. In my art class we don't just study architecture and interior design, we move in, submerging ourselves in fresh new arranging. Courtesy of fanciful art appreciation experiences offered by Louis Marx and other period American toy makers, children can visit and play in every period of design history. In fact, I am quite an entrepreneur, landlord of over 30 rentals, covering all major periods of American architecture and interior design. My buildings are available to rent by any appreciative player.

Childhood fascination with playing house and playhouses comfortably translates to an appreciation of beautiful architectural and interior forms. In friendly settings, play can be an important means of involving children in early forms of art appreciation. Building on many different toy collections, teachers of art classes can present memorable examples of the design arts. Our hands-on study of past styles extends to opportunities to place toy figures into period beds and cover them with a variety of exceptional doll quilts gathered from many regions of the country. We study a great American figurative sculpture—the history of dolls and fashion—by just seating and posing occupants of playhouses. We play in a Victorian home, but also sample authentic Victorian wallpapers and finely carved play chairs I collected. Starting in a "mod" 1970s home, we look back and touch on a toy scale the opulent history of televisions, radios, phones, beautiful American rocking horses, and doll carriages.

Sharing Beautiful Worlds

Before I spoke English, I learned about *Life* magazine. In our home, we looked at wonderful pictures of a new country that we did not at the time feel a part of. I remember my parents subscribing to *Life* magazine and my scrapbooking its pictures. Dad showed me cartoons from the *New Yorker*, and Mom pointed out pictures of "funny" abstract paintings. I fondly talk about our family outings to the great museums of New York City, generally on Sunday, when all the big museum doors were open and admission was free. My parents did not have a great knowledge of art, but they respected my arguments about what I liked. When my mother started taking photography classes, she let me use her camera to take my first color pictures. I learned to appreciate art because there was a feeling for beautiful things in our home, from the way Mom took care to set the table to how she saved each museum brochure.

The feeling for beautiful things may start at home, but appreciation needs to be exemplified each day in an art class. In the children's second visual home, the art room, the art teacher has to demonstrate a passion for saving, sharing, and visibly caring about all kinds of beautiful things. What children see each time they enter an art class matters. Art appreciation goes beyond the study of art history or the hammering home of art concepts and principles. It is sharing the breadth of the visual world and the excitement of making discoveries from it. The primary lesson each day is showing beautiful things that inspire students for the rest of the day. Parents provide the first museum of interesting things to look at in the home, but the museum with a lifetime of rewards must be kept open by an art teacher.

I stand before my first art class of the day with clippings from the "Design" section of the *New York Times*. I am holding an unusual fruit box I found at the market, and I am prepared to share an old flickering TV pencil sharpener. Each day my students are introduced to my art finds of the day and hear about the excitement of finding them. I tell students what I found in a toolbox and what I picked up on my way to class. Very soon students join in, coming to the art room to show what they found. Each class is an opportunity to unwrap and display beautiful things, to share aspects of our art loves.

Playing Marbles

In the art class, before sorting through containers of old glass marbles, we learn some of the rules of marble playing. You cannot play with beautiful marbles without learning to love beautiful glass. To appreciate glass, children take it into the light outside and play with it. An art class experience can nourish early appreciation instincts, sending students on their way to find the glint and glimmer of Tiffany's glass art or to look upward at the blazing glass windows of Chartres Cathedral.

Teaching art appreciation is getting beautiful things into children's hands. Starting with children's interests, the art world they know and appreciate, we can build lifelong connections to other artworks and art interests. Unforgettable contact with beautiful objects from the past—gently handling an antique play tea set, wearing an old wedding veil, pushing or pulling great toy sculptures—can all become a memorable art history experience. Providing a living art history for young art appreciators can begin with art teachers looking for toys they have kept. When few examples are left, it may require a passionate "buy back" of old favorites. Perhaps the art teacher's toy box needs refilling, but what a joyous task! It is a cheaper and better investment to build your own art history collection than to purchase expensive slide and poster sets. The popular art history posters may teach some facts, but they seldom lead to what we really want to accomplish: creating a lifelong "art affair" for children.

When children find out that they are playing with the toys their art teacher played with as a youngster, it promotes a special interest in preserving toy art. Building with a 1940s building set, printing with circus stampers from the 1950s or trying on a mid-century Halloween mask, creates a meaningful way to appreciate art history. And so I bring to class everything that comes out of vintage toy boxes, old toy carrying cases, and doll trunks. We study the history of teddy bears by having art sit on our laps. Children warm up the creaky mechanisms of old Fisher-Price pull toys by parading toy art along school hallways. Playskool puzzle classics and Lionel trains and accessories are put together as experiences in art history. Students share an instant appreciation for these artworks and cannot wait to talk to their parents about old toys.

When Art Walks In

On a rainy day when children parade their fantastic umbrellas to school, the celebration lingers in the art room. I am also prepared for rain by bringing in an old child's umbrella stand filled with vintage pieces. An impromptu umbrella store becomes a display theme for what the children brought, as well as for my vintage umbrellas. A circus tent–style children's umbrella was copyrighted in 1946. A plain dark blue umbrella from the 1930s has a surprise planetarium scene inside. A child about 75 years ago carried one of the umbrellas with wood shafts, Bakelite handles, and a "skylight window" which let in light from the top. My students learn to talk "Bakelite" because they have held old Bakelite umbrella handles. They use words like *Deco* and *streamlined* in conversations because they have participated in many classroom antique shows. Noticing when art walks in—the art kids wear, bring to class, what they currently collect and play with—is a key to appreciating many forms of childhood art. Encounters with extraordinary children's objects, old and new, elevate the appreciation and interest in beautiful everyday forms.

I am just as excited as the children when it comes to a back-to-school sale. Children start each school year carefully selecting the most interesting designs in school supplies. They know that the latest art will receive an enthusiastic reception in my class. In tune with the fall supply selection, an art room show-and-tell is held, featuring the history of pencil cases, erasers, old rulers, and pencil sharpeners. After admiring a new train lunch box chugging into class, I couple it to a visual history of the American lunch box. The children carry the old lunch boxes and create items to be placed inside. I recognize and offer the art room stage for the latest in children's object selections and use it as an opportunity to introduce relevant antiques that interest the class.

Children's Art History and Appreciation

Children experience the art in "home museums" long before they experience art in "art museums." In a recent interview, Yves St. Laurent spoke of his great antique cutout doll collection. Matisse fondly wrote of his old picture books. The appreciation for beautiful things is an early experience and an individual discovery. As art-making careers start at home and children's appreciation for great art also starts at home, it seldom begins with the first time showing of art masterworks. To receive masterworks with interest, children require a variety of preliminary experiences. We need to concern ourselves with children's experiences before they view masterworks, so they receive them as more than just facts or school pictures to learn.

Children need to develop a sense of interest to sensitively move toward great art when they encounter it. Indoctrination instead of sensitive starts turns kids away, just as early experiences with beautiful old things turn kids toward lifelong enjoyments. As the early art making of children is fostered by caring adults, early art appreciation and history interests also need nurturing. Caring for art is not only a process of learning; it is also the development of a feeling, a caring, and even a need for beautiful things. This happens early in young children and cannot be substituted by a later cramming of factual art knowledge. We need to learn more about how young artists develop art interests in beautiful things and how their taste and self-confidence in art views and choices are formed.

SHOWING HOME ART TO SCHOOL ART CLASSES

After years of being a follower of the latest trends in art school, I first noticed children's art in 1969 as a new elementary art teacher. It was incredibly refreshing to find artists not trying to imitate or fit into an existing art world. I was drawn to children's art immediately.

I filled my studio with children's drawings and exhibited my drawing and painting collaborations with children in Soho. I simply wanted the children in my classes to discover the wonders of their own art, to be as excited about it as I was. With freshman enthusiasm, I began to borrow children's works from the first art class of the day and share it with the next. To avoid jealousy or competition within a class, we looked at children's art from other classes, especially the art children started bringing from home. Later, when I became the parent of young artists and witnessed their unique art inscribed on every part of our house, I became a faithful importer of my children's home art. Working in home studios, the children became their own art teachers, independently producing an art vastly different from the art made in school settings.

A Slide Show

At first I just wanted to pick up everything from my children's room and bring it to class exclaiming, "Look at this incredible stuff, it's your art heritage, a testament to the artists you are when you come to school!" I will not forget my first experience showing children's art to a class. I was worried they would laugh and call it silly. Would they be interested or feel they had already made that, so why look at someone else's work? I decided on a slide show to remove the art from its daily context and to dignify the work by showing it the way I presented adult art. I had filled these carousel trays before, sharing the works of well-known artists that influenced my art. I wondered if I should have different standards for selecting children's work? I wanted to show beautiful art, but I was also trying to select pieces to demonstrate the unique nature of children's art. I felt more at stake in this premier, having high hopes for a slide show that would move students to remember their early works and see them as something groundbreaking and important. In other words, I really wanted my young students to feel about their art as I did when I first became an art teacher and a parent.

After much anticipation, finally the lights went out, and the first work appeared on the screen—"Napkins." It showed a napkin figure in a fancy gown. The figure was walking a dog. The piece, which I still keep on my dresser, was constructed at McDonald's from three napkins. This fragile form made from an everyday material was typical of children's art—finding art opportunities everywhere and elegantly shaping the most innocent materials. There was little response to the piece because students expected to see other kinds of art, yet there was mention of making things out of burger foil, and a student promised to bring in people he had built from straws. I moved the lever to the next slide.

Even in the dark I saw the smiles greeting the next image called "The Wedding." It depicted a white spoon bride dressed in a flowing white napkin gown, with the groom, a fork, elegantly fitted with a shiny burger-wrap tux propped up by a straw cane. Two young artists animated this action scene. Smiles became signals of recognition that this slide represented a favorite play-art category. The children talked about their fast-food and action figure setups, describing the settings and scenery they constructed. The friendly response eased me into the next slide and new stories from the children. I reminded the class that we were looking at exciting works of art, that young sculptors find their materials in all kinds of art-supply "stores," and that play setups and performances are part of the art.

The next slide was of my daughter Ana, using ketchup packets she found at the restaurant to paint a portrait series. Ana lined burger boxes with white napkin canvases, so she would be able to take home the wet drawings. Students responded to Ana's faces more joyously than to any adult art I have ever screened. One student jokingly said, "You will never find this in an art museum." The comment made for a wonderful centerpiece for our discussion of how children daily expand the list of accepted art media and materials and find amazing ways to make art using the most unexpected things. My students decided to make buttons declaring, "Kids invent the latest." Not bad for a slide presentation I was so worried about!

The slides were long remembered, and students began to refer to their home chores, plays, and collections as art, broadening our conversations about art in class. My conviction of the importance of showing children's art to children grew with the response to each show. Children welcomed the official recognition of their art. They saw how their creative inventions were respected and celebrated. Today, I often use video to share children's home art in class, capturing the performances, settings, artists' descriptions, and even some of the sound effects that can accompany a new art form. I've learned to place great trust in young artists' skills to present their own art on video without adults interpreting it. Over the years, testing and school accountability have often been interpreted as testing children's knowledge about adult art. This means that children are exposed to more adult art in their classes than ever before. Calling for a balanced presentation—showing examples of children's art to children—has become more urgent. In our classes I share the following media and themes discovered in children's art with children:

- Students view examples of art made as gifts for special persons and for special occasions in life. I bring in and wear to class the artworks my children have fabricated for birthdays and anniversaries. It gives us an opportunity to talk about some of the reasons children make art.
- I introduce children as beautifiers, decorating anything worn and every object in their room. I curate examples of children decorating their shoes and shoelaces, backpacks, notebooks, phones, mouse pads, boom boxes, light switches, bikes, and many other things to enhance the appearance of their environment.
- Familiar children's plays such as playing house, restaurant, store, post office, bank, and school result in artworks in many media. I show art classes examples of children setting up home furnishings and objects in complex play environments, modeling new worlds.
- I chronicle children's abilities to handcraft and make their own things in artworks from jewelry, watches, toys, purses, decorative shelves, and designs for many personal containers.
- I collect examples of the children's art of packing and wrapping from masterful ribbon art over fanciful birthday packaging and from videos of children packing a suitcase or stocking a refrigerator with groceries. I use slides to demonstrate the original art of decorating shopping bags and converting cereal boxes to painted gift boxes.
- I document nature artists in the park, surveying pine needle rooms, serving in outdoor restaurants, or excavating sand and water displays. Modifying nests or setting up unique outdoor playhouses is also part of the nature artist's repertoire.
- I introduce the original Bob the Builder toys beside a tower of lamp shades, next to a soft pillow bridge, or posing by a stretch of beanbag mountains. We look at the ingenuity of children constructing play dwellings with umbrellas, blankets, and other imaginative building materials.
- We view children as performance designers on videotape—young directors of large casts of play figures animate toy movements and lend voices to play actions. We picture the setup artists, dress-up artists, and

disguise artists working with flashlights and synthesizers. These artists orchestrate circuses, space launches, and Barbie aerobics classes often set up by rearranging home furnishings.

- The best parties are in the portfolio of events designers. I illustrate parades, fashion shows, and birthday parties that only children can imagine as part of an art form that utilizes many materials and media.
- I introduce children as home-chore artists, turning every home chore into a creative adventure. The ability to clean up, straighten up, and display objects in a drawer or on a shelf reveals the art of organizing many home canvases. Pictures of unique table settings and corkboard displays illustrate children in the act of design exploration.
- I introduce children as art inventors who discover new canvases, art tools, and materials. We illustrate looking freely through a trash can on a sidewalk, or into a kitchen cabinet, children's' boundless view of art supplies. We depict children's art inventions to broaden our notion of art.
- I explain children's' drawing history: the birth of a line from dotted marks and wiggly scribbles to far-shot arcs, to mystical ellipses from which a circular head emerges as children grin at the first drawing attempts of younger siblings.
- I show my students my own childhood art that my parents saved from the time I was 6 years old. Students are interested in their art teachers' early creations and an illustrated personal art story is well received. Children respond by seeking to discover and preserve their early artworks.

Each family has an interesting artistic past, generations of family members who pursued art. As I share the art of my uncle Telcs, a Hungarian sculptor, and my cousin Izzy, a Russian painter, I ask my students to research and share with pride their own family artists.

What we project as slides, or hold up in the art class is extremely influential in defining what is art, who is an artist, and the art that is welcome in a class. The examples we hold up to admire often define only the teacher's view of art. Children need to be a part of the examples we show. Our challenge is to convey to children the importance of their own art and artistic past. We need to teach children to preserve their youthful artistic freedoms to dream and freely explore unique art interests and pride in past accomplishments. I discuss with the children why we show art in class. For example, we can talk about how artists gather inspiration from all sources, from firsthand experiences with nature, sidewalk finds, and the works of other artists young and old. Children need to understand that artists look for ideas in the works of other artists, but that artists also look to themselves, and to their childhoods for ideas.

Why Show Children's Art to Children?

What do you hold up as wonderful art? What artworks do you get excited talking about to your class? Does sharing your favorite old master in an art book stimulate you? Are you animated in your talk about a piece of children's art? Do you discuss children's art in the same way you discuss the art of an old master? Or do your discussions about the art children have made reflect the subtle judgment that they are second-class creators reaching for unobtainable heights? Display children's art to children, call it valuable, unique, an art to be proud of and preserve. An artist lives in all of us; showing children's art to children demonstrates that an artist is not a remote individual, appearing only in books, posters, or adorning the walls of museums. Artists can also be children creating great art in home studios or in the classroom.

Art education textbooks today have fewer pictures of children's art than earlier textbooks which celebrated children and their art in virtual portfolios. Resource companies aggressively market poor reproductions of adult masterpieces, but offer no slides or posters celebrating children's accomplishments. Teaching can mislead when the content of art classes is viewing only adult works, guided by exercises of adult principles and ideas of art. No wonder children conclude that their art is unwelcome in school. Young art teachers who have not spent much time around children's art don't instantly recognize that the art children create at home is totally out of sync with what is purveyed as school art. Art teachers whose children are grown may fondly remember their children's home creations, but these same teachers are not supported in their training to appreciate children's art as a basis for teaching. Besides, only young parents have the ready access to the fresh art made daily by kids at home. There is something obviously missing from the school art we now show children.

Young artists accomplished at making adult-style art become media sensations. Recently an 11-year-old abstract expressionist sold her art for a fortune. She was interviewed as a CNN headliner, famous for making art like an adult. But, children creating great children's art are not news! What a topsy-turvy world we live in when truly significant news is a little known fact—that children's art has inspired most twentieth-century artists and art movements. Too often the headline is the same in school: Children able to mimic adult artworks are regarded as class artists, and their adult-style pieces adorn hallway display boards in a public acknowledgment of good art. When polished adult-style works are held up for emulation, children are not taught to value the art they make or to respect children's art in general.

Art teachers constantly search for adult art they believe children would like to see. Ironically, the most often selected artists are Miro, Paul Klee, and Alexander Calder, artists who eloquently spoke of children's art as their major influences. Why not "split the screen" of twentieth-century art shows, to hold up the muse with the masters? There is no shortage of child-wrapping artists to introduce the art of Cristo. Young table-setting artists abound to share the screen with the *Dinner Party*. Examples of young earthwork artists abound in all outdoor settings. Children are the original action artists, with no one portraying action and energy more convincingly than children. Adult artists who were able to dip into their childhoods emerging with youthful energy and expressive freedom will be of interest to children when seen in the context of children's art.

Few explanations are needed; children looking at children's art, "get" it. Children are drawn to children's art, and when looking at home art, they have a wealth of things to say about having done something similar. They feel an inherited expertise. But children viewing adult art in a museum or on classroom posters are often told what the art is about, as if the adult had a direct link to the artist. Then we all have witnessed the unfortunate next step—the copies of Picasso, Van Gogh, or Matisse appear in a school display. But when children see children's art, they do not feel compelled to copy adult art. Children seeing art made by other children see it as encouragement to pursue their own inventive ideas.

Art teaching is sharing with children the richness of the visual world. To be inspired by beautiful things is essential in the search for one's own art ideas. I share with children finds from nature, the man-made environment, masterpieces from museums, and art created by children. It is important to officially include children's art in the pantheon of art and artists, as well as celebrate children's art in many informal ways. I take home a bouquet of children's art from my art class each day. We can become too busy making sure that the children take their art home and neglect selecting our favorite pieces to enjoy. Taking art home daily reminds me of the art that inspired me to go into teaching children in the first place. Collecting children's art also shows my students that I feel honored and rewarded by their work. I show children's art to children because that is what I love and enjoy hanging in my home and studio.

Suggestions for Presenting Children's Art

My students were surprised when I struggled to bring into the room a heavily carved, gold-leafed, museum-quality frame surrounding a delightful child's drawing of a teddy bear. The surprise was not just the dignified frame but that it contained a child's drawing and not some great old masterpiece from a museum. I explained that the art was brought from the living room of our home and that it was one of my treasured pieces of original art. The point I was trying to make in sharing this work is that children need to see their art presented with respect. On other occasions I show children's art from a handsome brochure of artworks from a museum show of Russian children's art I curated many years ago. Yes, children's art can be in a museum or in a distinguished frame on a living room wall. Using the same formats we use to show adult art—books, slides, posters, or CD-ROMs—takes children's art showings beyond the refrigerator door status. I frame children's art to be presented in important locations in my school or on loan at community sites.

Visiting Artists Series. A poster on the door announces our visiting artists today. I prepare a clothesline in class for 8-year-old Sarah, a special guest, to share her series of clothespin figures she has been working on at home. Sarah's art is unwrapped with great anticipation, and interested viewers surround her. Children are the most inspiring spokespersons for their work, and they bring to class the complete story of a material idea, revealing an art find. Young artists make terrific guests and help demonstrate that children are artists, and their art is an important feature of an art class.

Studio Visits. It is common to have open-studio nights in our city where one can visit places where artists work. It should not be more difficult to gain access to children's home studios by seeing video presentations of how and where children create at home. In my class, children not only share their art, they also share the videos they make of their room's arrangement, special collection displays, and larger art projects that would be difficult to bring to school. Video takes us to the artist, so we can see and hear children talk about what they consider their important home art. While parents eagerly document the growing years with cameras, scrapbooks, and collections, children can be encouraged to preserve and document their creative life outside of school.

Exhibitions of Home Art in School. In a hallway corner, intertwined ropes hang like vines in a rain forest canopy. The ropes become a temporary home for a fantastic display of bugs made at home by one of our students. Exhibits of home art in school declare that the art children make on their own is important. Supporting home art, as an important mission of school art, is the point of one-person art shows I set up throughout the building. Some pieces look incomplete without the artist's words and playful demonstration of what it does or how it works, so we often add a statement from the artist or even an explanatory video of the children's voice to their art.

Active Viewing. Children's art is made by active bodies and playful hands. Their final products require a similarly active viewing. In our classes children look at children's art on a video screen with magnifying glasses. They peer through Saran Wrap-covered screens on which they can make instant tracings. They use Post-its stuck on computer monitors to create active notes and sketches. They look at the art, then actively shop for ideas they want to pursue. In this playful viewing, children find related paths in the art, visual connections that lend confidence to their own art. Our students view art with art materials by their sides, so they are ready to create themselves. Children make instant plans and find abundant ideas in other children's art relating to finds, experiences, and processes they encountered themselves. Viewing children's art inspires children to confidently set goals for their own art making, seeing all the unique methods and media they are shown verified as art.

Starting Class with Children's Art

How a class begins emphasizes what is important. Starting an art class with showing children's art demonstrates that an art class is about children's art. An art room needs to feel like a comfortable place where children can bring their art to show, and the art teacher can also share children's art. In my office from floor to ceiling, I store boxes of children's art—boxes labeled, Presents for Parents, Birthday Art, and Corkboard Art. All these boxes contain works from my own children and art gifts other children have given me. Looking through these boxes in class is an exciting unwrapping ceremony, accompanied by wonderful stories and recollections that each item triggers. Discovery stories tell of where and how the art was made, how it was found, and why I saved it.

Looking at Art as Change

In one of our classes, students look at large, "coffee table" art books highlighting the works of Mondrian. The students look at the artist's beginning works shown in the first sections of the art books, then they flip to the last pages to compare this early work to his later art. Children are interested in changes in artworks during the life of an artist, especially when children see these same changes occurring in their own art. We look at young children's early scribbles in a big book, on its way to becoming a controlled circle, to a smiling head sprouting a body. We conclude that art is always changing during every age, from a single work, or through the entire life of an artist. Children discuss the stages they like, yet come to the realization that one is not better than another. Great art can occur at each stage including their stage—the art of childhood. An open attitude to art can be fostered in children who study art as part of a constant process of change.

CHILDREN'S ART IS REAL ART

I enjoy demonstrating to future art teachers the enthusiasm their future students have for art. We walk into an elementary classroom and ask, "How many of you want to become artists?" Almost everyone's hand goes up. Then I hold up two pieces of art for my young audience: one a well-known Van Gogh painting of his bedroom and the other an imaginative child's drawing of her room. The children laugh as if it would be a "no brainer"— obviously only the Van Gogh is real art. My future art teachers immediately recognize the challenge of teaching art to young artists who don't think children's art is "real" art. After countless lessons in the appreciation of adult artists, why be surprised that children don't see their art as part of the art world? As children study the art of the great masters like Calder, Miro, and Picasso, these same students always need to be reminded that Calder, Miro, and Picasso were, themselves, the greatest fans of children's art.

Sample Lesson Plan: Sculpture on Wheels

Typically, art lesson plans are written plans, and follow formulas derived from other subject areas. These lesson plans specify objectives, required materials, and the time allotted for each segment of a lesson. They include a process for evaluating the lesson's outcome. The traditional art plan describes the teacher's original lesson idea and explains what will happen in class. Objectives for the lesson plan describe what an adult feels is important for children to learn about adult art, artists, and known art processes. In this action, the art teacher is the only one involved in planning, and by the time young artists enter the classroom, all major decisions regarding the art have already been made. The student's vision is not taken into account. In this unrealistic presentation of the creative process, whose art is really being made in an art class? There is an alternative, whereby artists—the students—and the teacher plan for an art class.

WHY TEACH THIS LESSON?

Early riding toys such as bikes, pedal cars, and toy carriages play an important part in children's early appreciation of moving sculpture. The lesson about sculpture on wheels refers to children's early art forms of taking imaginary rides in laundry baskets and customizing their remote-controlled toys to transport teddy bears. Students appreciate learning about the rich art history of wheeled toys. The challenge of designing sculpture on wheels expands early home experiences into a familiar school art.

CLASSROOM SETUP AND DISPLAY

School furniture will be moved aside to open the floor space. Tables without chairs will be used as workbenches. Students will wear shop aprons with buttons saying, "Art Is an Invention." Old trunks and suitcases filled with useful parts line the walls of the room and will be open to shoppers.

BACKGROUND STORY

I will pass around an old black and white photograph of myself standing next to my first bike. Before receiving the bike, I used to make many other riding toys. I will share a drawing I made as a child of my scooter, constructed from ball-bearing wheels and scrap wood, and the wicker laundry basket racer pulled by my dog Bundi. Other drawings will be added as students recollect vehicles they constructed.

PLANNING AT HOME

Art lessons start at home and come to class in idea books. The richness of home events yields many ideas, which are expanded by sketches, writings, and photographs, kept in each child's handmade book. Keeping an idea book states that practicing art is a personal search, and keeping track of their ideas changes children's view of school art. Students will collect pictures and make drawings of their favorite riding toys at home. They will ask parents about the carts, carriages, and bikes their parents owned and created as children. Students will sketch ideas for riding toys in their idea books, and search for objects and collect wheels to meet the specifications of their design.

PRIME TIME

The lesson will begin with what the students show and talk about. The first few minutes of an art lesson are prime time. It is not only the peak of students' attention, but these few minutes also define who is in charge of the lesson and whose art ideas are the most important. Who generally starts the art lesson? It is the art teacher taking attendance and explaining what the students will be doing. "Prime time" should be designated as the students' time, demonstrating that this class is fueled by student ideas. During an initial show-and-tell, students will express thoughts and plans, and show the objects they gathered at home.

PRELIMINARY PLAY

Planning active play starts is a familiar way for children to investigate art. Brief, moving introductions, instead of long lectures, immediately involve children. Play starts will move art to the floor. Preliminary plays are designed for fun, planned for fresh tool handling and playing with surfaces and forms. They are anything but routine.

I will bring my daughter Ilona's old bike to class. This is the same bike on which Ilona learned to ride. I will tell the class that I look forward to presenting this bike to her daughter Emilie. Ilona, however, wants me to throw out the old bike because she feels Emilie will want a fancy new one. As a group activity the students' ideas and help will be utilized to redesign and redecorate the old bike so Emilie will want to ride it.

ART HISTORY AND APPRECIATION

I will transport to class some wheeled toys my children played with and customized, including vintage baby carriages, rolling suitcases, and toy shopping carts. Students will view Ana's classic Schwinn bike, Jacob's 1940s Gong Bell motorcycle, and Ilona's 1950s ice cream truck and ride-on locomotive. Vintage bicycle horns, grips, and 1950s mud flaps from my collection and from the *Standard Catalogue of Schwinn Bikes*, will be discussed as design classics and placed in students hands.

CLASS SHOPPING

Everyone will be invited to open my suitcases, toolboxes, and parts drawers to shop for items to use in the bike's transformation. Students will bring their art toolboxes to class, filled with unusual materials.

The art teacher plans for interesting shopping sites filled with tempting, multipurpose materials awaiting discovery. Instead of waiting for delivery of identical school supplies, all students will have an opportunity to get up and shop for unusual items.

Children plan for the art class by freshly stocking their art boxes. Since the contents of each art box are unique, it contributes to each artist's ability to customize their work.

ART TALK

As the bike gets a face-lift, students talk about their design ideas. Students will share stories and pictures of their first bikes and relate stories of scooters, go-carts, and riding toys they dreamed about making.

The art teacher's talks set the classroom climate. Creative art talk will lead to creative artworks. There is room for playful stories, "silly talk," or exaggerated talk, which eases art-making tensions and opens the door to unexpected responses. Conversation will open up artistic freedom or define its limits. Class art needs a source. There is no better place to find this source than in student stories about their home art inventions and adventures.

PLANS FOR ART MAKING IN CLASS

Students will create a riding toy from found objects and materials they shopped for at home and found in class. They will design creative presentations of their models in the form of brochures, and posters, preparing to pitch their ideas at a mock sales meeting with toy executives.

AFTER-CLASS PLANS

We will discuss home plans for decorating and converting other student-owned toys. We will make plans to photograph or videotape and share on the Internet student's home inventions.

An art lesson plan should include art homework, something that will encourage students' collecting, thinking about art, or art making after class. Along with the artwork, what plans and ideas are taken home from an art class? How can art continue after school and become part of the child's life? Art teaching is planning for an artist's life at home. School art plans include teaching children how to be full-time artists again, as they used to be before entering school.

COPLANNING AN ART CLASS

I picked up my daughter Ana from her final class of the semester, and she said, "This was a great class; I got so many great ideas from the teacher." I would like my student's young and old to say that my class was also great, but then I would want them to add, "I can go anywhere now and find my own ideas for art. I can go to any store or backyard and discover dozens of art projects." Planning an art lesson is planning for students' artistic independence. To achieve this important goal, students have to be involved in all aspects of planning art. They need to be partners in the preparation of art lessons. A lesson plan involving students assures that students can pursue their ideas and develop their own art.

Select Bibliography

Amabile, T. M. (1989). *Growing up creative: Nurturing a lifetime of creativity*. New York: Crown Publishers.

Andrews, B. H. (2005). Art reflection and creativity in the classroom: The student-driven art course. *Art Education, 58*(4), 35–41.

Baker, D. (1992). The visual arts in early childhood education. *Design for Arts in Education, 91*(6), 21–25.

Beal N. (2001). *The art of teaching art to children*. New York: Farrar, Straus & Giroux.

Bressler, L., & Thompson, C. (2002). *The arts in children's lives: Context, culture and curriculum*. Boston: Kluwer Academic Publishers.

Bucknam, J. A. (2001). Express yourself: beginning at home with family stories. *Art Education, 54*(4), 38–44.

Duncum, P. (1999). A case for art education of everyday aesthetic experiences. *Studies in Art Education, 40*(4), 295–312.

Gardner, H. (1994). *The arts and human development*. New York: Basic Books.

Giroux, H., & Simon, R. (1989). *Popular culture, schooling, and everyday life*. New York: Bergen & Garvey.

Graue, M. J., & Walsh, D. J. (1998). *Studying children in context*. Thousand Oaks, CA: Sage.

Green, L. G. (1999). The return of the body: Performance art and art education. *Art Education, 52*(1), 6–13.

Greene, M. (2000). *Releasing the imagination: Essays on education, the arts, and social change*. San Francisco: Jossey-Bass.

Kindler, A. M., & Duras, R. (1994). Artistic development in context: Emergence and development of pictorial imagery in the early childhood years. *Visual Arts Research, 20*(2), 1–13.

Lai, A., & Ball, E. (2002). Home is where the art is: exploring the places people live through art education. *Studies in Art Education, 44*(1), 47–67.

Lark-Horovitz, B., Lewis, H. P., & Luca, M. (1999). *Understanding children's art for better teaching*. Reston, VA: National Art Education Association.

Lowenfeld, V. (1952). *The nature of creative activity*. New York: Harcourt, Brace & World.

Michael, J. (1982). *The Lowenfeld lectures*. University Park: Pennsylvania State University Press.

Noddings, N. (2002). *Starting at home: Caring and social policy*. Berkley: University of California Press.

Olson, J. (2003). Children at the center of art education. *Art Education, 56*(4), 33–45.

Paley, V. G. (1993). *Boys and girls, superheroes in the doll corner*. Chicago: University of Chicago Press.

Piaget, J. (1955). *The language and thought of the child*. New York: World.

Pile, N. (1973). *Art experiences for young children*. New York: Macmillan.

Sandell, R. (2006). Form + theme + context: balancing considerations for meaningful art learning. *Art Education, 59*(1), 33–38.

Silberstein-Storfer, M. (1982). *Doing art together*. New York: Simon & Schuster.

Smith, N. (1993). *Experience and art: Teaching children to paint*. New York: Teachers College Press.

Szekely, G. (1978). Art as a communication system. In B. Persky (Ed.), *Bilingual Education* (pp. 330–340). New Jersey: Avery.

Szekely, G. (1978). Uniting the roles of the artist and teacher. *Art Education, 31*(1), 17–21.

Szekely, G. (1979). Creative use of media in art instruction. *Educational Technology, 19*(2), 5–9.

Szekely, G. (1980). The art lesson as a work of art. *Art Teacher, 10*(3), 12–14.

Szekely, G. (1981). The artist and the child: a model program for the artistically gifted. *Gifted Child Quarterly, 25*(2), 67–72.

Szekely, G. (1981). Creative designs for classroom routines. *Art Education, 34*(6), 14–18.

Szekely, G. (1982). Conversations in the art class. *Art Education, 35*(3), 15–18.

Szekely, G. (1983). Preliminary play in the art class. *Art Education, 36*(6), 18–24.

Szekely, G. (1985). Teaching students to understand their own artworks. *Art Education, 38*(5), 38–44.

Szekely, G. (1988). The art exhibit as a teaching tool. *Art Education, 41*(1), 9–18.

Szekely, G. (1988). Art inspirations from the computer. *Technological Trends, 33*(5), 20–23.

Szekely, G. (1988). *Encouraging creativity in art lessons*. New York: Teachers College Press.

Szekely, G. (1989). Drawing innovations in the public school. *OAEA Journal, 28*(1), 14–24.

Szekely, G. (1990). An introduction to art: Children's books. *Childhood Education, 66*(3), 132–138.

Szekely, G. (1990). New approaches to secondary school art education. In B. Little (Ed.), *Secondary art education: An anthology of issues* (pp. 223–242). Reston, VA: National Art Education Association.

Szekely, G. (1990). Outdoor playing and art. *Journal of the Canadian Society for Education Through Art, 21*(2), 8–14.

Szekely, G. (1990). The teaching of art as a performance. *Art Education, 43*(3), 6–18.

Szekely, G. (1991). Discovery experiences in art history for young children. *Art Education, 44*(5), 41–50.

Szekely, G. (1991). *From play to art*. Portsmouth: Heinemann.

Szekely, G. (1991). Planning for the sharing of experiences and observations. *Art Education, 41*(3), 6–14.

Szekely, G. (1992). Play and art in the elementary school. In A. Johnson (Ed.), *Art education: Elementary* (pp. 165–176). Reston, VA: National Art Education Association.

Szekely, G. (1993). Adopting a school: Art education students in residence. *Art Education, 46*(5), 18–25.

Szekely, G. (1993). The Percy H. Tacon Memorial Lecture. *Journal of the Ontario Society for Education Through Art, 21*(2), 6–17.

Szekely, G. (1993). Visual arts areas of study: integration with other subjects. In J. Michael (Ed.), *Visual arts teacher resource handbook* (pp. 87–110). New York: Krauss International.

Szekely, G. (1994). From play to art: A visit to the Nova Scotia College of Art and Design. *NASCAD Papers in Art Education, 7*(1), 125–138.

Szekely, G. (1994). Shopping for art materials and ideas. *Art Education, 47*(3), 9–18.

Szekely, G. (1995). Art at home: Learning from a "Suzuki" education. In C. Thompson (Ed.), *The visual arts and early childhood learning* (pp.44–58). Reston, VA: National Art Education Association.

Szekely, G. (1995). Circus. *Art Education, 48*(4), 44–51.

Szekely, G. (1995). Observing children's artistic development. *Journal of the Canadian Society for Education Through Art, 24*(1), 29–39.

Szekely, G. (1996). Exploring art in middle school. In C. Henry (Ed.), *Middle school art: Issues of curriculum and instruction* (pp. 101–104). Reston, VA: National Art Education Association.

Szekely, G. (1996). Preparation for a new art world. *Art Education, 49*(4), 6–14.

Szekely, G. (1997). The art of writing in art education. *Journal of the Canadian Society for Education Through Art, 28*(1), 31–37.

Szekely, G. (1999). The art of convention presentation. *Art Education, 52*(2), 47–52.

Szekely, G. (1999). Children as architects. In J. Guilfoil & A. Sandler (Eds.), *Built environment education in art education* (pp. 163–177). Reston, VA: National Art Education Association.

Szekely, G. (1999). I would rather drive a cab than teach art. *Journal of the Canadian Society for Education Through Art, 30*(2), 28–32.

Szekely, G. (2000). Painting in the year 2000. *Art Education, 53*(5), 12–18.

Szekely, G. (2001). The display art of children. In B. Zuk & R. Dalton (Eds.), *Student art exhibits* (pp. 21–28). Reston, VA: National Art Education Association.

Szekely, G. (2003). Art homework. *Art Education, 55*(3), 47–53.

Szekely, G. (2003). The art teacher as a collector. *The Canadian Art Teacher, 2*(2), 13–22.

Szekely, G. (2003). *A retrospective: 1973–2003 essays for art teachers*. Boston: Pearson Education.

Szekely, G. (2006). Thirty years of planning: an artist-teacher's visual lesson plan books. *Art Education, 59*(3), 12–18.

Szekely, G., & Szekely, I. (Eds.). (2005). *Video art in the classroom*. Reston, VA: National Art Education Association.

Index

About the Author

For 35 years George Szekely has been a pioneer in developing creative changes and methodologies for art teaching. His work has been formulated in books, journals, unique performance-style keynote presentations, and teaching demonstrations through his nationally initiated Adopt-a-School projects. He was among the first art educators to emphasize the importance of children's play in art making and to advocate the study of children's home art as the foundation for school art practice.

He has been elected a Distinguished Fellow (2006) of the National Art Education Association. He is an Emanual Barkan Prize–winning author, and a Victor Lowenfeld Award recipient for his lifetime achievement in art education. A former Vice President of the National Art Education Association, he was named A National Treasure by student chapters of the NAEA. He has published over a hundred articles in major journals of education and has been a contributor to art education programs on public television. He has published nine books, among the most recent *Video Art for the Classroom, A Retrospective 1973–2003: Essays for Art Teachers, From Play to Art, The Art of Teaching Art* (also published in a Chinese edition), and *Encouraging Creativity in Art Lessons.*

He is a frequently invited guest speaker at national state/province-level art education meetings in the United States and Canada. A prolific painter, he has had 26 one-person shows in New York and throughout the United States and Europe. A graduate of the High School of Music and Art, Cooper Union, Pratt Institute, and Columbia University, he has taught in the New York City public schools and at the City University of New York. Since 1978 he has been Area Head and Senior Professor of Art Education at the University of Kentucky.